LIFE, LIBERTY AND DEATH
on the Appalachian Frontier

ROBERT B. SWIFT

Life, Liberty and Death on the Appalachian Frontier
by Robert B. Swift

Copyright © 2024

All rights reserved. Reproduction or utilization of this work in any form, by any means now known or herein after invented, including but not limited to xerography, photocopying and recording, and in any storage and retrieval system, is forbidden without permission from the copyrighted holder.

Library of Congress Control Number: 2024943856
International Standard Book Number: 978-1-60126-921-8

Cover Art: *Trees That Speak*. Artist: Robert Griffing. Publisher: Paramount Press Inc.

Masthof Press
219 Mill Road | Morgantown, PA 19543-9516
www.Masthof.com

Acknowledgments

My sincere thanks to the following individuals and institutions for their assistance in making this book possible: my wife Judy for technical assistance; my son Brian and daughter-in-law Kelly Munoz for editorial and technical assistance; my son David with travels; John L. Moore, a Northumberland, Pa. author, for editorial advice and technical assistance; and Joseph Dudick for research endeavors over many years. Brian, Kelly and John also provided photos.

Also Robert Emerson, executive director, Old Fort Niagara; Steve Smith, Public Service Librarian for the Historical Society of Pennsylvania; the Moravian Historical Society, Buffalo History Museum, Ontario Historical Society, Conococheague Institute, Welsh Run, Pa.; Morlatton Village, Historic Preservation Trust of Berks County PA; Congregation Shaarai Shomayim, Lancaster, Pa.; Lebanon Valley (PA) Chamber of Commerce, Tioga Point Museum, Athens, Pa., and Erin Greb of Erin Greb Cartography, Doylestown, Pa.

And a great debt is owed to the late Paul A. W. Wallace, author of *Indian Paths of Pennsylvania* published by The Pennsylvania Historical and Museum Commission. Wallace's diligence in tracking the course of ancient Indian paths, interviewing and corresponding with people who lived along those paths and giving talks to local historical societies is a 20th-century odyssey in itself. He is an inspiration to anyone trying to reimagine the wilderness journeys of the 18th century.

Table of Contents

Acknowledgments. iii
Preface ix
Introduction. xiii

CHAPTER 1
From Okehocking to the Cornplanter Tract 1
    Okehocking 3
    Cornplanter Tract. 6
    Gayantgogwus and Seneca Women. 11
    The Quaker-Seneca Relationship 14
    Cornplanter Seneca Adopt Pennsylvania Gov. James. 15
    Lappawinsoe and Tishcohan. 17
    Nanticoke Migration 19
    Tuscarora Migration. 24

CHAPTER 2
The Onondaga-Philadelphia Connection 33
    Palatine Migration to Pennsylvania. 43
    Destination London: Native American Leaders Feted There. .47
    Cadwallader Colden and Jane Colden. 50
    Canasatego 52
    Sir William Johnson and the Mohawk River Gateway 55
    Rattlesnake Adventures. 59

CHAPTER 3
Squatters in the Susquehanna River Valley 65
    Scots-Irish Emigrants Drawn to Limestone Springs 75
    Donegal 77
    Paxton 78
    Silver Spring Presbyterian Church. 80
    Meeting House Springs. 81
    Big Spring. 82
    Falling Spring 83
    Augusta Stone Defiance 83
    Shamokin Is Magnet for Schuylkill Fur Traders 84
    Traders on the Frankstown Path 88
    Joseph Simon 94
    Barnabas and Elizabeth Hughes .96
    A Journey to Lake Erie 98

CHAPTER 4
Cherokee Warriors on the Pennsylvania Frontier. 105
    French Build Portage Road South From Lake Erie 116
    British Army Nurse Weathers Braddock Campaign 119
    Christopher and Thomas Gist: An Eye for Land 122
    General Forbes Last March. 125
    Massy Harbison 127

CHAPTER 5
Job Chilloway and His World. .131
    John Martin Mack and Jeanette Mack 141
    Great Island 144
    David Brainerd. 146
    Tree Paintings Tell a Story. 149
    The Great Runaway 152

CHAPTER 6

Seneca Ordeal at Fort Niagara.................159
    Colonel Bolton at Fort Niagara...................169
    Catharine Montour 172
    Old Smoke....................................174
    Mary Jemison at Gardeau Flats....................175
    Three Captives Shape Genesee History...............179
    Cherry Valley and Stone Arabia 181
    Stone Arabia..................................182
    Joseph Brant Leads Exodus to Canada 183
    Jemima Wilkinson—The Public Universal Friend.......187
    Buffalo Creek Reservation........................188
    Passenger Pigeons 192

Bibliography...................................199
Index 207
About the Author 219

Preface

*L*ife, Liberty and Death on the Appalachian Frontier* tells the stories of the men and women who ventured through the mountains and forests and along the rivers of the Appalachian frontier in Pennsylvania and New York during the 18th century.

For Native Americans in this region—the Haudenosaunee or Iroquois, Delaware, Shawnee, Nanticoke, Tuscarora and others—the journey was not always about getting from point A to point B.

They went on a generational journey from birthplace to burial ground trying to preserve a way of life and culture that could be passed onto future generations. Displaced by war, Seneca refugees faced sheer tragedy in the ice caves at Fort Niagara during the bitter winter of 1779.

Native American culture was under attack by those acting in the name of God, King and Country to fulfill imperial designs drafted in London and Paris. Emissaries from Philadelphia, Albany, Williamsburg and Quebec sought to keep the peace with the Iroquois at Onondaga who held the balance of power in the region for a time.

"When in the year 1737, I was sent for the first time to Onondago, at the request of the Government of Virginia, I left home at the end of February quite inconsiderately to undertake a journey of 500 English miles through a wilderness where there were neither highways nor paths, neither men nor, even at that time of the year, even animals to be found to stay our hunger," wrote the Pennsylvania diplomat Conrad Weiser about a grueling winter journey to the Iroquois seat.[1]

Idealism motivated others to tread on unfamiliar ground. Quaker, Presbyterian and Moravian missionaries sought to extend the writ of a secular experiment in religious toleration in Pennsylvania or lead willing religious converts along a new path of life.

Missionaries of the Moravian Church in particular provided vivid descriptions of the terrain they encountered in the journals and diaries they kept. They observed Native American customs closely because they were trying to win converts and write bilingual dictionaries.

"After a few miles ride we struck the base of Second Mountain, at a point where it butts down to the river's edge, which point is a line with the northern limit of the Proprietaries' land, as fixed in the last purchase," wrote Moravian Bishop John Christopher Frederick Cammerhoff of another winter journey in 1748 to the multi-ethnic village of Shamokin at the Forks of the Susquehanna River. "We were now in the Indian country. The rain continued to beat down, and as we toiled through the snow in the Narrows, we occasionally lost the Indian trail, where it had led into the Susquehanna, which had overflowed its banks."[2]

A few such as John Bartram and Jane Colden considered it their life's work to collect, dissect and classify the species of plant and animal life in the New World. It was the Age of Reason after all.

Many journeyed in pursuit of wealth, whether measured in land tracts, bales of fur or in a search for gold and silver that often disappointed.

Surveyor Christopher Gist was under instructions from the Ohio Company to note the conditions of the land he traveled. Gist reported that after leaving the Delaware village of Shannopin's Town at modern Pittsburgh, Pa., that he found "good Land for Farming, covered with small white and red Oaks and tolerable level; fine Runs for Mills &c."[3]

While a forested wilderness of towering trees defined much of the region, it would be a mistake to think that's the only thing the 18th-century traveler encountered.

All around was evidence of an established civilization—of Native American villages with their scattered huts and bountiful gardens, the old town sites left by a migrating tribe, a cluster of painted trees along a trail relating the exploits of a party of warriors through symbols, a lean-to with a hunk of dried meat for the next passerby.

Bartram described passing the site of the old Shawnee village of Chillisquaque in 1743: "Our way from hence lay through an old Indian field of excellent soil, where there had been a town, the principal footsteps of which are peach-trees, plums and excellent grapes."[4]

The Appalachian region described in this book was located in the eastern one-third of the future United States and drained by a number of great waterways: the Delaware, Schuylkill, Susquehanna and Juniata Rivers in eastern and central Pennsylvania, the Allegheny and Ohio Rivers in western Pennsylvania and the Mohawk, Genesee and Niagara Rivers in New York.

The modern traveler familiar with interstates and airport hubs may not think of a world as defined by rivers. Yet, rivers were the main highways of the 18th-century. The trail network developed by the Native Americans and later modified by traders and soldiers follows the course of rivers and their tributaries. The town of Water Street in central Pennsylvania takes its name from a riverbed used as a trail through a gap in Tussey Mountain.

Not only does an 18th-century geographical map hold different meaning than today's maps, so does the political map. After all, would you give it much thought if a friend told you he was traveling from Philadelphia to Syracuse, N.Y.? In the 18th century this was the diplomatic route used by Pennsylvania officials and the Iroquois Confederacy.

This book relies on contemporary first-person accounts in journals, diaries and reports to help capture this fascinating period in our history. The spellings, punctuations and abbreviations used by those authors are maintained.

Endnotes

1. Conrad Weiser, "Notes on the Iroquois and Delaware Indians," *The Pennsylvania Magazine of History and Biography* Vol. 1, No. 2 (1877), 163-164.

2. John W. Jordan, ed., "Bishop J. C. F. Cammerhoff's Narrative of a Journey to Shamokin, Penna. in the Winter of 1748," *The Pennsylvania Magazine of History and Biography* Vol. XXIX, No. 2 (1905), 165.

3. William A. Darlington, ed., *Christopher Gist's Journals* (Salem, NH: Ayer Company Publishers, Inc., 1991), 34.

4. John Bartram, Lewis Evans and Conrad Weiser, *A Journey from Pennsylvania to Onondaga in 1743* (Barre, MA: The Imprint Society Inc., 1973), 39.

Introduction

This book is divided into six chapters each anchored with an essay about the 18th-century frontier and accompanying pieces about people, places and events that tie in.

Chapter 1 looks at how the Native Americans were dispossessed of their land in Pennsylvania over the course of a century. The Delaware were pushed out of eastern Pennsylvania through land deals and encroachment by white settlers. They fought unsuccessfully in the French and Indian War to regain their land. The Nanticoke and Tuscarora facing war in Maryland and North Carolina migrated north through Pennsylvania seeking new homes. The Seneca at century's end held a tract of land in northwestern Pennsylvania granted to Chief Cornplanter.

Chapter 2 focuses on a wilderness trail linking the Iroquois seat at Onondaga in New York State and Philadelphia and the diplomatic journeys between the two capitals. The duo of the Pennsylvanian Conrad Weiser and Iroquoian Shikellamy faced threat to life and limb in the winter of 1737 traveling to Onondaga to avert a war.

The folk migration of the Palatine Germans down the Susquehanna River to reach the fertile Tulpehocken Valley, the trials of the Onondaga orator Canasatego and efforts by Sir William Johnson to open the Mohawk River Gateway to British control are covered in this chapter.

Chapter 3 examines how Scots-Irish settlers pushed across the Susquehanna River despite boundary lines set between Pennsylvania and Native Americans. This chapter also looks at why the Scots-Irish located Presbyterian churches by limestone springs and how fur traders ventured from the Schuylkill and Susquehanna Rivers into the interior.

Chapter 4 starts with the exploits of Cherokee warriors on the southern Pennsylvania frontier during the French and Indian War and how a British-Cherokee alliance fell apart. The obstacles facing a French invasion army in western Pennsylvania, Matron Charlotte Browne's ordeal during the 1755 Braddock expedition to the Forks of the Ohio and British General John Forbes' last march to Philadelphia after victory at the Forks are covered.

Chapter 5 starts with a search for historical details about Job Chilloway, the so-called friendly Delaware. This chapter also explores the journeys of Moravian missionaries, the mystique of Great Island on the West Branch of the Susquehanna River and the Native American tradition of tree painting.

Chapter 6 tells the grim story of the Seneca at Fort Niagara during the winter of 1779 following the Sullivan campaign. Related pieces look at how Catharine Montour, Mary Jemison and Joseph Brant coped with the impact of the Revolutionary War in New York State.

CHAPTER 1

From Okehocking to the Cornplanter Tract

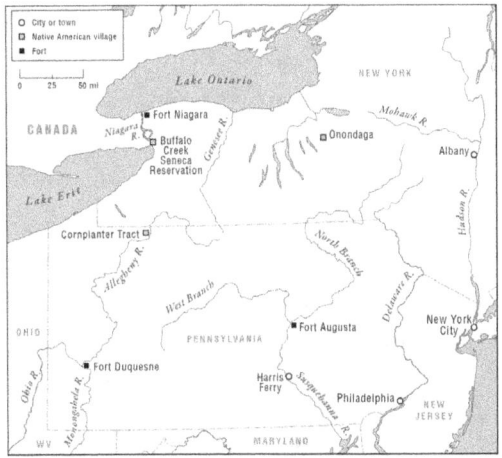

Map showing key features of Pennsylvania/New York frontier by Cartographer Erin Greb.

The journey from Okehocking, a short-lived Delaware "reservation" in southeastern Pennsylvania, to the Cornplanter Tract in northwestern Pennsylvania is not linear.

It covered a century's worth of time, a period when Native Americans were gradually dispossessed of their territory in Pennsylvania through warfare, land sales, trickery, westward migration to escape white encroachment and finally in the 20th century by eminent domain.

It wasn't obvious at first that dispossession would be the result of all the interactions between the Conestoga, Conoy, Delaware, Shawnee and Seneca and the successive waves of English, Quakers, Scots-Irish, Germans and French Hugenots arriving in Pennsylvania.

Pennsylvania founder William Penn followed his practice of buying tracts of land from the Native Americans he encountered during two short stays in the province even though the parties to those deeds held vastly different conceptions of what land ownership actually meant.

The more powerful Iroquois Confederacy (including the Seneca) or Haudenosaunee centered in the Finger Lakes to the north overruled the Delaware or Lenni Lenape on some land deals, including ordering their leaders to accept the notorious Walking Purchase of 1737. The Delaware were in a tributary position with regards to the Iroquois.

Several men hired by Penn's two sons to mark the purchase boundaries at the Forks of the Delaware River ran the distance rather than walk it as customary. Therefore, the Delaware gave up more land in the transaction than they bargained for. Their resentment over this fraud eventually led to war two decades later.

Even before a tract of land was formally "purchased" by the Penn family, white squatters didn't hesitate to pick choice spots along the waterways to settle and start farming regardless of whether the land was good for hunting game.

The westward migration in reaction to the advancing white settlers, loss of hunting opportunities for food and changes to a traditional way of life led to the establishment of Shamokin at the Forks of the Susquehanna River in the 1720s as a hub of displaced people.

The Shawnee and many Delaware moved to villages along the Allegheny River like Chartier's Town and Kittanning and later to the Forks of the Muskingum River in the Ohio Country.

The French and Indian War from 1755-63 and Pontiac's War in 1763-64 accelerated the pace of Native American dispossession. The bitterness of those wars made Penn's idea of a peaceful coexistence with Native Americans impossible. The Treaty of Fort Stanwix in 1768 led to the loss by Native Americans of a major swath of territory stretching from the northern reaches of the Susquehanna River to the Forks of the Ohio River at modern Pittsburgh.

The American Revolution threatened the survival of both the relocated Delaware in the Ohio Country and the Seneca, keepers of the Iroquois western door, in the region of the Upper Allegheny River and Genesee River. The Seneca allied with the British and suffered devastation during the American invasion of their homeland in 1779. The Seneca lost most of their territory through a series of land sales in the decades following the Revolution, but managed to retain ownership of several reservations in New York State.

The Okehocking "Reservation" and granting of the Cornplanter Tract to a Seneca leader are somewhat unique in the interactions between Native Americans and Pennsylvanians. These were specific land grants by the government to groups of Native Americans for land they once regarded as belonging to their own people. Neither was a reservation in the terms of those Indian reservations established during the 19th century in New York and the Great Plains states.

Okehocking

By the time the Okehocking Grant was made in 1702, the various bands of Delaware or Lenni Lenape had been dealing with Swedish, Dutch and English settlers for more than half a century.

Coexistence proved difficult for the Delaware with white settlers chopping down forests, competing for game, damming streams and interfering with fish migrations, letting free-ranging swine damage cornfields and erecting fences that hindered their hunting and seasonal movements between the uplands and riverbank camps. The influx of European settlers along the Delaware River increased dramatically during the 1680s, thus putting even more pressure on the Okehocking and other Delaware bands to move inland.

Penn concluded some 17 separate land deals with various Delaware leaders between 1682 and 1701 in southeast Pennsylvania.[1]

During this period, the Okehocking moved further north along Ridley Creek to escape the settlers, but they expressed fear to provincial officials of being pushed even further away.

The Okehocking band petitioned Penn's officials in 1702 for land in the area of Ridley Creek, which "under certain Metes and Bonds, that they Might live no more like Dogs, as they expressed themselves."[2]

They were given a tract of vacant land for themselves and their descendants with the understanding it would revert to Penn if they departed. Located within the tract is a symbolic turtle-shaped rock outcrop. But a land tract couldn't compensate for the disruption to the Okehocking way of life. The game they hunted became scarce. Their seasonal migrations to fishing spots were jeopardized. The Okehocking became dependent on European goods.

The band, numbering roughly 30 people, lived in modern-day Willistown Township in Chester County for several decades. Not much is known about the individual members except for the names of Pokais, Sepopawny and Muttagooppa mentioned in a legal warrant to survey a 500-acre tract for them. Notable Quaker James Logan signed the warrant as well.[3]

Penn described the Delaware homes. "Their Houses are Mats, or Bark of Trees set on Polies, in the fashion of an English Barn, but out of the power of the winds, for they are hardly higher than a Man; they lie on Reeds or Grass. In Travel they lodge in the Woods about a great Fire, with the Mantle of Duffels they wear by day, Wrapt around them, and a few Boughs stuck around them."[4]

The Okehocking land wasn't regarded as being valuable for agriculture, and by 1710 a road was built across the tract. Willistown Township was created in 1704.

The Okehocking likely bartered for food from the Quaker farmers moving into Willistown Township with such homemade items as baskets, brooms and bowls.[5]

By the 1730s, the Okehocking had left the land grant on a seasonal basis and moved westward. They were part of a great Delaware migration that ultimately ended up in Oklahoma in the 19th century. A Quaker had owned the tract before it was granted to the Okehocking and the Penn family later sold it after their departure to Quaker brothers Mordecai and Amos Yarnell.[6]

The Pennsylvania Historical Commission and The Chester County Historical Society erected a monument to the Okehocking Indian Town in 1924 using a "tall native time-stained boulder" with a bronze tablet. Today 155 acres of the land grant is part of the Okehocking Preserve, a green space offering woods and trails for recreation along Ridley Creek.

Located within nearby Ridley Creek State Park, the fieldstone Quaker Joseph Pratt house is the centerpiece of the 112-acre colonial Pennsylvania plantation. It's the size of an average colonial farm. This living history museum offers a fine example of the Quaker farming settlement patterns that supplanted the Okehocking way of life.

The original owner, Thomas Duckett, acquired this property in the 1680s. The current stone farmhouse was enlarged numerous times over the decades by Pratt and his descendants. The colonial plantation interprets the 1760s era, four decades after Pratt purchased the property.

It deserves mentioning that several Native Americans became private owners of small land tracts in 18th-century Pennsylvania for a short period of time. But these grants were rare exceptions given to individuals in good graces with the province.

The Delaware negotiator Tatamy was granted a 300-acre tract near the Delaware Forks by the General Assembly in the 1730s. Interpreter Andrew Montour of a prominent Algonquian family was likewise given the

Okehocking monument

green light in 1752 to select a tract along the New Path north of the Blue Mountains. Gov. John Penn granted the Delaware scout Job Chilloway a patent to land at Wyalusing in 1774. He sold it to Henry Pawling of a prominent Philadelphia family a year later.

Cornplanter Tract

While our knowledge of the Okehocking band is limited, that can't be said for the Seneca leader Cornplanter and his descendants who lived for 173 years on the Cornplanter Tract along the Allegheny River in Pennsylvania just south of the New York State border.

Frontiersmen, missionaries, agriculturalists, teachers, merchants, ethnologists, a governor and finally engineers visited the tract and wrote about what they saw. But the enduring legacy of the Cornplanter Tract rests with the legends and traditions that the Seneca ascribed to the places and natural features of the landscape along the Allegheny. These gave rise to both creation myths and a new religion.

A classic example is Dyoshaisde"on, where the snake slid down referring to a Seneca belief that a giant snake slid down a hillside amidst falling timber to the river after a lightning strike. It's a place south of the New York State line marked by a ravine.[7]

Another example is Dyonyonwai'ntge'on where the streamlet empties referring to a sacred place where the prophet Handsome Lake, a half-brother to Cornplanter, rose to preach after a vision in 1799 and started a new religion.[8] These places visited by the ethnologist William Fenton in the 1930s are submerged under a reservoir today.

The Rev. Timothy Alden, a missionary to the Seneca, described Cornplanter's town of Jennesadaga in 1827. "The site of this, which comprises about a half dozen buildings, is on a handsome piece of first rate bottom land, a little within the limits of Pennsylvania," wrote Alden. "It was grateful to notice, from the many enclosures of thrifty maize, buckwheat and oats, the peaceful agricultural habits

Left: Cornplanter, Seneca chief (Library of Congress Prints and Photographs Division) Right: Grave of Cornplanter near Kinzua Reservoir (Author)

of the inhabitants. As further evidence of the recent melioration of conditions, there was a considerable show of oxen, cows and horses; and likewise of logs brought from the adjacent forest, designed for the sawmill and the Pittsburgh market."[9]

During the 1790s, about 400 people lived on the Cornplanter Tract. The Allegany Seneca reservation was just across the New York border. Alden's description offers evidence that the ideas guiding the formal establishment of Cornplanter's Tract in 1791 were put into practice.

During a 1790 visit to Philadelphia, Cornplanter asked President George Washington for assistance to help his people develop a land-tilled agricultural economy, grind corn and build schools, sawmills and forges on land they settled on the Allegheny River following the American Revolution.

It was recognition on his part that the Seneca faced a difficult time sustaining themselves with hunting and seasonal agriculture due to the loss of most of their territory.

The Pennsylvania General Assembly granted Cornplanter title to three tracts of land in 1791—Jennesadaga and two smaller parcels, which he later sold. These land grants were in recognition for Cornplanter's help to the United States government in post-Revolution negotiations with Ohio Indians.

Cornplanter (1750-1836) was born along the Genesee River, the son of a prominent Seneca woman and Albany Dutch trader John Abeel (also spelled O'Bail). Cornplanter sided with the British during the Revolution and led raids on American settlements in the Mohawk and Wyoming Valleys.

The 1779 American campaign led by Gen. John Sullivan then destroyed some 40 Seneca villages in the Genesee River region. The final British defeat in 1783 left the Seneca without a powerful ally. The Seneca dispersed with one group migrating to Canada and others living in several reservations in New York established after large land sales in western New York to American speculators.

Cornplanter's policy of helping the Americans following the Revolution bore fruit at the 1794 Treaty of Canandaigua affirming Seneca sovereignty.

By 1798, Quaker missionaries arrived at Jennesadaga to help deliver the education and economic assistance sought by Cornplanter. The Philadelphia Yearly Meeting of the Quakers formed an Indian Committee in 1795 to help the Seneca adapt to changing times. "We wish them (children) to be instructed to read and to write, and such other things as you teach your children," wrote Cornplanter to the Quakers.[10]

Quaker missionary Halliday Jackson wrote how his associate John Pierce told Cornplanter's people "of our intentions to Sojourn amongst them, & teach them to Plow to Sow, & to reap that they might eat the Goodly things of the land, and also to instruct them in the use of mechanical Instruments, and how to take care of their Flocks and Herds that they might have meat in abundance & bread without scarcity."[11]

Halliday Jackson witnessed something extraordinary—the birth of a new religion based on the visions of Handsome Lake, Cornplanter's half-brother.

Handsome Lake had an initial vision in the spring of 1799 while lying in a coma at his cabin following a heavy bout of drinking. His nephew Blacksnake arrived and found a warm spot on what appeared the lifeless body of Handsome Lake. So did Cornplanter. Handsome Lake eventually awoke and told his vision of meeting three angels or messengers who warned against drinking whiskey, practicing witchcraft and abortion. Being weak still, Handsome Lake asked Cornplanter to relay his vision at a council.[12]

Handsome Lake preached the Iroquois must stay united, become economically self-sufficient, not be dependent on white society and avoid alcohol because it was having a destructive effect upon their society.

Here is Jackson recounting what Handsome Lake said about a later vision involving the angels, "He (Great Spirit) thinks a great Pity that the Indians shall lose all their Land-- that their Children and generations to come should have no land to Sit down upon...."[13]

Corplanter and his sister Gayantgogwus, a medicine woman, gave early support to Handsome Lake. Handsome Lake said the three messengers directed that she provide medicine to help his recovery.[14]

The Iroquois were divided over Handsome Lake's teachings with some following him into what is now known as the Longhouse religion, some keeping traditional beliefs and others becoming Christian.

The Quakers eventually established a school at Tunesassa near the Allegany Seneca reservation. In 1805, a young Quaker couple, Rachel and Benjamin Coope, or Cope, traveled from Chester County in southeast Pennsylvania to teach at Tunesassa.

In her diary, Rachel wrote about their goal of instructing the Seneca in agriculture, spinning and dairy. Rachel described how Cornplanter's sister greeted them and said she was glad the Great Spirit had brought them safe through their long journey.

"He (Cornplanter) wanted to see some of our linnen, or Manufacturing, and said if two or more of their Women could get in the way of making they could learn the others," wrote Coope.[15]

Cornplanter eventually turned against the Americans and Quakers as white settlers came to the region, but he lived long enough to board a steamboat on the Allegheny River.

For six decades the Kinzua Dam posed a real threat to Cornplanter's descendants living on the tract with its potential to inundate their land.

Talk of a dam at the headwaters of the Allegheny River surfaced in the early 20th century as Pittsburgh industrialists sought protection from floods. A devastating flood in 1936 gave the project new life. Demand for electric generating power and water releases to abate pollution was also a catalyst.

The Cornplanter Seneca appealed to Pennsylvania archaeologists and historians for help. In 1939, Iroquois anthropologist William Fenton surveyed the bounty of medicinal plants along Cornplanter Run with the help of Seneca herbalists Charlie Gordon and Havey Jacobs.

"Cornplanter Run is a singularly beautiful spot," wrote Fenton. "Along its margins and in the adjoining thickets and timber grow all kinds of medicinal plants. Small wonder that the Cornplanter Seneca became famous herbalists." Fenton wrote that Iroquois from Tonawanda and Canada sought Manroot, a tuber that grew along Cornplanter Run.

He added: "We stopped beside an elderberry bush (Sambucus), o'tgo"da' in Seneca, while Charlie (Gordon) showed us how to select the green 'whips' and slit them to extract the pith. In preparing a beverage for persons suffering from 'heart disease,' he put two handfuls of pith in three quarts of warm water. Elder has been called aptly a whole pharmacy in itself, and the Indians have many uses for it."[16]

Fenton also recorded boneset and mints to cure colds, angelica to treat pneumonia, plantain for an upset stomach, wire grass for sore muscles, "rattlesnake killer" to make a poultice for snake bites and fireweed for consumption among other medicinal plants.

Fenton, an anthropologist and author employed by both the federal government and New York State during a long career, visited Cornplanter Tract several times and became well acquainted with its residents in the late 1930s and 1940s.

He wrote a remarkable article "Place Names and Related Activities of the Cornplanter Seneca" that appeared in *Pennsylvania Archaeologist* in 1945-46. He described the lore and legends of key sites along the Allegheny River that are now part of a vanished world.

World War II delayed the Kinzua Dam project, but a new push started in the 1950s with congressional funding authorizations. The Philadelphia Quakers provided the Cornplanter Seneca with legal assistance and joined protests against the dam construction by the U.S. Army Corp of Engineers.

The Seneca said the taking of their land through eminent domain violated the 1794 Treaty of Canandaigua. But Seneca appeals to the U.S. Supreme Court and President Kennedy to block the project went unheeded.

The Kinzua Dam was completed in 1964 and most of Cornplanter's Tract was flooded except for an isolated section. The Seneca lost one-third of the Allegany Reservation land. The residents were given compensation and relocated to new housing subdivisions in New York. Cornplanter's grave was moved to a new cemetery on higher ground.

The memory of a submerged river valley that nourished a new religion and medicinal plants remains vivid today for the exiled Cornplanter Seneca.

Gayantgogwus and Seneca Women

The half-sister of Handsome Lake plays a major role in his June 1799 vision that laid the foundation of a new religion. As he awoke from a coma, Handsome Lake outlined plans for the distribution of a medicine—new strawberries that will heal the people of Cornplanter's village and give them strength.

"We will appoint Odjiskwathe and Gayantgogwus, a man and wife, to make the medicine. Now they are the best of all the medicine people," wrote Seneca archaeologist Arthur C. Parker in his English translation of Handsome Lake's Code. "Early in the morning you will see them and at that time you will have the medicine for your use, and before noon the unused medicine will be cast away because you will have recovered."[17]

The Seneca consider the early strawberries of June to be sacred and of great medicinal value. Not much is known about Gayantgogwus and her husband. She is said to have lived a long life and died at age 101 in 1846 at the Cattaraugus reservation.[18]

Gayantgogwus as a medicine woman occupied an important position in a matrilineal society. She is considered important to helping win support especially among women for Handsome Lake's visions of a self-sufficient Iroquois society.[19]

"Our Seneca women give birth to our nation, and therefore the children receive their clan from their mothers," said the Seneca Iroquois National Museum in Salamanca, N.Y.[20]

The eight Seneca clans are based on the kinship of extended families and named for a totemic animal such as a bear or turtle. They are linked through the maternal line. Clan members could live in different villages in the 18th century. Clan members were expected to provide hospitality to another member traveling between villages.

This social structure gave Seneca women an important and nuanced, if not always visible role, in political affairs. The senior woman in a clan could name a new chief after consultation with other women and even remove him. They didn't speak at council meetings where consensus was sought on important issues like war and peace, but they would get men to speak for them.[21]

During the 1794 Treaty of Canandaigua, the prominent Seneca

orator Red Jacket told the Americans he was speaking for the women at one point, according to an account by the Quaker representative William Savery. Three Seneca women had asked to be admitted to the council and have Red Jacket speak for them.

"He was then desired to act as orator for the women and deliver to the council what they had to say," wrote Savery. "The substance of this was, that they felt a deep interest in the affairs of their nation, and having heard the opinion of their sachems, they fully concurred in them, that the white people had been the cause of all the Indians' distresses; that they had pressed and squeezed them together, until it gave them great pain in their hearts, and that the whites ought to give back the lands they had taken from them."[22]

The women raised the main subsistence crops of corns, beans and squash that fed the whole village, while the men hunted and fished to add to the diet. A young married couple would live with the wife's family. Men helped with the clearing of land and building homes, a continual process with villages relocating to more fertile grounds every few years.

Historian Elisabeth Tooker explains that the Seneca valued items in accordance with those who used them. Women used the basic farming tools while men used the hunting weapons. Mary Jemison, the white captive who lived most of her life with the Seneca, described the women's agricultural work in her narrative.

> "In the summer season, we planted, tended and harvested our corn, and generally had all our children with us; but had no master to oversee or drive us, so that we could work as leisurely as we pleased. We had no ploughs on the Ohio, but performed the whole process of planting and hoeing with a small tool, that resembled in some respects, a hoe with a very short handle."[23]

The crowding of the Seneca onto reservations after the British loss in the American Revolution led to upheavals in the social order. Men lost access to the vast hunting lands and were encouraged by the whites to take up farming regarded until then as the job of women. Women fared better in coping with the cultural shock as they remained family-oriented and had less contact with whites, wrote Martha Champion Randle in *Iroquois Women, Then and Now*.[24]

The Quaker-Seneca Relationship

A 34-year-old Rachel Coope or Cope wrote about her journey through the Pennsylvania wilderness in 1805 to reach the Quaker settlement of Tunesassa near the Cornplanter Tract and her bouts with melancholy as she and her husband Benjamin taught the arts of agriculture, weaving and dairy farming to the Seneca. Coope was the daughter of Quaker elder Joshua Sharpless who helped establish the Quaker Allegany mission in 1798.

"…after going over a hill, had a very rough swampy road along a Valley between great Mountains, though such an amazing thicket of Pines &c," she wrote about encountering the wilderness after having traveled west through the towns of Elizabethtown (where they lodged at the still-standing Sign of the Bear Tavern), Middletown, Harrisburg and then north along the east bank of the Susquehanna River to Williamsport.[25]

On June 14, 1805, Rachel and her husband attended a council at Cold Spring on the Allegheny River where "we went into the council house where were a large number of Indians 10 chiefs and a good many women."[26]

She wrote: "We felt peace of Mind in being with them, and hoped that our sisters the Indian Women, when we became a little more acquainted would be willing to be instructed."[27]

At Tunesassa, Rachel wrote in January 1806 about the schoolhouse being built and her teaching women knitting, spinning and soap making. She died in childbirth in 1807.

These entries from Coope's journal were transcribed and posted by Haverford and Swarthmore Colleges in an interesting on-line collection titled *Beyond Penn's Treaty, Quaker and American Indian Relations* about Quaker journeys to the Indian country.

Quakers were involved with the short-lived Okehocking reservation at the start of the 18th century. They forged a relationship with the Seneca following the Revolution that extended into the 20th century with assistance in trying to block the Kinzua Dam project.

The vehicle for involvement from 1795 on was the Indian Committee of the Philadelphia Yearly Meeting. The committee sent teachers to educate the Seneca at the Cornplanter Tract and the Allegany and Cattaraugus Reservations in New York, monitored legislation and treaties affecting Native Americans and from 1852 to 1938 ran a boarding school at Tunesassa.

The role of boarding schools has come under scrutiny in recent years with assertions they caused significant damage by separating Native American children from their families and culture and trying to assimilate them into western culture. In recent years the *Friends Journal* has published articles about the legacy of Quaker Indian boarding schools in this regard.

The Indian committee provided legal assistance to help the Seneca overturn a fraudulent 1838 land sale treaty that threatened to dispossess them of all their reservations in western New York and brokered a compromise treaty in 1842.

The committee launched a campaign in 1961 to stop the Kinzua Dam. Quakers held a silent vigil at the construction site that year.[28]

Cornplanter Seneca Adopt Pennsylvania Gov. James

The motorcade of Gov. Arthur James left clouds of dust as it traveled dirt roads into a remote corner of Pennsylvania on an August afternoon in 1940. James was on his way to be officially adopted as a member of the Seneca Nation at a ceremony attended by 3,000 people at the Cornplanter Tract on the Allegheny River.

It was an unusual journey for James. He described himself as a "red-headed breaker boy from Plymouth," referring to his roots in Pennsylvania's anthracite region. James had been a favorite son candidate for the Republican presidential nomination just two months before in Philadelphia.

As part of the adoption ceremony, James was asked where he is going and what he is going to do. "I am a friendly traveler who has come many, many miles to see if I can do many, many things for your people," replied James. He was given the name o-dahn-got, meaning Sunlight by a Wolf Clan mother.[29]

The adoption ceremony was cast as a story where a traveler appears at a Seneca campsite. The ceremony featured an adoption song and several dances. After the ceremony, James placed a wreath with the legend "To a Friend of the State" at the state monument marking Cornplanter's grave at a nearby cemetery.

The cemetery and Cornplanter's monument were relocated a quarter-century later to the Riverview-Corydon Cemetery on higher ground to escape Kinzua Dam's reservoir. The proposed federal Kinzua Dam wasn't mentioned at the adoption ceremony, but it was certainly a worry of the Cornplanter Seneca at the time.

The Pennsylvania Federation of Historical Societies formed a committee in 1940 to examine the impact of a dam on the Cornplanter Seneca. William Fenton, an Iroquois anthropologist, made a field survey of the Cornplanter Tract at the request of the Pennsylvania Historical Commission. Fenton's account published in *Pennsylvania Archaeologist* in 1945-46 shows the Allegheny River's importance to the Seneca as a source of creation myths and sacred sites linked to Handsome Lake's visions and habitat for fish, wildlife and medicinal plants.

"The Allegheny River in northwestern Pennsylvania traverses a singularly wild and beautiful area that comprises wooded hills that rise upwards of 2100 feet," wrote Fenton. "These hills are the heaps of earth, say the Cattaraugus Senecas, that the Creator had left over when he finished making the earth."[30]

Lappawinsoe and Tishcohan

Two iconic portraits of Native American leaders evoke an infamous land sale that dispossessed the Delaware or Lenape of their lands around the Forks of the Delaware River in eastern Pennsylvania. The Swedish-American portrait artist Gustavus Hesselius painted Lappawinsoe and Tishcohan on separate canvasses in 1735 and was paid for his work by the Penn family. This pair and other Delaware engaged in a preliminary talk on May 9, 1735, about the sale of the Forks lands with Pennsylvania proprietors John and Thomas Penn at the family estate at Pennsbury.

These talks led to the notorious 1737 Walking Purchase where the Penns extended the boundaries of the purchase tract as far as possible. Instead of having men measure the boundaries in a leisurely walk during a day and a half as was customary, the Penns hired runners who covered territory to a point north of the Blue Mountains.

The Penns pressed their case for the tract with a dubious 1686 deed suggesting the land had once been sold to William Penn and a map showing waterways that proved confusing to the Delaware.[31]

Left: Lappanwinsoe Delaware Chief portrait by Gustavus Hesselius (Wikipedia. org) Right: Tishcohan Delaware Chief portrait by Gustavus Hesselius (Library of Congress Prints and Photographs Division)

In August 1737, Nutimus, Lappawinsoe, Tishcohan and Menakihikon (there are numerous spellings of their names) signed the Walking Purchase deed agreeing to the sale.

Most of the Delaware living at the Forks had migrated there from New Jersey to escape white encroachment. The exodus started in the late 17th century and by the mid-1800s only a couple hundred Delaware were left in that state.

Lappawinsoe's and Tishcohan's village of Hockendaqua near modern Northampton happened to be where the first day "walk" by Penn's runners finished on Sept. 19, 1737. Two of the Indians accompanying the runners had dropped out and the Penn agents asked Lappawinsoe to provide replacements. He refused reportedly saying the Penns had already taken the best land and they might "go to the Devil" for the bad land, according to testimony taken years later from runner Edward Marshall.[32]

The Delaware sought the help of the powerful Iroquois to stop the purchase, but the Iroquois having struck an alliance with Pennsylvania, told the Delaware to leave their villages and relocate to the Susquehanna and Wyoming Valleys.

Lappawinsoe moved to the Susquehanna Valley and there is a reference to Tishcohan being in the Ohio Valley in the 1750s.[33] The two would be lost to history if not for Hesselius' oil portraits. These portraits are widely reproduced and attract attention from anthropologists for such realistic details as the tattoo on Lappawinsoe's forehead and the fur pouches around both men's necks. They are considered Hesselius' masterpieces especially for the way he captures the expressions on his subject's faces and their own persona.[34]

Lappawinsoe is seen as older with greying hair, a wearied look and blue blanket around his torso; Tishcohan is middle-aged and has hair on his chin and a half-smile on his face. He also wears a blue blanket and necklace of blue beads and has an English pipe in his pouch.

Hesselius (1682-1755) benefited from court ties having done an earlier portrait of James Logan, the Pennsylvania official who was a driving force in the Walking Purchase. He came to America from Stockholm in 1712 with a pastor brother and lived mostly in Philadelphia for the rest of his life. Hesselius was drawn to the Moravians for a while but later in life he painted the Pastor Israel Acrelius of the Holy Trinity Old Swedes Church in Wilmington, Del.

The Swedish naturalist Peter Kalm described how Hesselius used pyrites to make a reddish undercoat for his paintings. "Mr. Hesselius has several pieces of this kind of stone which he used in his paintings," wrote Kalm. "He first burnt them, then pounded or ground them to a powder and at last rubbed them still finer in the usual way and this gave him a fine reddish brown color."[35]

Nanticoke Migration

For the Nanticoke, the people of the tidewater, a good portion of the 18th century was spent in a northbound migration that started at their ancestral home on a tributary river of the Chesapeake Bay and ended at the post-Revolutionary War reservation of the Iroquois in Grand River, Ontario and other scattered places.

The Nanticoke were described as good hunters and fishermen and skilled at making wampum, beads made from the purple and white parts of shells, and valued as a guide in oral story telling.

The Nanticoke met English explorer Captain John Smith in 1608 as he journeyed around the Bay in the *Discovery Barge*. Most of them left Maryland nearly 150 years later to escape the pressure of land encroachment by English settlers. They lived at several locations along the Susquehanna River in Pennsylvania prior to the French and Indian War. They were among the refugees at British-held Fort Niagara during the American Revolution. A small number of Nanticoke were counted in a tribal census at Grand River following the Revolution.

But importantly, too, a number of Nanticoke remained at their homeland in the Bay region throughout the centuries and their descendants today form the Nanticoke Indian Tribe of Delaware and the Nanticoke-Lenni Lenape Tribal Nation in New Jersey.

In his *A Map of Virginia,* Smith described traveling on a "pretty convenient river on the East called Cuskarawaok," the home of the Nanticoke, near modern Vienna, Md.

Some of the Nanticoke climbed trees and fired arrows at Smith's ship while he made gestures of friendship. The next day a group approached the ship dancing and carrying baskets, but Smith's men suspecting a trap fired a volley into the reeds and later found discarded baskets and much blood. On the third day tensions eased and several thousand Nanticoke in Smith's estimation clustered around the party in a welcoming mood.[36]

Smith was followed by thousands of English colonists who settled on the Eastern Shore and cleared and fenced land for farms with little regard for Nanticoke habitation. The English settlers let their livestock roam and that provoked complaints from the Nanticoke when cattle invaded their cornfields.

These steady incursions led to Nanticoke uprisings in the 1640s and 1670s against the Maryland colony. At the start of the 18th century, Maryland created two reservations for the Nanticoke—one called the Chicony Reserve and the other at Broad Creek in the Nanticoke Creek watershed—that existed for a number of years.[37]

Yet expecting the Nanticoke to live on a defined tract of land was at odds with their traditional seasonal migrations in search of food, whether for shellfish, crabs and oysters at the Bay, game animals in the woods or nuts, roots, berries and corn.[38]

The matter came to a head in 1723 when settlers Capt. John Rider and Issac Nicholls claimed possession of a Nanticoke village because it was deserted except for one older man.

The two burned the village and built their own house. The Nanticoke returned and then took the matter to a Maryland court. The court ruled the white men were trespassers, a rare victory in an otherwise losing struggle.[39]

The Nanticoke like other eastern tribes had become tributaries while retaining autonomy of the Iroquois Confederacy in the early 18th century. By the 1740s, most decided to follow invitations from the Iroquois to settle along the Susquehanna River in Pennsylvania. The catalyst for the move was Nanticoke participation in an abortive Shawnee-led uprising against Maryland authorities. The Nanticoke gathered at Winnsoccum Island in swamplands along the Pocomoke River to make war preparations, but Maryland officials got wind of the plot and arrested the leaders.

This Nanticoke migration occurred over the course of decades as various groups of Nanticoke moved northward sometimes staying at one place for several years and then setting out again.

One important trip in this regard came when a Nanticoke delegation went to the Iroquois capital at Onondaga in 1743. They encountered the Pennsylvania emissary Conrad Weiser there on his own diplomatic journey to ease tensions on the Virginia frontier. "In the Morning I went to see the Nantikokes; there was six in Number, none could speak a word of the Language of the united Nations. I found there besides Canasetego (the Onondaga leader), his brother Zilla Woollie; and others; they desired me to stand Interpreter for the Nanticokes (they heard us talk English together), to which I consented," wrote Weiser.[40]

Naturalist John Bartram at the scene reported the Nanticoke presented a number of Wampum belts to the Iroquois, "a seventh, to request them to let them settle on a branch of the Susquehanah."[41]

A year later a body of Nanticoke were living on Juniata Island (now Duncan Island) where the Juniata River enters the Susquehanna. The Protestant missionary David Brainerd stopped there in 1745 and was discouraged that he didn't have an opportunity to preach to them since preparations for a dance were underway.[42]

By 1748 the Nanticoke had moved to the site of the modern Nanticoke in the Wyoming Valley on the north branch of the Susquehanna.

A bronze monument in Lancaster County marks the site of another Nanticoke village on Indiantown Rd. off Route 322 north of modern Ephrata, Lancaster County, Pa. The red sandstone boulder erected in 1932 by the Lancaster County Historical Society has a bronze plaque with a map showing the village site. The monument is on a rise one half mile west of Indian Run near the Indiantown Mennonite Church.

The monument says the Nanticoke lived here from 1721 to 1748, but the first date is long before the accepted start of the migration. A story told by a local family said the Nanticoke once returned to the site to bury a chief and invited them to attend.

Left: Nanticoke Village monument

Below: Nanticoke Village site near Indian Run (Author)

This location is twenty miles east of the Nanticoke Path, described by historian Paul A. W. Wallace, as a north-south path linking Nanticoke on the Susquehanna River with the Chesapeake Bay. The Nanticoke used this path to return to the Chesapeake Bay to fish and harvest oysters. The path followed modern Route 10 for part of the way in Pennsylvania.[43]

The Nanticoke drew attention for an unusual burial practice—the carrying of the bones of their ancestors for burial back in old villages or with a move to a new one.

The Moravian missionary Rev. John Heckewelder wrote that he saw the Nanticoke loaded with the bones of their ancestors as they moved through the town of Bethlehem from 1750 to 1760. The Nanticoke scraped the bones clean of flesh prior to taking them on a journey, said Heckewelder, but fresh bones could create a stench.[44]

Moravian missionaries at Friedenshuetten at Wyalusing on the Susquehanna River recorded the movements of Nanticoke during the 1760s in their mission diary:

> May 16, 1766 "Muschkoss, a notorious Nanticoke powwow, who stands charged with having been privy to the death of several Indians of his tribe, and who is in bad repute even at Zeninge (Osteningo), left to-day to our relief. He passed the winter here."

In September 1767, the missionaries reported that two Nanticoke told them that 55 of their nation were enroute from Maryland and they asked for corn and the loan of canoes to the aged and infirm. The Nanticoke arrived two weeks later and feasted on roast ox and cornbread.

> March 20, 1769 "Twenty Nanticokes arrived from Zeninge. They report a scarcity of food, almost a famine, up the river, and bring the blankets and strouds which were apportioned among them at the late treaty, to barter away for corn."[45]

From Osteningo at modern Binghamton, N.Y., the migratory Nanticoke continued to western New York. After American independence, some went west to Ohio while others joined the Six Nations reservation in Ontario. And the Nanticoke remaining in Maryland have retained their identity to this day.

The Nanticoke Indian Museum in Millsboro, Del., features exhibits about the tribal culture and history.

Tuscarora Migration

Like the Nanticoke, the Tuscarora engaged in a decades-long northbound migration in the 18th century from their southern homeland in North Carolina to the realm of the Haudenosaunee or Iroquois Confederacy. The outcome of this migration was different for the Tuscarora though. It led to the establishment of a Tuscarora Nation reservation of more than 6,000 acres in the Niagara River region that exists to this day.

The Tuscarora were related to the Iroquois and that kinship provided them a safe haven after a brutal war with the English in 1711-13. Numbering some 5,000 in population, the Tuscarora in 18th-century North Carolina subsisted on fish and shellfish, raised the staple crops of corn, beans and squash and cultivated orchards. They had contact with European colonists as early as the late 16th century.

As the 18th century began, the Tuscarora faced greater white encroachment and resulting problems with kidnappings and dishonest traders on their territory along the Neuse River emptying into Pamlico Sound.

Tensions increased when the Tuscarora accused John Lawson, the surveyor general of North Carolina, of taking their land. The Tuscarora seized Lawson and the Swiss explorer Baron Christoph De Graffenried who were on an expedition in 1711 checking for navigation along the Neuse River. Lawson was killed while De Graffenried was released.

"Through the wonderful and glorious providence of the Most High, I have at last escaped out of the barbarous hands of the wild Tuscarora Nation, and have arrived at my little dwelling at New Bern; but yet half dead," wrote De Graffenried about his experience.[46]

Lawson is also known today as the author of *A New Voyage to Carolina*, a natural history of the region and account of his journey among several Indian nations, including the Tuscarora, published in 1709.

Lawson's death prompted Tuscarora warriors living in the lower towns to attack the settlements of Swiss and Palatine Germans around New Bern. Colonial forces from South Carolina then invaded Tuscarora territory twice capturing their forts at Narhantees and Neoheroka. Cherokee and Yamasee warriors aided the colonials.

A year before war broke out a group of Tuscarora had met Pennsylvania officials at Conestoga to discuss getting permission to settle on lands overseen by the Iroquois.[47] After the war, North Carolina established a reservation for the Tuscarora that existed until 1803.

The Tuscarora migration from North Carolina began in earnest in 1714; it would collectively take various bands of Tuscarora more than 60 years to reach the nation's new homeland on the Niagara Escarpment in western New York.

One large organized group settled near Onaquaga or Oquaga, a multi-ethnic Oneida town on the Susquehanna River at modern Windsor, N.Y., where they lived until the American Revolution. The Tuscarora became the sixth nation of the Iroquois Confederacy in 1722.

Traces of this migration are seen in place names like Tuscarora Mountain and Tuscarora Creek in central Pennsylvania and Tuscarora Creek, a tributary of the Monocacy River in central Maryland.

The Tuscarora Path went up the Shenandoah Valley, cut through Path Valley near modern Fort Loudon, Pa., crossed the Juniata River and went to Shamokin at the Forks of the Susquehanna River and then roughly followed the Susquehanna to Onaquaga, according to historian Paul A. W. Wallace in *Indian Paths of Pennsylvania*.[48]

Pennsylvanian Indian negotiator Conrad Weiser estimated the number of Tuscarora warriors at 150 in the 1740s.[49]

During the American Revolution, the Tuscarora were ensnared in the split among the six Iroquois nations over supporting the Americans or British. While nominally pro-American, the Tuscarora suffered also when American forces destroyed Onaquaga in 1778 because British-allied Mohawk leader Joseph Brant made his headquarters there.

The Tuscarora fled westward to Oneida country and by 1780 some of them were among the refugees miserably huddled at Fort Niagara after the Sullivan campaign. The return to Niagara was a homecoming of sorts since the Tuscarora had lived there before going to North Carolina.

The Seneca gave the Tuscarora land on the Niagara Escarpment, an ancient rock ridge, near modern Lewiston, N.Y. The 1797 Treaty of Big Tree affirmed the Tuscarora right to this land. The current Tuscarora Nation Reservation consists of three tracts of land: one granted by the Seneca, the second a gift from the Holland Land Company and the third land purchased by the U.S. government for them in 1803.

During the War of 1812, the Tuscarora were steadfast allies of the United States and they paid a price for that. In December 1813 a British-Canadian force invaded Lewiston and the residents fled along Ridge Road towards the Tuscarora Reservation. The Tuscarora created a diversion by blowing horns to give the British the impression that the defenders were greater in numbers than they actually were. The Tuscarora helped the Lewiston residents to safety but they lost most of their own homes to British torches.[50] On the bicentennial in 2013, a monument to the Tuscarora Heroes was dedicated in Lewiston.

The Tuscarora faced a modern challenge in the late 1950s when

Path Valley Tuscarora migration landmark

the New York State Power Authority seized 557 acres of reservation land through eminent domain to build a reservoir and transmission lines for the Niagara Power Project.[51]

The controversy took a toll on the Tuscarora with legal battles that went to the U.S. Supreme Court, protests and passive resistance in front of surveyors' vehicles and some internal division among the residents of the reservation.

In 1960, the Supreme Court ruled that the targeted land could be used for the power project. The building of the reservoir caused the relocation of 29 homes while others were demolished or burned down.[52]

"The news (of the land taking) was like an explosion on the reservation and it traveled around like the fuse on a firecracker," wrote

Ted C. Williams in *The Reservation*. "It was like looking out your window and seeing a stranger pull boards off your house and saying, 'I bought your house last night.'"[53]

Williams ends his tale of the fight over the reservoir by noting that a medicinal plant, a symbol of Mother Earth's power, still grew along Gill Creek near the reservoir.

Endnotes

1. Charles S. Keyser, *Penn's Treaty with the Indians* (Philadelphia: David McKay, 1882), 22-26.
2. Marshall J. Becker, "The Ockehocking: A Remnant Band of Delaware Indians," *Pennsylvania Archaeologist* Vol. 46., Issue 3 (1976), 33.
3. Ibid., 33.
4. Albert Cook Myers, ed., *William Penn's Own Account of the Lenni Lenape or Delaware Indians* (Somerset, NJ: The Middle Atlantic Press, 1970), 27.
5. Becker, op cit., 40.
6. Willistown Township Historical Commission, Excerpt from *"Acres of Quakers"* compiled by John Charles Nagy and Penny Teaf Goulding. April 30, 2021 accessed. https://www.willistown.pa.us/DocumentCenter/View/739/Native-American-History-excerpted-from-Acres-of-Quakers?bidId
7. William N. Fenton, "Place Names and Related Activities of The Cornplanter Senecas," *Pennsylvania Archaeologist* Vol. 15, No. 1 (Jan. 1945), 26-27.
8. William N. Fenton, "Place Names and Related Activities of The Cornplanter Senecas," *Pennsylvania Archaeologist* Vol. 15. No. 2. (April 1945), 42.
9. Timothy Alden, *An Account of Sundry Missions Performed Among the Senecas and Munsees; in a series of letters. With an appendix* (New York: J. Seymour, 1827), 11.
10. Letter from Cornplanter to Quakers. 1791. *Beyond Penn's Treaty: Quaker and American Indian Relations.* Quaker & Historical Collections at Haverford College and Friends Historical Library at Swarthmore College. July 4, 2021 accessed. https://pennstreaty.haverford.edu/manuscripts/SW_Letters_1791_02_10.pdf
11. Anthony F. C. Wallace, ed., "Halliday Jackson's Journal to the Seneca Indians, 1798-1800," Part I, *Pennsylvania History* Volume XIX, No. 2 (April 1952), 127.
12. Anthony F. C. Wallace, *The Death and Rebirth of the Seneca* (New York: Alfred A. Knopf 1970), 240-241.
13. Anthony F. C. Wallace, ed., "Halliday Jackson's Journal to the Seneca Indians, 1798-1800," Part II, *Pennsylvania History* Volume XIX, No. 3 (July 1952), 344.
14. David Swatzler, *A Friend Among the Senecas* (Mechanicsburg, PA: Stackpole Books, 2000), 126.
15. Some Account of Rachel Coope (Journal B). 1805. *Beyond Penn's Treaty: Quaker and American Indian Relations.* Quaker & Historical Collections at Haverford College and Friends Historical Library at Swarthmore College. July 5, 2021. accessed. https://www.pennstreaty.haverford.edu. 33.
16. Fenton, No. 2. op cit., 46-48.
17. William N. Fenton, ed., *Parker on the Iroquois* (Syracuse, NY: Syracuse University Press, 1968), 24-25.

18. Rochester Museum & Science Center. March 26, 2023 accessed. https://www.rmsc.org.
19. Wallace, *Death and Rebirth*, op cit., 248.
20. Seneca Iroquois National Museum. Seneca Culture & Women Exhibit. March 26, 2023 accessed. https//www.senecamuseum.org.
21. Wm. Guy Spittal, ed. *Iroquois Women An Anthology* (Ontario, Canada: Iroqrafts Ltd., 1990), 112-113.
22. G. Peter Jemison and Anna M. Schein, eds., *Treaty of Canandaigua 1794* (Santa Fe, NM: Clear Light Publishers, 2000), 272.
23. June Namias, ed., *A Narrative of the Life of Mary Jemison* (Norman and London: University of Oklahoma Press, 1992), 84.
24. Spittal, op cit., 142.
25. Coope, op cit., 14.
26. Ibid., 28.
27. Ibid., 28.
28. Joy A. Bilharz, *The Allegany Senecas and Kinzua Dam* (Lincoln: University of Nebraska Press, 1998), 55-56.
29. "Governor James Adopted Into Seneca Nation," *Pennsylvania Archaeologist* Vol. X, No. 4 (October 1940), 75-77.
30. Fenton, Vol. 15, No. 1, op cit., 25.
31. Anthony F. C. Wallace, *King of the Delawares Teedyscung 1700-1763* (Syracuse, NY: Syracuse University Press, 1990), 25.
32. William J. Buck, "Lappawinzo and Tishcohan Chiefs of the Lenne Lenape," *The Pennsylvania Magazine of History and Biography* Vol. 7, No. 2 (1883), 216.
33. Ibid., 218.
34. Ian M. G. Quimb, ed., *American Painting to 1776 A Reappraisal* (Charlottesville: The University Press of Virginia, 1974), 130.
35. Adolph B. Benson, ed., *Peter Kalm's Travels in North America Volume 1* (New York: Dover Publications Inc., 1964), 46.
36. Karen Ordahl Kupperman, ed., *Captain John Smith A Select Edition of His Writings* (Chapel Hill & London: The University of North Carolina Press, 1988), 90-91.
37. Nanticoke Lenni-Lenape Tribal Nation. Our History. March 30, 2023 accessed. https://www.nlltribe.com
38. Frank. W. Porter III, "A Century of Accommodation: The Nanticoke in Colonial Maryland," *Maryland Historical Magazine* Vol. 74, No. 2 (Summer 1979), 182.
39. Ibid., 183-184.
40. John Bartram, Lewis Evans and Conrad Weiser, *A Journey from Pennsylvania to Onondaga in 1743* (Barre, MA: Imprint Society, 1973), 119.

41. Ibid., 77.
42. David Brainerd, *The Project Gutenberg eBook of the Life of Rev. David Brainerd, Chiefly Extracted from His Diary,* by Jonathan Edward, March 30, 2023 accessed. https://www.gutenberg.org 170.
43. Paul A. W. Wallace, *Indian Paths of Pennsylvania* (Harrisburg: The Pennsylvania Historical and Museum Commission, 1971), 107-109.
44. John Heckewelder, *History, Manners, and Customs of the Indian Nations Who Once Inhabited Pennsylvania and the Neighboring States* (Arno Press & The New York Times, 1971), 92.
45. William C. Reichel, *Wyalusing and the Moravian Mission at Friedenshuetten* Moravian Historical Society: Transactions of the Moravian Historical Society. Vol. 1. No. 5 (1871) March 30, 2023 accessed. https://www.jstor.org. 196-200.
46. Vincent H. Todd, *Christoph Von Graffenried's Account of the Founding of New Bern* (Bowie, MD: Heritage Books Inc., 1999), 261.
47. Anthony F. C. Wallace, *Tuscarora A History* (Albany: State University of New York Press, 2012), 67.
48. Paul A. W. Wallace, op cit., 168-170.
49. Paul A. W. Wallace, *CONRAD WEISER Friend of Colonist and Mohawk* (New York: Russell & Russell, 1971), 200.
50. Leo Simonson, *Tuscarora Heroes* (Lewiston, NY: Historical Association of Lewiston, Inc., 2014), 49-53.
51. Bryan Printup and Neil Patterson Jr. *Tuscarora Nation* (Charleston, SC: Arcadia Publishing, 2007), 9.
52. Ibid., 114-115.
53. Ted C. Williams, *The Reservation* (Syracuse, NY: Syracuse University Press, 1976).

CHAPTER 2

The Onondaga-Philadelphia Connection

Most modern travelers have little reason to journey between Syracuse, N.Y., and Philadelphia, Pa., despite a good network of highways connecting the cities from north to south.

During the first part of the 18th century, however, there was plenty of foot traffic between the Haudenosaunee or Iroquois Confederacy's capital at Onondaga near Syracuse and Philadelphia, the capital of provincial Pennsylvania.

This traffic was due to a diplomatic and strategic partnership between the Iroquois and Pennsylvania starting in the 1730s and lasting four decades. It provided benefits to both powers.

The Iroquois based in central New York wanted to protect their southern door by exercising influence over a host of displaced tribes and directing where they could settle in the Susquehanna River Valley. They were also steering northbound migrating tribes like the Tuscarora to new homes in New York.

Pennsylvania wanted to conduct its Indian relations and negotiate land sales with one powerful entity rather than a multitude of tribes and spokesmen. William Penn had engaged with various tribes over the initial land sales in the 1680s, but his sons pursued a different policy.

The Iroquois Confederacy was likely created in the 15th century as five related Nations situated in territory from east to west—the Mohawk, Oneida, Onondaga, Cayuga and Seneca—and living south of Lake Ontario agreed to halt intertribal warfare among themselves and act in concert as one political unit while still having a wide degree of autonomy.

The Onondaga were the last to join the Confederacy, and with their lands holding the central territory, the council fire or seat of the Confederacy was located there.

The League enabled Iroquois expansion in a series of wars with neighbors like the Huron, Erie and Susquehannocks and ultimately with the French over control of the fur trade. But the Iroquois also suffered great losses of young warriors during those wars.

By the start of the 18th century, Iroquois leaders resolved to stay neutral for the most part in the emerging imperial wars between the French and British and exert leverage through a middleman's role. They accepted European encroachments on their land with the French Fort Niagara guarding the Niagara Portage and Fort Oswego, a British post north of Onondaga.

The stage was also set for an alliance in 1732 between Pennsylvania and the Five Nations. A treaty that year opened the way for the governing Penn family to purchase lands west of the Susquehanna River. The Iroquois overruled the tributary Delaware or Lenape on the sale of land tracts, including the controversial Walking Purchase of 1737 that led to the removal of the Delaware from the Forks of the Delaware River.

The Iroquois sent an overseer named Shikellamy to influence the affairs of the displaced tribes gathered at Shamokin at the Forks of the Susquehanna River. He formed a diplomatic duo with Conrad Weiser, Pennsylvania's chief Indian negotiator.

Starting in 1727, Shikellamy (?-1748) had looked after the affairs of the displaced Delaware, Tutelo, Conoy, etc., gathered at Shamokin. His roots are uncertain. He is thought to be either a Cayuga or Oneida or possibly even having a French father.

Weiser (1696-1760) was among the emigrants from the Palatinate in Germany who first settled in New York and then migrated to the Tulpehocken Valley. Weiser lived with the Mohawks for several years and learned their language. He came to the Tulpehocken Valley in 1729 and steadily gained in prominence on the frontier starting as an interpreter for the Iroquois at conferences.

Together, Shikellamy and Weiser engaged in shuttle diplomacy between Onondaga and Philadelphia for the next decade on matters involving land sales, threats of war between the Iroquois and southern Catawba tribe, the activities of white squatters on the frontier and threats to peace when a trader or Indian was murdered in a frontier altercation.

Their stopovers included the meeting places of the provincial council in Philadelphia, the Georgian-style mansion of Pennsylvania colonial Secretary James Logan at Germantown, Weiser's home at Womelsdorf, Shikellamy's seat at Shamokin, Ostonwakin, home of the interpreter Madame Montour; Tioga, the southern gateway village for the Iroquois; and Owego, a Cayuga village.

The journey between Onondaga and Philadelphia could be rough in the winter when food was scarce in the villages as Weiser and Shikellamy found out in 1737. Large parties of Iroquois journeyed to conferences in Philadelphia in the summer months.

From Philadelphia, Pennsylvania negotiators would follow the Schuylkill River to Weiser's home on Tulpehocken Creek south of the Blue Mountain. They took the Tulpehocken Path across gaps in the mountain ranges to Shamokin. A party then followed the Sheshequin Path from Ostonwakin to Tioga, fording Lycoming Creek and Towanda Creek along the way and then went to Owego and Osteningo where the Susquehanna headed in a northeast direction. A party would continue straight north crossing Gooseberry Hill to reach Onondaga.

Moravian bishops and missionaries also took the path starting in the 1740s. They went to Onondaga to smooth the way for their plans to build Pennsylvania missions populated with Delaware and Mahican religious converts.

A round trip to Onondaga in the winter could last six weeks.

Left: Oneida Chieftain Shikellamy oil on canvas, 1820 (Wikipedia.org)
Right: Tulpehocken Path marker (Author)

Travel times were measured in days in better weather. The 40-mile Tulpehocken Path, linking Weiser's and Shikellamy's homes, has a place in frontier lore. The Path cut through Pennsylvania's ridge-and-valley terrain, but made use of gaps to avoid climbing four steep mountains.

The Tulpehocken Path is noted for place names: Pilger Ruh (Pilgrim's Rest) given by the Moravians for a still-flowing mountainside spring; the Double Eagle for an ancient carving of an eagle into a large tree and stone monuments denoting two frontier forts.

One of the most treacherous locations on the journey to Onondaga was an area on the Sheshequin Path known as Windfall. Here the path was blocked by stands of trees blown down in windstorms.[1]

"The forest is so dense that for a day the sun could not be seen, and so thick you could not see twenty feet before," wrote Moravian Bishop Augustus Spangenberg about his trek along Lycoming Creek. "The path, too, is so bad that the horses were often stuck, and had to be extricated from the bogs; and, at other points, it lay full of trees that had been blown down by the wind."[2]

The mapmaker Lewis Evans traveling in the summer of 1743 described the final leg of the journey: "From Gooseberry-hill, traveling N.N.E. through a moist, beautiful and fruitful country about eight and forty miles, we reached the first town of the Onondaga Indians. This country is varied with pleasant swelling knolls, brooks and little lakes."[3]

Philadelphia naturalist John Bartram described Onondaga as situated in a valley in 1743:

> "The fine vale of Onondago runs north and south, a little inclining to the west, and is near a mile wide, where the town is situated and excellent soil. The river that divides this charming vale is 2, 3 or 4 foot deep, very full of trees fallen across or drove on heaps by the torrents. The town in its present state is about 2 or 3 miles long, yet the scattered cabins on both sides the water are not above 40 in number; many of them hold 2 families, but all stand single and rarely above 4 or 5 near one another; so that the whole town is a strange mixture of cabins interspersed with great patches of high grass, bushes and shrubs, some of pease, corn and squashes…"[4]

The alliance was forged in 1732 when a delegation of Iroquois came to Philadelphia accompanied by Weiser and met the newly arrived proprietor Thomas Penn. An even larger delegation came in 1736 staying first at Logan's home of Stenton where they camped for several days and then going to Philadelphia where they negotiated a sale of land west of the Susquehanna River.

Showing hospitality with food, drink and gifts was part of the diplomatic convention of the day. Logan met with considerable personable expense providing accommodations for delegations from Onondaga that included whole families.

Weiser and other northbound travelers could expect a good

meal, often of boiled corn and beans, sometimes of roasted game, upon their arrival at Onondaga before any business was done.

The most harrowing journey for Weiser and Shikellamy came when they set off for Onondaga in late winter 1737 thinking the worst of the season was behind them. Both men had close calls with death. This was an urgent trip on behalf of Pennsylvania and Virginia officials seeking to avert another war between the Iroquois and the Catawba tribe based in the southern Appalachians.

The pair and several companions soon found that winter's grip was still on the land with a heavy snow pack, overflowing streams and submerged fords and near famine in the Indian villages along the way. Food scarcity was often a problem for Native Americans in late winter and early spring with wild game scarce, dwindling supplies of dried corn and beans from last fall's harvest, berries not yet available and sap from sugar maple trees sometimes the only recourse for sustenance.

Shikellamy's close call came when he fell off a steep cliff on the trail along Lycoming Creek. His fall was broken when the strap of his pack caught on a small tree.

At one point in the middle of a "dreadful thick wilderness" within several days of Onondaga, Weiser exhausted to the core by little food and fatiguing marches sat down under a tree waiting to die. Shikellamy's words of encouragement helped Weiser get back on his feet.[5]

The return trip went better and Weiser reached home on May 1 six weeks after he left.

In 1742, Weiser accompanied the Moravian Church leader Count Nicholas Ludwig Von Zinzendorf via the Tulpehocken Path on a trip to visit Shamokin and Ostonwakin.

At Ostonwakin where Madame Montour lived, Zinzendorf met her son Andrew Montour and wrote a famous description of him being half European and half Indian.[6]

Zinzendorf's party eventually reached Onondaga as they

sought tacit approval for the Church's plans to build mission settlements.

Also in 1742 a large Iroquois party from Onondaga led by Canasatego arrived in Philadelphia to negotiate outstanding issues relating to the 1736 sale of lands west of the Susquehanna River. It was here that Canasatego delivered a personal rebuke to a Delaware delegation complaining about the Walking Purchase of 1737. The Iroquois numbered nearly 200 on this 1742 visit with their ranks swelled by family members seeking to escape a local famine. It cost Logan plenty to feed them during a stopover of just one day.[7]

A 1743 journey to Onondaga by Weiser, botanist John Bartram and mapmaker Lewis Evans with Shikellamy on yet another peace mission produced some of the best descriptions of the interior countryside.

Their keen powers of observation led Bartram to publish his observations of the journey in 1751 and Evans to print *A Map of Pennsylvania, New Jersey, New York and the Three Delaware Counties* in 1749.

The trio was well aware of the geopolitical significance of the trip. Evans carried surveying equipment and Bartram wrote about the need to find the sources of rivers in order to extend a beneficial trade to the Ohio and Mississippi regions.[8]

After reaching Onondaga, they hired a guide to take them to a nearby salt spring where Indians dug holes about two feet deep to collect brine and boil its contents until only the salt remained. Bartram describes one salt spring as glittering "like flakes of Ice or Snow in a Sunshiny Day."[9]

The death of Shikellamy in 1748 after he fell ill during a trip to Bethlehem signaled the end of an era. Weiser's attention and those of provincial officials turned increasingly to the Ohio country and the activities of the resident Mingo, Shawnee and Twightwee. Weiser made a groundbreaking trip without Shikellamy in 1748 to Logstown, a new seat of Native American power on the Ohio River.

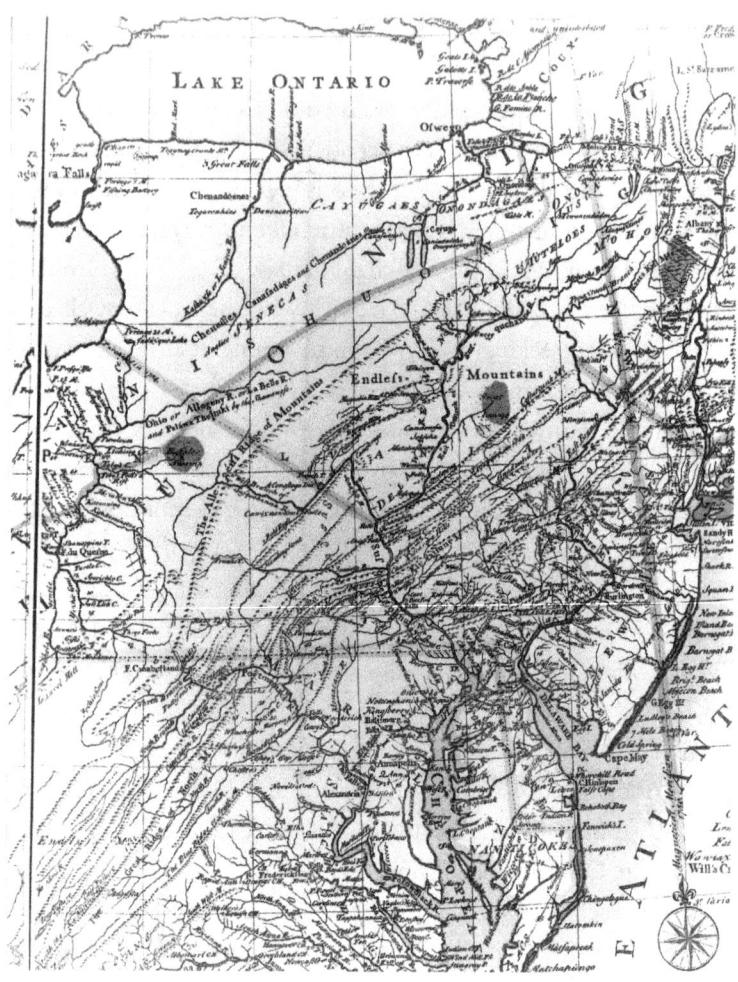

A General Map of the Middle British Colonies by Lewis Evans 1755 (Pennsylvania State Archives MG-11. No. 116. Section One 8X10)

Without Shikellamy's presence, Weiser and Moravian missionaries took new routes to reach Onondaga. In 1750, Moravian Bishop John Christopher Frederick Cammerhoff and missionary David Zeisberger left Bethlehem, entered the Wyoming Valley and then headed north by canoe along the Susquehanna and Chemung Rivers and finally walked overland to Onondaga arriving in June.

Cammerhoff wrote about an old village at Wyalusing, the site of the future Moravian mission of Friedenshuetten:

> "We came to a place called Gahonto (Wyalusing) by Indians. It is said to be the site of an ancient Indian city, where a peculiar nation lived. The inhabitants were neither Delaware nor Aquanoschioni, but had a language of their own…We could still notice a few traces of this place in the ruined corn pits…"[10]

At Onondaga, he described the house of Canasatego as having a "large pole before it with an English flag on it."[11]

Canasatego was a proud host, reported Cammerhoff. "This morning soon after we arose, we were served with a bountiful meal," he wrote. "On the whole they were very particular, in Onondaga, that we should not feel the need, of anything, and were anxious for us to relish their fare. (Canasatego's) manner was very kind and cheerful, he considered it an honor to entertain us in his house."[12]

Three months later in September 1750, Weiser and Christian Daniel Claus, a future British Indian agent, arrived in Onondaga to a much different reception. Canasatego had died a few days before. "Riding quite a stretch in the bush, we met an Indian hunter with the message that Canasatego, the chief of the 6 nations, had grown pale in death a few days ago," wrote Claus. "Mr. W was alarmed and considered our journey in vain because in such a case no council would be assembled."[13]

The Iroquois went ahead with the council realizing that Weiser and Claus had come a great distance to meet with them. But as Weiser's biographer Paul A. W. Wallace has noted, Tohashwuchdionny, Canasatego's successor, was pro-French and a Roman Catholic convert. The rising French sentiment lessened the value of Onondaga as a destination for diplomatic ventures from the south.[14]

This development points to the Iroquois role in the mid-18th century as being officially neutral between the British and French even if the Iroquois had engaged in productive diplomacy on the side with Pennsylvania officials.

Weiser and Claus had traveled to Onondaga through the Delaware Water Gap and along the Delaware River north to the Hudson Valley to Albany where they headed west along the Mohawk River to Onondaga. Weiser met with Sir William Johnson, the then-New York Indian agent, at Fort Johnson along the way.

Due to a variety of factors, Weiser's mission of getting the Iroquois to agree to attend a conference in Fredericksburg, Va., sought by the Virginia governor was not successful. This accelerated the interest of both Pennsylvania and Virginia in the rivalry with the French over the Ohio region.

The Iroquois lost much of their leverage with the defeat in the French and Indian War. The start of the American Revolution in 1775 put great strains on the Confederacy and ultimately led to a breakup. A council at Onondaga couldn't reach the unanimous decision needed to choose between the British or rebellious Americans.[15]

The Seneca, Mohawks, Cayuga and Onondaga allied with the British while the Oneida and Tuscarora sided with the Americans. The specter of Iroquois warriors fighting on opposide sides occurred at the 1777 Battle of Oriskany near the Mohawk River Valley.

In April 1779, American General Goose Van Schaick led an attack against Onondaga, a prelude to the Sullivan campaign into the Seneca heartland that summer. Many of the Onondaga had fled in advance, but Van Schaick's troops burned the long house and 50 other houses and took prisoners. The surviving Onondaga fled to British-held Fort Niagara as did the Seneca following the economic devastation of the Sullivan campaign.[16]

After the Revolution ended with American Independence, the Iroquois council moved from Onondaga to Buffalo Creek on the Niagara River, the new geographic center of the Confederacy. Unity was elusive, however, as Iroquois who migrated to Canada at the invitation of the British started their own council at Grand Reserve in 1803.

The territory of the Onondaga and other Iroquois nations shrank dramatically during this period through land sales to the Americans, some legitimate and others of dubious legality. A reservation was established at Onondaga in 1788 and the council returned there in 1847.

An important event at Onondaga happened in 1815 when Handsome Lake, founder of the Longhouse religion, died during a visit there. A granite monument marks the area of his grave near the council house.[17]

Philadelphia remained a destination for Native American leaders during the time it served as the first capital of the United States.

Palatine Migration to Pennsylvania

In the spring of 1723, fifteen Palatine German families embarked on a folk journey in the truest sense of the word from their homes in New York's Schoharie Valley to new lands in Pennsylvania's Tulpehocken Valley.

These were the people of Conrad Weiser, the future Pennsylvania diplomat. He wasn't with them on the inaugural journey, but came six years later. Weiser provided a rare written account of the peaceful journey through unbroken wilderness in a short autobiography.

"The people received word of the land at Schwadara and Tolpehaken in Pennsylvania," he wrote. "Many of them came together, cut a way from Schohary to the Susquehanna and brought their goods hither and made canoes and journeyed down to the mouth of the Swatara Creek and drove their cattle overland which happened in the spring of 1723. Then they came to Tulpehocken and settlement."[18]

The Palatines were Protestants from the Palatinate, an area in the Rhine River Valley in Germany, and many earned their living as farmers and small shopkeepers.

The trek to Tulpehocken, a Delaware phrase for land of the turtles, was part of a longer journey that started in 1709 when the Palatines left their homeland to finally escape a century of warfare and natural disasters. The grim times started with the Thirty Years' religious war between Catholics and Protestants in the mid-17th century. Spanish and Bavarian troops ransacked the region and then dynastic wars brought invading French forces.

A severe winter in 1708 prompted thousands of Palatines to accept English offers to help them migrate to America. They first went to England where Queen Anne gave sustenance and shelter to her fellow Protestants, numbering some 13,000 by 1709.

A large group of several thousand Palatines sailed the next year to New York where Gov. Robert Hunter promised them employment in an ill-fated project to produce tar and hemp for the Navy. They were established in camps along the Hudson River on Patroon Robert Livingston's Manor. Making tar in the quantities needed was more difficult than first thought and the land wasn't much good for farming either.

Palatine volunteers joined an unsuccessful English attempt in 1711 to seize French-held Quebec, and then in 1712 with conditions worsening in the tar camps, a number of them accepted a Mohawk offer to move west to the Schoharie River. Others moved to the Stone Arabia area in the Mohawk River Valley.

Weiser and his family were among the Palatines leaving the Rhineland in 1709. His father, John Conrad Weiser, was a prominent leader of the migration. Weiser endured the tar camps as a teenager and then moved to Schoharie. His father arranged for Weiser to live with the nearby Mohawk for a number of months to learn their language. This experience set the course for Weiser's long life as an interpreter and diplomat. Weiser wrote in his autobiography that he mastered the Mohawk language completely and used that skill to interpret when Mohawk hunting parties passed by.[19]

At Schoharie, the Palatines lived and prospered in seven villages or dorfs, but they lacked clear title to their land and faced the prospect of paying rent on it. This aggravated their dealings with New York authorities and land speculators and led to new migrations to Tulpehocken and Stone Arabia in 1723.

Weiser's level of involvement with the 1723 Tulpehocken trek is uncertain, but he moved there with his wife and family in 1729. Other Palatines joined the original group and their descendants live in modern Berks County today.

The Tulpehocken journey has been much explored by Palatine historians despite the sparse written record. Pennsylvania Gov. William Keith negotiated with the Palatines about settling in the Tulpehocken Valley when he visited Albany in 1722. Keith struck the deal even though the Penn family had yet to purchase that land from the Delaware. That wasn't done until 1732.

The Palatine families traveled south from Schoharie and built dugout canoes on Charlotte Creek, a tributary of the Susquehanna

Swatara Creek with kayakers (Lebanon Valley Chamber of Commerce)

River. They floated down the Susquehanna to Swatara Creek at modern Middletown, Pa., and then went up Swatara Creek to reach the Tulpehocken Valley. A justice of the peace at Donegal reported word of the passage to Pennsylvania authorities. There is dispute over what route the settlers' cattle took on the journey with some speculation focusing on the Delaware River.[20]

"One may still venture a reconstructed scene of that well-timed departure in its forest setting of early spring awakening," wrote historian Frank E. Lichtenthaeler in the 1940s. "They were a stalwart folk, ever hopeful and of unyielding will to do, that storm blown seed of Schoharie. They faced an undertaking of untold hazard and staked upon it all they had and those best loved."[21]

The reality of the early years for the Palatines was messier. Once again they lacked title to their new homes while the Penn family, colonial secretary James Logan and the Delaware engaged in maneuvers over the ownership of the land. At one point, the elderly Dela-

Conrad Weiser Homestead (Pennsylvania Historical and Museum Commission/Kyle Weaver)

ware leader Sassoonan complained the Palatines were settled on land that hadn't been paid for.

The Penns' 1732 land purchase from the Delaware and agreements between the Palatine settlers and Logan settled the matter until the French and Indian War broke out 23 years later. French-allied Delaware warriors conducted numerous raids in the area during that war.[22]

Weiser built a stone house near the southern end of the Tulpehocken Path, the trail to the multi-ethnic Native American village at Shamokin that was an important stopping point for his diplomatic journeys. The homestead and grounds at the foot of Eagle Peak near modern Womelsdorf, Pa., are maintained as a state historic site.

Destination London: Native American Leaders Feted There

On several notable occasions during the 18th century, Native American leaders from British-friendly nations visited London where they met the King or Queen, visited the city's sights and entertainments and were celebrated in song and portrait.

The first time happened when three Mohawk sachems and one Mahican sachem, or kings as they were called, arrived in London in 1710 on a diplomatic trip to forge stronger ties with the British and enlist support for a colonial assault on French-held Quebec.

They were Hendrick, Brant, John and Etowaucum. Peter Schuyler, the Mayor of Albany, accompanied them on the transatlantic journey.

The four kings had an audience with Queen Anne where they asked her to provide military support for the Quebec expedition. They presented Queen Anne with wampum and she in return presented them with a set of communion plates.

The kings traveled along the Thames River on the Queen's barge, saw a review of the Guards, watched a performance of Shakespeare's play *Macbeth* and were the honored guests at several banquets. The kings were escorted by crowds of Londoners on their visits and welcomed by Pennsylvania founder William Penn living his final years in his native country.[23]

Queen Anne commissioned portraits of them attired in regal Western clothing. "For all the appearances, it was not enough to be Indians: the essential characteristic of the four Indian kings in these contexts was that they be kings. They were treated as agents of state power and clients of the crown, roles Native Americans had never before been asked to play for an English audience," wrote historian Eric Hinderaker.[24]

The failure of an expedition to take Quebec in 1709 had prompted the visit; in 1711 another bungled invasion of Quebec sowed doubts about British resolve. But Queen Anne followed through on promises to build Fort Hunter and the Queen Anne Chapel for use by the Mohawk. Historic signs at modern Fort Hunter, NY, mark the site.

Twenty years later, it was the turn of the Cherokees to receive honors during a visit to London. The visit in 1730 affirmed an alliance between the Cherokees, the largest of the southern Native American tribes, and the British. The alliance had its roots when the Cherokees helped North Carolina troops defeat the Tuscarora in 1713.

Seven prominent Cherokees went on the transatlantic journey, including Attakullakulla, or Little Carpenter, who later fought against the British. They met with King George II at Windsor Castle, visited the Tower of London, Westminster Abbey and Parliament, and like their Mohawk predecessors, were followed by large crowds. They signed articles of agreement spelling out trade rules, guaranteeing white men accused of crimes in Cherokee lands a trial in English court and defining military obligations.[25]

When a Cherokee delegation returned to London in 1762, the world had changed dramatically. The Cherokees had sent warriors in 1758 to fight for the British on the Pennsylvania frontier during the French and Indian War; within several years the Cherokees were fighting the British in their own southern Appalachian homeland. The war went badly for the Cherokees and they sued for peace in 1761.

The 1762 visit was an impromptu event. Visiting Virginia's capital at Williamsburg with a Cherokee delegation, the negotiator Ostenaco saw a portrait of King George III and expressed a desire to meet him. Virginia Gov. William Francis Fauquier made the arrangements and Ostenaco and several others sailed for England within a matter of weeks.[26] There they met King George III, saw the London attractions and were painted in a group portrait by Sir Joshua Reynolds.

"They (Cherokees) were struck with the youth, person, and grandeur of his Majesty, and conceived as great an opinion of his affability as of his power, the greatness of which may be seen on my telling them what manner to behave; for finding Ostenaco preparing his pipe to smoak with his Majesty, according to the Indian custom of declaring friendship, I told him he must neither shake hands or smoak with the King, as it was an honour for the greatest of our nation to kiss his hand," wrote British Lt. Henry Timberlake who accompanied them.[27]

When the Mohawk leader Joseph Brant visited London for a six-month period in 1775-76, he sought British help to protect Mohawk lands from rebellious American colonists. Brant went with a group of loyalists, including Guy Johnson, seeking to keep his job as Superintendent of Indian Affairs.

Brant met with King George III and had discussions with government leaders about using his influence to line up Iroquois support to help put down the rebellion. Like others before him, Brant was introduced into the top layers of society and posed dramatically in war garb with a tomahawk for painter George Romney.[28]

Cadwallader Colden and Jane Colden

Cadwallader Colden has much in common with Benjamin Franklin. Both were active in public affairs and politics. They were accomplished writers and made significant contributions to science in the 18th century. Both men knew each other and corresponded over the years. Yet Franklin is remembered today as a Founding Father of the American Republic while Colden is consigned as a relic of the colonial era. Colden's scientific interests extended to the study and cultivation of plants. His daughter Jane is recognized as the first female botanist in America.

Colden (1688-1776) is also known for a historical work *The History of the Five Indian Nations Depending on the Province of New-York in America*. This book examines the role of the Iroquois Confederacy in holding the balance of power between New France and the American colonies up to 1688. Colden's position as surveyor-general for New York gave him insight into the Iroquois' strategic position.

He surveyed land in the Mohawk River Valley and accompanied New York Gov. William Burnet in 1721 to a meeting with Iroquois leaders there. He drew a map of the Five Nations indicating the lands of each member nation in 1724.

In 1727, Colden's history of the Iroquois was published and today it's considered a classic of early American literature. It was one of several regional histories of the early American colonies published in that period. Colden describes how the Confederacy worked:

> "Each Nation is an absolute Republick by its self, govern'd in all Publick Affairs of War and Peace by the Sachems or Old Men, whose Authority and Power is gain'd and consists wholly in the Opinion the rest of the Nation have of their Wisdom and Integrity."[30]

He recognized the importance of Onondaga to the Confederacy.

"Their affairs of Great Consequence, which concern all the Nations, are Transacted in a General Meeting of the Sachems of every Nation. These Conventions are generally held at Onondaga, which is nearly in the center of all the Five Nations."[31]

Son of a Scots-Irish Presbyterian minister, Colden was a graduate of the University of Edinburgh. He emigrated to America in 1710. His appointment as New York Surveyor-General led to a post on the governor's council where he engaged in the political controversies of colonial New York. Colden finished his public service as Lieutenant Governor of New York from 1761-76, but he was a staunch loyalist and tossed aside by the revolutionary currents during the last few years of his life.

Starting in the 1720s, Colden built an estate called Coldengham at the edge of the frontier near modern Montgomery west of the Hudson River. Here he wrote scientific papers on medicine and physics and classified plants according to the classification system

Left: Cadwallader Colden (Library of Congress Prints and Photographs Division http://hdl.loc.gov/loc.pnp/cph.3a05862.jpg)

Right: Bishop Cammerhoff grave, Bethlehem, PA (Author)

devised by the famous Swedish botanist Carl Linneaus. Colden also built a small canal on his property and was an early advocate for what eventually became the Erie Canal.

Colden corresponded on matters of scientific interest with Franklin; Pennsylvania official James Logan; Peter Collinson, a leading British botanist; American naturalists John and William Bartram; Johann Friedrich Gronovius, a Dutch botanist; and Peter Kalm, a Swedish naturalist and protege of Linnaeus, who toured North America from 1747 to 1751.[32] Kalm visited Coldengham and refers to Colden's scientific observations in a journal of his travels.

Jane Colden (1724-66) benefited from these contacts. John Bartram, the father of American botany, looked at her botanical notes during a visit and corresponded with her about various plants.

Jane Colden learned botany at Coldengham under her father's tutelage. He translated the Latin writings of Linneaus into English for her. Jane engaged in the practice of exchanging seeds and plant specimens with those in the botany field. She wrote a work using Linnaeus' system to describe and draw more than 300 plants found in New York. The manuscript is preserved at The British Museum.

Jane Colden sought knowledge from Native Americans about the medicinal uses of native plants found around Coldengham.[33] She was most active in her botanical pursuits during the 1750s before her marriage at the decade's end. She died relatively young at age 42 and her contributions were only rediscovered in the late 19th century.

Jane Colden is getting more recognition for her botanical achievements in recent years. A natural plant sanctuary in her name has been established at Knox Headquarters State Historic Site in Vails Gate, N.Y.

Canasatego

For at least a decade, Canasatego was the chief spokesman for the Iroquois Confederacy at the treaty proceedings, councils and negotiations that marked the world of diplomacy between the Haudenosaunee and the colonies of New York, Pennsylvania, Maryland and Virginia.

Canasatego (?-1750) lived at Onondaga, the traditional seat of the Confederacy. We actually have a good description of him provided by Witham Marshe, a Maryland official who kept a journal of the 1744 Treaty of Lancaster.

> "The first of these sachems (or chiefs) was a tall, well-made man, had a very full chest and tawny limbs. He had a manly countenance, mixed with a good-natured smile. He was about sixty years of age, very active, strong, and had a surprising liveliness in his speech."[34]

Canasatego is remembered as an orator. He is the subject of considerable debate among historians. His speeches at various councils about the role of the Delaware in relation to the Iroquois and the nature of the Iroquois Confederacy have come in for plenty of interpretation. It should be noted that Conrad Weiser and other provincials interpreted Canasatego's speeches. We don't hear his actual voice.

In 1742 at Philadelphia, Canasatego ordered the Delaware to vacate territory at the Forks of the Delaware supposedly sold to the Penn family as part of the infamous Walking Purchase in 1737. He said the Iroquois had made women of the Delaware, and therefore, they couldn't sell land. He told them to relocate to Shamokin or the Wyoming Valley, both areas outside the French orbit of influence.

Canasatego's directive was in line with the alliance between the Iroquois and Pennsylvania. The diplomatically isolated Delaware complied, but resentment at the loss of the land led to their joining the French in attacks on Pennsylvania border settlements in 1755.

Canasatego's use of the word women here, viewed as pejorative by colonial listeners, didn't accurately reflect the relationship between the two tribes. Historian Francis Jennings describes this as more of an uncle-nephew relationship using the Native American lexicon.[35]

The next year, Weiser, Shikellamy, John Bartram and Lewis Evans went on a diplomatic journey to Onondaga to ease tensions resulting from a backwoods skirmish in Virginia. Weiser described a private sidebar meeting with Canasatego in the midst of several conferences with Iroquois chiefs:

> "I with Shikellimo visited Canasatego, desired him to meet Us in the Bushes to have a private Discourse, which he approved of. We met a little way distant from the Town; I brought with me my Instructions and the Wampums I had, and told him that as he was our particular Friend and well acquainted both with Indians, & white People's Affairs and Customs, I would tell him all my Business, and beg his Advice how to speak to everything when the Council should be met. He assured me of his good will and Affection to the Governor of Pennsylvania and all his People, and that he would do for me what lay in his power."[36]

The Lancaster Treaty of 1744 gave Canasatego his greatest stage yet. He attracted the attention of Marshe as he led more than 200 Iroquois, including families, in a procession to the county courthouse. The Treaty reaffirmed the Iroquois-Pennsylvania alliance even as King George's War broke out between Great Britain and France.

Yet, that war only deepened British-French rivalry over the Ohio Valley and led Pennsylvania to cultivate ties with the Mingo and Twightwee who had settled there removed from the Iroquois orbit.

Canasatego is also remembered for a July 4 speech urging the colonies to emulate the Confederacy:

> "We have one Thing further to say, and that is, We heartily recommend Union and a good Agreement between you our Brethren. Never disagree, but preserve a strict Friendship for one another, and thereby you as well as we, will become the stronger. Our wise Forefathers established Union and Amity between the Five Nations; this has made us formidable; this has

give us great Weight and Authority with our neighbouring Nations. We are a powerful Confederacy; and, by your observing the same Methods our wide Forefathers have taken, you will acquire fresh Strength and Power, therefore whatever befalls you, never fall out one with another."[37]

Six years later, as Weiser approached Onondaga on another mission, he received word that Canasatego had died just a few days before. His successor was pro-French and a Roman Catholic convert. There's some speculation that Canasatego was assassinated perhaps by poisoning due to his pro-English views.[38]

Sir William Johnson and the Mohawk River Gateway

The importance of the Mohawk River as a gateway to the interior of the North American continent, to the strategic position of the Iroquois Confederacy and to the contest between Great Britain and France cannot be overstated.

The Mohawk provided the only entrance through the mountainous Appalachian Plateau into the western Plains between Georgia and the St. Lawrence River in Canada, wrote Codman Hislop in *The Mohawk*.[39]

The river flows eastward 110 miles from its start with two streams merging near modern Rome, N.Y., to its junction with the Hudson River north of Albany. The Oneida Carry, a land portage between the Mohawk and Wood Creek, was part of a strategic water route that connected the Mohawk to Oneida Lake and the Oswego River flowing north to Lake Ontario at Oswego, N.Y.

Native Americans long used the Oneida Carry while the Dutch were the first Europeans to encounter it as they looked for fur trade routes. Harmen Meyndertsz van den Bogaert on a Dutch mission to the Iroquois in 1634-35 refers to Oneida Lake and the Oswego River without mentioning either by name.[40]

Above: Johnson Hall (Author)

Right: Sir William Johnson, Major General of the English forces in America (Library of Congress Prints and Photographs Division http://hdl.loc.gov./loc.pnp/cph.3a06347)

The colonial American who best understood the river's importance and shaped events along it for several decades was Sir William Johnson. An Irishman, Johnson (1715-1774) arrived in the Mohawk Valley in 1738 to manage the landholdings of his uncle. He quickly mastered the fur trade due to his willingness to adopt Mohawk customs and learn their language. His Mohawk name was Warrahijagey ("he who does much").

Johnson's trading activities took him often to the English post established at Oswego in 1727 as a counter to French Fort Niagara.

These ties led to Johnson becoming Indian agent for the province of New York.

Johnson eventually became the largest landowner in the Mohawk Valley. He built fortified homes first at Fort Johnson and then at Johnson Hall. Both were the nucleus of small settlements and are now maintained as historic sites. Both homes were the site of many important conferences with Native Americans.

The outbreak of the French and Indian War in 1755 made the Mohawk Valley a battleground and speeded Johnson's rise to prominence. He won a victory against a French army at Lake George at a time of demoralizing British defeats on other fronts.

The Rev. John Ogilvie accompanied Johnson during the 1755 Lake George campaign and described in a diary how Johnson used his persuasive powers on the Iroquois. "He first gave them an Historical Acct. of all that had passed between their Ancestors & the Eng-

Fall of Cohoes, of the River Mohawk (The Miriam and Ira D. Wallach Division of Arts, Prints and Photographs: Print Collection, The New York Public Library (1777-1890) https://digitalcollections.nypl.org/items/510d47d9-3do5-a3d9-e040-e300a18064a99))

lish to this date Time: How friendly the English had treated them, & never spilt any of yr. Blood. How faithful yr. Forefathers had been to the Covenant, and how bravely they had distinguished themselves in all yr. Wars," wrote Ogilvie in an entry for June 24, 1755.

> "He likewise repeated the many Acts of Cruelty the French had been Guilty of to yr. Forefathers and how ready the English were in bringing them Succour. Then he shewed them the Encroachments of the French upon his Majesty's Territories, and the barbarous Murder of many of his Subjects. He informed them, that now the King yr. Father was determin'd to assert his Rights, & scourge the French for yr. Cruelty and Breach of Faith: That now he expected they would immediately take up the Hatchet and join us in our intended Expeditions, & that he hoped they would give a speedy & Catagorical Answer."[41]

Johnson rose to his greatest prominence yet with appointment in 1756 as British Superintendent of Indian Affairs.

A French invasion of the British-held Oneida Carry in 1756 led to the fall of Fort Bull guarding one end of the portage. Later that year the French captured a recently built Fort Ontario at Oswego and the English and Dutch settlements along the Mohawk were open to deadly attack. The British reoccupied the Oneida Carry in 1758 and built Fort Stanwix at Rome.

In 1759, Johnson scored one of the war's major victories capturing Fort Niagara at the juncture of Lake Ontario and the Niagara River after a siege.

Johnson faced new diplomatic challenges in the years after the conclusion of that war in 1763. The outbreak of Pontiac's War, a pan-Indian uprising led by the Ottawa Chief Pontiac, was a new threat to British supremacy. Johnson held a council at Fort Niagara in 1764 to bring some of the rebellious tribes, including the Seneca, in Pontiac's War back to the British fold. The Seneca personally ceded islands in the Niagara River above Niagara Falls to Johnson, but he transferred them to the Crown.[42]

In 1768 at Fort Stanwix, several thousand Native Americans from many tribes gathered along with Johnson and provincial governors to draw a boundary line to keep Native American territory separate from newly ceded lands to the colonies. Westward bound settlers ignored the boundary line.

Johnson died suddenly in 1774 while speaking at an Indian conference at Johnson Hall, thereby being spared the impending chaos and destruction to his colonial world brought by the American Revolution.

Rattlesnake Adventures

When Jacob Yaple, Isaac Dumond and Peter Hinepaugh built cabins for their families in 1789 at the site of the future Ithaca, N.Y., they encountered an unwelcome surprise. The Hinepaugh cabin at the head of Cayuga Lake was in an area infested with rattlesnakes.

The newcomers killed thirty rattlesnakes in the vicinity and then found several more snakes on the floor of the completed cabin that were then killed. That night a bonfire was built with one person staying around to watch for snakes. The next day the settlers discovered a snake den nearby and killed a great many more.[43]

The three veterans of the Revolutionary War endured many hardships to travel from Kingston, N.Y., to their new home, but they like many 18th-century travelers remembered the plentitude of rattlesnakes on the frontier. Encounters with rattlesnakes highlight the travel journals of the era. Some frontiersmen wore leggings to guard their legs from bites. Benjamin Franklin popularized the defiant rattlesnake in 1775 as a symbol of America.

On a diplomatic journey to Onondaga in 1743, the naturalist John Bartram used his skills to describe the death of a rattlesnake blocking his path near the top of a ridge:

Rattlesnake Natural History of Carolina, Florida and the Bahama Islands (v2. Tab 46 Mark Catesby. The Public Domain Review. Publicdomainreview.org)

"At this place we were warned by a well known alarm to keep our distance from an enraged rattlesnake that had put himself in a coiled posture of defence within a dozen yards of our path, but we punished his rage by striking him dead on the spot. He had been highly irritated by an Indian dog that had barked eagerly at him but was cunning enough to keep out of his reach, or nimble enough to avoid the snake when he sprung at him. We took notice that while provoked, he contracted the muscles of the scales so as to appear very bright and shining, but after the mortal stroke his splendor become much diminished."[44]

"We named the mountains on this side of the Susquehanna *Snake Mountain*, because we saw snakes in great numbers lying on the stones and rocks near the shore, basking in the sun," wrote Moravian Bishop John Christopher Frederick Cammerhoff during a 1750 journey to Onondaga.[45]

The famed hunter Philip Tome (1758-1814) devoted a whole chapter to the danger from rattlesnakes in his classic *Pioneer Life or Thirty Years a Hunter* published in 1854. Like those Ithaca settlers, Tome described how he helped build fires to keep rattlesnakes away from his father's cabin in Pine Creek Valley in northcentral Pennsylvania.

In 1816 while living near Cornplanter's Town on the Allegheny River, Tome had a conversation with the Seneca chief Cornplanter about coping with rattlesnakes:

"He said all the traveling in summer had to be done in canoes, on account of them. The way they destroyed them was to burn the woods in the same manner as we did…When they were obliged to lie out at night in a place which was infested by rattlesnakes, they drove four crotches into the ground, upon which they placed poles, and across which these they laid pieces of bark. In this manner they avoided sleeping on the ground."[46]

On a tour of America and Canada in the 1790s, Isaac Weld Jr. showed a fascination with rattlesnakes that he observed infesting the islands in Lake Erie:

"Two kinds of rattlesnakes are found in this part of the country; the one is of a deep brown colour, clouded with yellow, and is seldom met with more than thirty inches in length. It usually frequents marshes and low meadows, where it does great mischief amongst cattle, which it bites mostly in the lips as they are grazing."[47]

Franklin wrote about the rattlesnake as a symbol in 1775 in the *Pennsylvania Journal*.

"I observed in one of the drums belonging to the marines now raising, there was painted a Rattle-Snake, with the modest motto under it, 'Don't tread on me.'"

He recounted how a rattlesnake's eye excelled in brightness. The rattlesnake doesn't attack until giving notice even to her enemy, wrote Franklin, saying this represents magnanimity and true courage.

"Was I wrong, Sir, in thinking this a strong picture of the temper and conduct of America?" he asked.[48]

Endnotes

1. Paul A. W. Wallace, *Indian Paths of Pennsylvania* (Harrisburg: The Pennsylvania Historical and Museum Commission, 1971), 5-6.
2. Rev. Wm. M. Beauchamp, ed., *Moravian Journals Relating to Central New York, 1745-1766* (Bowie, MD: Heritage Books, Inc., 1999), 10.
3. John Bartram, Lewis Evans and Conrad Weiser, *A Journey from Pennsylvania to Onondaga in 1743* (Barre, MA: The Imprint Society, 1973), 110.
4. Ibid., 59.
5. Paul A. W. Wallace, *Conrad Weiser Friend of Colonist and Mohawk* (New York: Russell & Russell, 1971), 89.
6. William C. Reichel, *Memorials of the Moravian Church* (Philadelphia: The Moravian Book Association, J.B. Lippincott & Son, 1870), 95-96.
7. Wallace, *Conrad Weiser*, op cit., 116.
8. Robert B. Swift, *By Great Rivers Lives on the Appalachian Frontier* (Charlestown, SC: America Through Time, 2019), 36.
9. Bartram, Evans and Weiser, op cit., 61-62.
10. Beauchamp, op cit., 30.
11. Ibid., 46.
12. Ibid., 53.
13. Helga Doblin and William A. Starna, eds., *The Journal of Christian Daniel Claus and Conrad Weiser: A Journey to Onondaga, 1750* (Philadelphia: The American Philosophical Society, 1994), 42.
14. Wallace, *Conrad Weiser*, op cit., 211.
15. Fred R. Wolcott, *Onondaga Portrait of a Native People* (Syracuse: Syracuse University Press and Everson Museum of Art, 1986), 17.
16. Richard Berleth, *Bloody Mohawk The French and Indian War & American Revolution on New York's Frontier* (Hensonville, NY: Black Dome Press Corp., 2009), 272.
17. Wolcott, op cit., 20-21.
18. Frederick S. Weiser, ed. *John Friederich Weiser's Buch Containing The Autobiography of JOHN CONRAD WEISER (1696-1760)* (Hanover, PA: The John Conrad Weiser Family Association, 1976), 49.
19. Ibid., 29.
20. John W. and Martha B. Harper, "The Palatine Migration-1723 from Schoharie to Tulpehocken," 1723-1973 Anniversary Magazine of the Tulpehocken, *Historical Review of Berks County* (Womelsdorf: The Tulpehocken Settlement Historical Society, 1973), 39.
21. Frank E. Lichtenthaeler, "Overland Barriers of the Susquehanna Corridor," 1723-1973

Anniversary Magazine of the Tulpehocken, *Historical Review of Berks County* (Womelsdorf: The Tulpehocken Settlement Historical Society, 1973), 32-33.

22. Francis Jennings, "Incident at Tulpehocken," *Pennsylvania History* Vol. XXXV, Nov. 4 (October 1968), 335-355.

23. Morris Bishop, "Four Indian Kings in London," *American Heritage* Vol. XX111, Number 1 (December 1971), 62-65.

24. Eric Hinderaker, "The 'Four Indian Kings and the Imaginative Construction of the First British Empire," *The William and Mary Quarterly* Vol. 53, no. 3 (July 1996), Sept. 5, 2022 accessed. https://www.jstor.org. 494.

25. Grace Steele Woodward, *The Cherokees* (Norman and London: University of Oklahoma Press, 1963), 64-66.

26. Ibid., 80-82.

27. Duane H. King, ed., *The Memoirs of Lt. Henry Timberlake The Story of a Soldier, Adventurer and Emissary to the Cherokees, 1756-1765* (Cherokee, NC: Museum of the Cherokee Press, 2007), 71-72.

28. Isabel Thompson Kelsay, *Joseph Brant 1743-1807 Man of Two Worlds* (Syracuse, NY: Syracuse University Press, 1984), 167-69.

29. Seymour I. Schwartz, *Cadwallader Colden A Biography* (Amherst, NY: Humanity Books, 2013), 35-36.

30. Cadwallader Colden, *The History of the Five Indian Nations* (Cornell University Press, 1964), xx.

31. Ibid., xx.

32. Schwartz. op cit., 44.

33. Beatrice Scheer Smith, "Jane Colden (1724-1766) and Her Botanic Manuscript," *American Journal of Botany* Volume 75, No. 7 (July 1988), 1090-96.

34. Witham Marshe, *Journal of the treaty at Lancaster in 1744, with the six Nations.* William Henry Egle, ed. (Lancaster, Pa.: The New Era Steam and Job Print, 1884) April 11, 2023 accessed. https://www.loc.gov. 12.

35. Jennings, op cit., 344.

36. Bartram, Evans and Weiser, op cit., 116.

37. James M. Merrell, ed., *The Lancaster Treaty of 1744* (Boston and New York: Bedford/St. Martin's, 2008), 85-86.

38. William A. Pencak and Daniel K. Richter, eds., *Friends and Enemies in Penn's Woods* (University Park, PA: The Pennsylvania State University Press, 2004), 162.

39. Codman Hislop, *The Mohawk* (New York and Toronto: Rinehart & Company, Inc., 1948), 3.

40. Charles T. Gehring and William A. Starna, eds., *A Journey into Mohawk and Oneida Country, 1634-1635* (Syracuse, NY: Syracuse University Press, 1988), 12-13.

41. Milton W. Hamilton, ed., "The Diary of Reverend John Ogilvie, 1750-1759," *The Bulletin of the Fort Ticonderoga Museum*, Volume X, No. 5 (February 1961), 354.

42. Lloyd Graham, *Niagara Country* (New York: Duell, Sloan & Pearce, 1949), 61-62.

43. Yaple family documents.

44. Bartram, Evans and Weiser, op cit., 30-31.

45. Beauchamp, op cit., 28.

46. Philip Tome, *Pioneer Life or Thirty Years a Hunter* (Mechanicsburg, PA: Stackpole Books, 2006), 35.

47. Isaac Weld Junior, *Travels Through the States of North America and the Provinces of Upper & Lower Canada*, Volume II (New York: Augustus M. Kelley Publishers, 1970), 162.

48. J. A. Leo Lemay, ed., *Benjamin Franklin Writings* (NY: The Library of America, 1987), 744-46.

CHAPTER 3

Squatters in the Susquehanna River Valley

A confiscated surveyor's compass symbolized the tensions between colonial agents and land squatters on Pennsylvania's frontier during the 18th century. The year was 1741 and Pennsylvania officials were preparing to draw the boundaries for the Manor of Maske at the Scots-Irish settlement of Marsh Creek west of modern Gettysburg. Pennsylvania proprietor Thomas Penn had directed them to reserve a 30,000-acre land tract for use by his family in the midst of the Marsh Creek Settlement.

The surveyors encountered two dozen angry and armed settlers determined to stop the land survey. The settlers believed establishing the manor would make it more expensive for them to secure legal title to their land. One of them, Thomas Hosack (or Hooswik), seized one of the surveyors' tools of the trade—a compass—and threatened to stop the party from using their chain as well.[1]

During the 18th century, a compass was used to measure horizontal angles in order to determine the corner boundaries in a land parcel. The Gunter's chain, consisting of brass rings, links and steel pins, was used to mark a line of latitude.

The Pennsylvania officials retreated after this altercation. In a letter to Proprietor Thomas Penn, Deputy Surveyor General Zachary Butcher described the precarious situation he was in:

"I was designed about two weeks ago to have Laid out the Manor at Marsh Creek, but the Inhabitants are got into such Terms, That it is as much as man's life to go amongst them, for they gather'd together in companies, and go in Arms every Time they Expect I am anywhere near about, with full resolution to kill or cripple, me, or any other person, who shall attempt to Lay out a mannor there."[2]

The stalemate over land ownership at Marsh Creek lasted for decades.

In the 1750s, Provincial Secretary Richard Peters and Surveyor General William Parsons headed another surveying party that also met with resistance from Marsh Creek settlers. They broke the chain as it was being laid out.

In 1754, Deputy Surveyor George Stevenson in a letter to Peters warned at the potential for more broken surveyor's instruments at the hands of Marsh Creek settlers:

> "if I were to ask information of any of the Inhabitants; they would immediately suspect my Intentions, & probably use me ill, or break some of my Instruments, as they did to you and Mr. Parsons formerly..."[3]

Marsh Creek is not the only case where squatters tangled with authorities on the Pennsylvania frontier during the 18th century.

Tomb of James Agnew who disrupted Marsh Creek survey. (Author)

These land disputes cropped up continually triggered by the desire of Scots-Irish, German, English and other European immigrants to homestead on land that could be obtained cheaper than in the more settled parts of southeastern Pennsylvania, the need to placate Native Americans wary of intrusions by white settlers onto lands they viewed as their own and the govern-

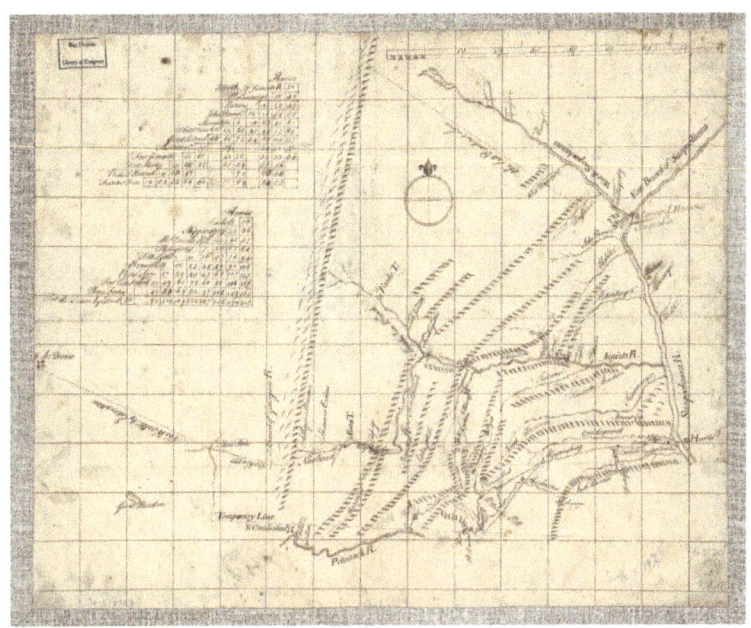

Top: John Armstrong's rough draft of the country to the west of Susquehanna. (Library of Congress Geography and Map Division http://hdl.loc.gov/loc.gmd/g3820.ar130300)

Bottom: Marsh Creek Cemetery west of Gettysburg, PA (Author)

ing Penn family's often confused land policies brought upon by archaic notions of landlord-tenant relationships.

Land squatters put down roots in the bottomland of the river valleys and alongside the trails that served as transportation networks through the densely forested Appalachian Ridge and Valley landscape. They often advanced beyond the westward boundaries of the land deals that William Penn and his sons reached with Native Americans in stages until the eve of the American Revolution.

The colonists and Native Americas held different conceptions of what land ownership meant. This greatly aggravated tensions on the frontier. The colonists thought of possessing land with deeds and fixed boundaries. They believed those legal mechanisms gave them the right to do what they wanted with a land parcel.

Native Americans generally thought of land in terms of communal use with respect for hunting rights and passageway rights. They would relocate villages to suit the season (no chilly winter winds along riverbanks for them) and to places where soil wasn't worn out from years of crop plantings.

The Penn family's practice of dealing with the Iroquois on land sales starting in the 1730s, rather than the less powerful Delaware actually inhabiting the land, generated friction. The 1737 Walking Purchase at the Forks of the Delaware River bred resentments that led the Delaware to ally with New France twenty years later in the French and Indian War.

William Penn viewed his royal grant of Pennsylvania in semi-feudal terms. He invited the Palatine Germans fleeing decades of war and religious persecution, the Scots-Irish fleeing privation in Ulster and French Hugenots fleeing Catholic France to settle in Pennsylvania.

Penn as the colony's proprietor planned to charge these settlers rent. He also transported the feudal concept of manors to Pennsylvania. He reserved thousands of acres of choice land for these manors under his control in which land could be sold on special terms. This would be different terms than the sale of common land on a fixed price per acre.

In all, 80 manors were created in Pennsylvania totaling 600,000 acres, but most existed in name only. None of them developed to their fullest extent with the establishment of manor courts and barons with jurisdiction over property issues. Penn didn't get the rent money he felt was owed him.

Penn established a land office to handle the sale of both common and manor land, but this office basically didn't function from 1718 when William died until 1732 when his son Thomas arrived in Pennsylvania. It took that long to settle legal disputes over Penn's inheritance.

The normal process for legally obtaining land in colonial Pennsylvania involved these steps: 1) Apply for a warrant to have a survey made; 2) A warrant is issued authorizing a survey for a tract of land; 3) The survey determines the boundaries of the land tract and total acreage; and 4) A patent from the Penn family or Pennsylvania government conveys clear title and all rights to a private owner. Not all individuals getting a warrant took the step of getting a land patent.

Land disputes arose between squatters and the Penn family over two reasons: objections to the manorial policy and the desire to settle on lands west of the Susquehanna River that were not yet purchased from Native Americans.

As early as 1721, Gov. William Keith issued a proclamation to ban white settlement west of the Susquehanna River and ordered removal of several settlers already there so as not to encroach on Native American hunting grounds. However, Keith's action didn't stop Maryland inhabitants from moving into the trans-Susquehanna territory, a subject of boundary dispute between the governing Penn and Calvert families.

In 1722 at a conference with the Conestoga and Shawnee at Conestoga, Keith won acceptance for his proposal to create Springettsbury Manor, named for Penn's grandson Springett Penn, on the

Susquehanna River's west bank. Keith said the manor would create a barrier to both illegal Pennsylvania and Maryland settlers, but it didn't prove a useful deterrent any more than a proclamation did.[4]

A decade later the Penn heirs faced another headache with squatters at the Conestoga Manor on the east side of the Susquehanna River. Conestoga Manor had been established in 1719 to keep prime farmland in the hands of the Penns and also provide a haven for the dwindling Conestoga tribe.

Scots-Irish settlers flooded into the region in search of cheaper land. The Provincial Secretary James Logan first steered them to the Donegal area north of Conestoga. He wanted to create a frontier stronghold to ward off incursions by Marylanders and eventually by the French from the Ohio Country.

In 1727 Logan wrote a letter to James Steel outlining his views on this matter:

> "I therefore thought it might be prudent to plant a Settlem of such men as those who formerly had so bravely defended Derry & Inniskillen (Ulster Protestants) as a frontier in case of any Disturbance."[5]

By the end of 1730, however, Logan learned that other Scots-Irish who were part of a continuing wave of migration from Ulster had illegally occupied the Conestoga Manor. He directed the sheriff of newly established Lancaster County and local magistrates to evict them.

Writing to John Penn in early 1731, Logan said,

> "December last a body of Irish were resolved all together to settle Conestogoe Mannor by force alleging that it was against the Laws of God and Nature that so much Land should be idle while so many Christians wanted it to labour on and raise their Bread. We took measures effectually to defeat their purpose & by the Sherif of that County with a sufficient force had pulled down & burnt about 30 of their structures."[6]

In addition to Conestoga Manor, provincial authorities faced new problems with squatters west of the Susquehanna River. Native Americans were vocal about white squatters on the west side of the Susquehanna. Captain Civility, the spokesman for the Conestoga tribe, relayed a message through an interpreter expressing his displeasure in October 1731 during a meeting in Lancaster.

"That William Penn had promis'd them (the Conestoga) they Should Not be Distrubed, by any Settlers on the West side of Susquehanah, but now, Contrary thereto, Several Marylanders are Settled by the River at that side, at Conejohela; and One Crissop, is Very Abusive to them when they pass that way," wrote Surveyor Samuel Blunston about Civility's complaint.[7]

Pennsylvania authorities eventually captured Marylander Thomas Cresap after a skirmish at his west shore cabin in 1736. Pennsylvania and Maryland agreed on a temporary border in 1738 and the Mason-Dixon survey mapped a final boundary in 1765.

In November 1731, Blunston wrote Shawnee leader Peter Chartier about his plan to lay out a tract of land on the west shore between Conodoguinet Creek and Yellow Breeches Creek in modern Cumberland County to "accommodate the Shawnee or such others who may think it fit to settle there."

He added: "And we have also orders to Dispossess all Persons Settled on that side the River, That Those woods may Remain free to ye Indians for Planting & Hunting."[8]

The Shawnee moved west instead. Starting in 1734 Blunston issued nearly 300 licenses, a pre-step to getting a warrant, to settlers in the area while the Penns negotiated another land sale with the Iroquois.

The Juniata River was another Susquehanna tributary that attracted squatters. The first were Germans from the Mohawk Valley in New York. Frederick Staring or Starns and a small group settled at Big Juniata at modern Mexico, Pa., in 1741.

Delaware spokesmen complained the Staring group had settled

on good hunting grounds and they were pressured to leave two years later. But new squatters came to the area. In 1749 Pennsylvania Indian negotiator Conrad Weiser wrote to authorities:

> "the Indians are very uneasy about the white people Setling beyond the Endless mountains on Joniady (Juniata), on Sherman's Creek and else where; they tell me that above 30 families are settled upon the Indians' land this spring, and dayly more goes to setle thereon; some have setled all most to the heads of the Jonaidy River along the path that leads to Ohio; the Indian says, (and that with truth,) that that Country is their only Hunting ground for dears..."[9]

The best documented of the squatter disputes in Pennsylvania in terms of the individuals being evicted or dispossessed of their land stakes occurred at the Manor of Maske in 1741 and during the Burnt Cabins affair in 1750. We know the names of the settlers who disrupted the surveyor's work at the Manor of Maske. We know the reactions of some of the evicted settlers as recorded by provincial officials at Burnt Cabins.

The circumstances behind the standoff at the Manor of Maske in 1741 are much different from the Conestoga evictions a decade earlier. In the former case, settlers crossed the Susquehanna River and settled in the Marsh Creek area. The Penn family had struck a deal with the Iroquois in 1736 to purchase land west of the Susquehanna River and east of the Blue Mountain barrier.

The Penns urged mainly Scots-Irish homesteaders to settle at Marsh Creek. They started to filter in between 1736 and 1741. The Scots-Irish believed they would be able to purchase their land tracts on common terms.

When Thomas Penn ordered his surveyors to establish the 30,000-acre Manor of Maske in the midst of their settlement, the settlers stopped them believing they would either lose their land or end up paying a much higher price for it through a manor sale.[10]

In the ensuing years, the settlers wouldn't budge and the Penns lacked the manpower to complete the survey and drive them out. The names of 29 Marsh Creek settlers are listed in the Pennsylvania Archives under the heading "settlers at Marsh Creek who obstructed ye survey." Next to Thomas Hooswick's name is the notation "declared if ye Chain be spread again he wou'd stop it and then took ye Compass from ye Surv. Gen."[11]

Logan sounded a familiar theme in a 1743 letter written to the proprietors from his seat at Stenton in modern Germantown. After denigrating the Scots-Irish, Logan urged a policy of benign neglect while expressing hope the settlers would eventually turn against each other.

> "As to the Mannor of Maske, It is pretty full of ye poorest soil of ye Irish, who declare themselves determined to keep possession & prevent a Mannor being run out, & considering our present inability to enforce ye execution of ye civil power, & ye pains taken to propagate & improve a factious Spirit in ye People, it may be not amiss to suffer them to feel ye Inconvenience of Lawless force a little longer, for they begin to practice it upon one another...."[12]

Logan's wishful timeline of a "little longer" lasted a dozen years. In 1765, Gov. John Penn and the Marsh Creek settlers reached an agreement where the survey could proceed in return for allowing residents who settled on tracts prior to 1741 to purchase the land on common terms. But litigation over some land titles dragged on until 1802.[13]

With Native American complaints over land encroachment increasing, provincial authorities resolved in 1750 to take a coordinated approach to evict squatters in order to avert a war. Secretary Peters, Weiser, a sheriff and six magistrates from the newly formed Cumberland County and two sons of the late Iroquois spokesman Shikellamy traveled to a half-dozen locations west of the Susquehanna. They evicted squatters, burned some of their cabins to discourage a return and read legal charges against them.

Peters wrote a report of their activities for Gov. James Hamilton providing a look from an official standpoint of how things went. The first stop was at Big Juniata where they took William White, David Hiddleston and George Cohoon into custody while George and William Calloway escaped. The two called out, "You may take our Land and Houses and do what you please with them, we deliver them to you with all our Hearts, but we will not be carried to Goal," according to Peters. The Calloway cabin was burned.[14]

Andrew Lycon figures prominently in Peters' account. He wasn't home when the party stopped at his cabin and White, Hiddleston and Cohoon agreed to put up a bond to secure Lycon's eventual appearance in court.

Peters caught up with Lycon the next day on May 24:

"he presenting a loaded Gun to the Magistrates and Sheriff said he would shoot the first man that dar'd to come nigher. On this he was disarm'd convicted and committed to the Custody of the Sheriff. This whole Transaction happened in the Sight of a Tribe of Indians who by Accident had in the Night-time fixed their Tent on that Plantation, and Lycon's Behavior giving them great Offence the Shickealamies insisted on our burning the Cabbin or they would burn it themselves. Whereupon, when every thing was taken out of it (Andrew Lycon all the while assisting) and Possession being deliver'd to me, the empty Cabbin was set on Fire by the Under-Sheriff and then Lycon was carried to Gaol."[15]

Similar encounters played out with squatters living at the mouth of the Juniata River, Sherman's Creek, Path Valley, Aughwick and the Big Cove. On the west side of Tuscarora Mountain, many settlements were found and "some ordinary Log Houses to the number of eleven were burned to the Ground -- the Trespassers, most of them cheerfully and a very few of them with reluctance carrying out all their Goods," wrote Peters.[16] The name of the modern town of Burnt Cabins on Route 522 in Fulton County refers to this event.

Peters went to lengths to help the evicted squatters allowing them to stay temporarily on his properties (he was a major land speculator) and giving them money so they could resettle on purchased lands. In the end a few burnt cabins didn't stop the squatters from moving further westward as the Pennsylvania frontier receded. A new concept known as settlement rights made it easier for a squatter who had improved his land to make first claim as a purchaser.

There would be pauses in the land rush during the French and Indian War and the American Revolution. Yet the quest for new and cheap land would continue unabated as a new nation supplanted the Penn proprietorship. The revolutionary government divested the Penn family of their vast lands in 1779 while allowing them to keep ownership of unsold Manor land.

Scots-Irish Emigrants Drawn to Limestone Springs

A line of Presbyterian churches built beside limestone springs denotes the migration of the Scots-Irish beyond the eastern seaboard into the Great Valley of Pennsylvania and Virginia during the 18th century. Their sturdy stone churches situated along an arc south of the Blue Mountain range are a testament to the strongly held religious beliefs of the Scots-Irish, the name for the lowland Scottish natives who embarked on three great migrations in the 17th and 18th centuries.

The first migration starting in the first decades of the 17th century went from Scotland to Ulster in northern Ireland as part of King James I's resettlement scheme to supplant the Gaelic Irish. The second migration from Ulster to America started in 1718 as land-hungry Scots-Irish reacted to rising land rents in Ulster and other economic problems.

Donegal Church spring (Author)

Pennsylvania was an early destination for many of these emigrants. They pushed westward from Philadelphia into Lancaster County and eventually migrated south along the Great Valley into Virginia and the Carolinas.

The Scots-Irish brought with them their Presbyterian religion offering an independent outlook and strict morality that often placed them at odds with the established Anglican Church. They often moved in search of better land to farm or herd animals. This practice sometimes earned them the appellation of squatters when they didn't obtain legal ownership of a tract.

In Pennsylvania, the Donegal Presbyterian Church in Lancaster County; Derry Presbyterian Church and Paxton Presbyterian Church in Dauphin County; Silver Spring Presbyterian Church, the site of Meeting House Springs Presbyterian Church, Big Spring Presbyterian Church and Middle Spring Presbyterian Church in Cumberland County; and Falling Spring Presbyterian Church in Franklin County are reminders of the Scots-Irish migration.

These springs were a source of fresh water for both humans and domesticated animals. There are numerous large springs in Pennsylvania's Ridge and Valley region discharging water from carbonate rock such as limestone.

Donegal

The spring at Donegal forms a beautiful tree-lined pond just below the 1740 church sanctuary on a hill near modern Mount Joy. The Scots-Irish were steered to Donegal Township in 1721 by Pennsylvania Secretary James Logan. He wanted them to act as a buffer against incursions by the French or attacks by Native Americans against the colony.

The first church thought to be located at the cemetery was made of logs. Donegal is associated with the Lowrey family of fur traders who ventured into the Ohio country—the father Lazarus and sons James, John, Daniel and Alexander. John was killed in a gunpowder explosion in 1749 while trading in the Ohio. James escaped from capture by Native Americans in Kentucky.[17]

Alexander Lowrey Sr. (1727-1805), who partnered with Lancaster fur trader Joseph Simon and merchant Barnard Gratz, is buried at Donegal. He was a guide on the military expeditions of British Gen. John Forbes in 1758 and Col. Henry Bouquet in 1764.

Alexander Lowrey's name is carved on the Donegal monument to Revolutionary War veterans recognizing his service as a battalion commander of the Pennsylvania Militia at Brandywine and other battles. He was a member of the Pennsylvania General Assembly and an early advocate for American independence.[18]

During the American Revolution, worshippers at Donegal Spring gathered around a witness tree outside the church upon learning of a British army invasion of the Philadelphia area in 1777 and pledged support for the American patriots.

Paxton Church (Author)

Paxton

This stone church on a hill in suburban Harrisburg with a nearby spring is several miles east of the Susquehanna River. It's in the vicinity of a Delaware village named Paxtang or Peshtang that existed at the start of the 18th century. The 1740 church building replaced a log church.

The church graveyard surrounded by a stone wall contains the graves of such notables as John Harris Jr., founder of Harrisburg; U.S. Sen. William Maclay, author of a famous congressional diary and the Rev. John Elder (1706-1792), known as the "fighting parson" for his military exploits on the frontier and during the Revolution.

Born and educated in Scotland, Elder was parson for more than 50 years during a defining period for Paxton Presbyterian Church. The frontier community developed a siege mentality because of the onslaught of Native American raids in the area during the French and Indian War and Pontiac's War.

Elder was a colonel of the Paxton Rangers, an authorized provincial force that patrolled the area. He also became a defender or apologist for the Paxton Boys, an offshoot vigilante group of about 50 men that carried out a horrific massacre of the Conestoga Indians in Lancaster in December 1763.

The Paxton Boys first killed a half-dozen defenseless Conestoga at their village and returned two weeks later to kill 14 surviving tribe members who were lodged in the Lancaster jail ostensibly for their own safety.

The Conestoga were a remnant group living in a historic treaty town behind the lines of white settlement during Pontiac's War and their numbers were down to a handful. The Paxton Boys viewed them as a fifth column giving aid to warriors allied with Pontiac.

Elder had urged Gov. John Penn some months prior to move the Conestoga closer to Philadelphia to no avail. He indicated his awareness of plans for an attack while suggesting he tried to prevent it in a letter to Penn after the massacre. In this letter, Elder said the massacre was the culmination of a storm that exploded after gathering for a long time.[19]

A larger group of Paxton Boys marched on Philadelphia two months later with a petition of grievances that included greater representation for frontier counties in the provincial assembly. Benjamin Franklin condemned the Paxton Boys calling them the "Christian White Savages of Peckstang and Donegall!" and debate over their actions has been intense during the 270 years since the event.[20]

The Conestoga massacre was the death knell for William Penn's policy of peaceful coexistence with Native Americans. Conestoga was the scene of treaty conferences between Pennsylvania officials and Native Americans at the start of the 18th century. After 1763, it was known as a massacre site.

Silver Spring Presbyterian Church

During the 1730s the Scots-Irish migration moved west across the Susquehanna River and Silver Spring Presbyterian Church was established to meet the religious need of "The People Over the Susquehanna."

The 1783 stone church, adjoining graveyard and nearby spring stand today near Route 11, the colonial Great Road, north of modern Mechanicsburg, Pa.

James Silver (?-1776) may have crossed the river as early as 1724 as part of a fur trading operation. Silver was appointed in 1735 to a committee that charted the course of the Great Road from Harris Ferry (future Harrisburg) to the Potomac River. It went by Silver's house near the church. Silver was also appointed tax collector, petitioned for the formation of Cumberland County and was captain of a local militia unit. The area saw a few Indian raids during the French and Indian War.[21]

George Croghan, the King of the Traders, operated a nearby fur trade operation with a tannery and blacksmith shop along Conodoguinet Creek during the 1740s. It was near the New Path, a westward trading path crossing the Blue Mountain and Tuscarora Mountain.

Silver Spring Church and spring (Author)

Meeting House Springs

A fieldstone-walled graveyard marks the site of Meeting House Springs Presbyterian Church north of modern Carlisle, Pa. On a spring day with Blue Mountain in view to the north, this is a tranquil spot yet it's being encroached upon by development.

The Meeting House Springs congregation started in the 1730s in a log church built by Scots-Irish settlers. The church was built on a bluff overlooking a spring located on Conodoguinet Creek.

The church's early years were marked by doctrinal splits over qualifications of ministers and continual threats of attack by Native

Right: Grave of Ranald Chambers, road surveyor, Meeting House Springs (Author)

Below: Meeting House Springs Church Cemetery (Author)

Americans during the French and Indian War. Many settlers in the Carlisle area fled east across the Susquehanna River after the first attacks in 1755. Church services were sporadic during this period.

The Meeting House Springs congregation moved to Carlisle in 1758 where a church was built on the town square. The remaining graveyard is surrounded by the wall built in 1860. The inscription on the gravestone of Ranald Chambers (1686-1746) says he was appointed by the court at Lancaster in 1735 to lay out the road leading from Harris Ferry toward the Potomac River. The oldest grave is of Janet Thompson, wife of the church's first minister, who died in 1744.

Big Spring

Big Spring Presbyterian Church is located on a hill overlooking Big Spring, the fifth largest spring in Pennsylvania, at modern Newville, Pa. The present stone church was built in 1789 while a plaque in the graveyard marks the location of the first log church dating to 1737.

The Allegheny Path connecting Philadelphia with the Forks of the Ohio and Delaware village at Kittanning crossed Big Spring Run. Big Spring Run flows into Conodoguinet Creek, a tributary of the Susquehanna River. The circa 1762 Laughlin Mill stands on the east bank of Big Spring.

Most of the first Scots-Irish settlers in this area (then called Great Spring) were holders of Blunston Licenses, issued by Penn family land agent Samuel Blunston in the 1730s for tracts of land. These licenses were a first step in obtaining title to the land once the Penns had purchased this region from Native Americans. The building of the Great Road in the 1750s spurred settlement, too.

The church graveyard contains many marked and unmarked graves. The oldest marked graves date to the Revolutionary War period. Twenty-four veterans of that war as well as church pastors are buried there. The inscription on the grave of William Lusk reads "In memory of William Lusk A soldier of the Revolution. Member of the Order of Cincinnati. He freed his slaves. Died June 1790."

Falling Spring

Falling Spring Presbyterian Church in Chambersburg, Pa., is associated with Benjamin Chambers (1708-1808)—early settler, mill owner, fort builder and founder of Chambersburg. Chambers donated the land for this church overlooking Falling Spring. The current church was built in 1808 and a log church occupied the site in the 1730s.

Chambers built a fortified stockade at the confluence of Falling Spring and Conocacheague Creek in 1756 at the start of the French and Indian War. The stockade enclosed Chambers' residence, a gristmill and water-powered saw. The fort site is marked near an 18-foot waterfall on Falling Spring Creek. On a bluff behind the church is the cemetery with Chambers' grave and tradition holds the graves of Delaware Indians.

Augusta Stone Defiance

The line of Presbyterian Churches beside springs extended south into Virginia and the Carolinas, which also saw westbound Scots-Irish migration. One of them, Augusta Stone Presbyterian Church, is at modern Fort Defiance, Va., in the Shenandoah Valley. This limestone church was built in 1749 atop a hill and has distinctive architectural features including drooping gables.

The Rev. John Craig came to America from Scotland in 1738 and arrived in Virginia's Augusta County in 1740 to lead the Scots-Irish settlers in worship. During the French and Indian War, Craig built a stockade around the church where families could gather for protection from raiding parties. A church museum contains Craig's possessions.[22]

Shamokin Is Magnet for Schuylkill Fur Traders

During the 1720s, licensed Pennsylvania fur traders based on the Schuylkill River in the eastern part of the state expanded their operations to the Susquehanna River and beyond. The 126-mile Schuylkill River was an early gateway to the western waterways and the Native American tribes that lived along them.

Pennsylvania's founder, William Penn, saw the potential of the Schuylkill River describing it as "being a hundred miles boatable above the falls, and its course northeast toward the foundation of the Susquehanna…it is like to be a great part of the settlement of the age" in a letter to the Society of Free Traders in 1683.[23]

Even before Penn, Swedish and Dutch traders had ventured from trading posts on the Schuylkill to trade for beaver pelts from the Minquas or Susquehannock. The pelts were desirable for clothing in Europe.

The fur trade had dramatic impacts on Native American society. The Native Americans neglected agriculture to concentrate on hunting for the animal furs that could be traded for necessities, wrote historian Francis Jennings in "The Indian Fur Trade of the Susquehanna Valley."

"The Indians new and urgent concern was with hunting for the market, the international European market into which the Indians' product were now integrated," he wrote.[24]

The Great Minquas Path linked future Philadelphia and the lower Susquehanna River. Shamokin, the multi-ethnic Native American village that developed at the Forks of the Susquehanna (modern Sunbury, Pa.) during the 1720s, became a magnet for the Schuylkill fur traders. The Delaware and other tribes migrated to this strategic point after being dispossessed of land and facing encroachment from white settlers in the Delaware Valley.

Shamokin was the most prominent Native American village in

Pennsylvania during the mid-18th century. The Delaware chief Sassoonan or Allummapees relocated there from the east. The Iroquois negotiator Shikellamy arrived there about 1727 to undertake diplomatic forays with his partner Conrad Weiser.

Shamokin was the radius of a dozen Indian paths spreading in every direction. The most famous was the Tulpehocken Path extending southeast from Shamokin to Weiser's home at Womelsdorf and linking to the Schuylkill River and Philadelphia.

Visiting in 1743, naturalist John Bartram expressed hope Shamokin would be a gateway for English trade to the Ohio Country and Mississippi River.

"The town…lies partly on the east side of the river, partly on the west, and partly on a large island in it, and contains upwards of fifty houses, and they tell me, near three hundred persons, although I never saw much more than half that number in it; but of three different tribes of Indians, speaking three languages wholly unintelligible to each other," wrote missionary David Brainerd in 1745.[25]

The Moravians established a blacksmith shop at Shamokin in 1747. The trading posts of Schuylkill traders James Letort and John and Nicholas Scull II are located on a rough 1727 map of the Susquehanna River.[26] James Letort, the son of French Hugenot fur traders Jacques and Anne Letort, later moved west like so many of his contemporaries.

Nicholas Scull II (1687-1761) later became a cartographer and Pennsylvania Surveyor-General. His survey work includes the infamous 1737 Walking Purchase from the Delaware. Scull's masterpiece is a 1759 map of Pennsylvania showing the area east of the Allegheny Mountains. Scull came from a family of surveyors—including his father Nicholas I and three sons, Edward, John and Nicholas III. A grandson, William Scull III, published an even more detailed map of Pennsylvania in 1770.

Anthony Sadowski, a Polish émigré, was a contemporary who traded at Shamokin. He reportedly fled Poland to escape religious persecution and eventually bought land in Pennsylvania along the Schuylkill and founded Amity Township. Fluent in languages, Sadowski engaged in the fur trade opening a trading post at Shamokin and then extending his operations to the Allegheny River and Ohio country. He also served as an interpreter at conferences with the Native Americans. Sadowski's grave and a state historical marker are located at Saint Gabriel's Episcopal Church in modern Douglassville, Pa.

Another Schuylkill trader, French Hugenot Peter Bezellon, located a trading post further south on the Susquehanna by a Conoy village at modern Bainbridge, Pa. His trading path became known eventually as Old Peter's Road.

A surviving legacy of the Schuylkill fur trade is the Mouns Jones House, situated by a ford on the Schuylkill's east bank. The house and surrounding beautiful riverside area is part of Old Morlatton Village, owned by the Historic Preservation Trust of Berks County in Douglassville, Pa.

Mouns Jones House, Old Morlatton Village, PA (Gene Delaplane)

Jones was the son of Jonas Nilsson, an emigrant to New Sweden and early fur trader in Kingsessing. Jones moved with other Swedish families from Philadelphia to the Manatawny area around 1700. He built the sturdy two-story red sandstone house with a 1716 date stone.

Jones was a licensed Indian trader and could have served as a middleman in the fur trade possibly having a warehouse for goods on the site. His location at a river ford meant that Native Americans passed through there as colonial records show.[27]

In 1728, Shamokin traders Sadowski and Nicholas and John Scull helped ease tensions over an interracial killing that threatened peace on the frontier. Pennsylvania Gov. Patrick Gordon dispatched the trio with messages of condolence and gifts to Shamokin after two white brothers, John and William Winter, killed an Indian man and two women in colonial era Chester County. They acted in a vigilante manner after reports of menacing Indians seen near white settlements, including the French Creek iron furnace. Provincial authorities determined that the killings by the Winter brothers were unjustified. They were indicted, tried before a jury and then hanged for the death of an Indian woman known as Quilee or Hannah.[28]

Gordon held conferences with Sassoonan and others to offer more presents and assurances to keep the peace.

"I now mourn with you the unhappy Accident that followed by the Madness of these furious wicked men, who could so inhumanely destroy our good Friends & their neighbors," Gordon told Sassoonan at a June 4, 1728 conference. "The Criminals are now in Dungeons with Iron Chains on them, & they are to be tried in about fourteen days at Chester, by the laws of our Great King."[29]

Interracial killings and disputes over proper justice periodically shook the frontier. In 1722 prominent traders John and Edmund Cartlidge of Lancaster County were implicated in the killing of a Seneca named Sawantaeny. They lost their local government positions and were briefly imprisoned, but escaped capital punishment due to intercessions by the Iroquois and Conestoga.

Shikellamy and Weiser were called upon to keep the peace after the killing of Indian trader Jack Armstrong by a Delaware named Mushemeelin at Jack's Narrows near modern Mount Union, Pa., in 1744. Mushemeelin was hung for that crime in Philadelphia, but the Delaware were not happy that the King's justice was applied in this case.

Traders on the Frankstown Path

From atop the Thousand Steps Trail, a stone staircase carved by quarry workers, you are treated to a panoramic view of Jack's Narrows where the Juniata River squeezes between Jack's Mountain near modern Mount Union, Pa. This is considered the deepest gorge in Pennsylvania. On a warm sunny fall day, a steady stream of hikers climb the steep grade of the thousand steps.

Jack's Narrows is a strategic point on the Frankstown Path and scene of the murder of Shamokin fur trader Jack Armstrong and two companions in 1744, which stirred tensions on the Pennsylvania frontier. The Juniata River is a natural gateway from the Susquehanna River to the Allegheny River region.

Armstrong's killing by a Delaware from Shamokin named Mushemeelin raised

Jack's Narrows Overlook, scene of Jack Armstrong's murder (Brian Swift/Kelly Munoz)

the thorny question of whether the latter would be tried by white man's justice or by Native American customs. Mushemeelin was hanged for the crime after a jury trial in Philadelphia. Shikellamy and Conrad Weiser had to deal with resentment among the Delaware for that outcome ahead of an important conference in Lancaster. The murder occurred months before the start of King George's War between the British and French bringing even more tension on the frontier.

The death of Armstrong stemmed from a dispute over a debt of animal skins that escalated when Armstrong seized one of Mushemeelin's horses. Mushemeelin picked the Narrows as the site for an encounter with Armstrong to get the horse back. Two Delaware from Shamokin named John and Jimmy went with him for what they thought was a hunting trip. There are different accounts of who is responsible for the death of Armstrong's companions and how the sequence of events actually transpired.

With rumors circulating about the crime, a group of frontier settlers including Armstrong's brother Alexander went from Paxton to Shamokin to find out what happened. This group and a number of Delaware then traveled from Shamokin to the Narrows to search for evidence where they suspected Armstrong had camped. They discovered the remains of three bodies and buried them. The white settlers gave court depositions of what they found. Shikellamy then apprehended Mushemeelin and John.

Shikellamy's sons had the task of taking the pair to Lancaster, but John was released enroute so only Mushemeelin was delivered to Pennsylvania authorities. Eventually Pennsylvania's chief justice interviewed John and Jimmy in Philadelphia and declared them innocent. David Hsiung gives an excellent account of how different accounts by Shikellamy, Weiser and others about the affair can be interpreted in "Death on the Juniata: Delawares, Iroquois, and Pennsylvanians in a Colonial Whodunit."[30]

Pennsylvania Gov. George Thomas was busy in the wake of the

murders trying to maintain good relations with the Six Nations and Delaware as King George's War beckoned. He recalled the 1728 execution of the Winter brothers for killing two Indians in a speech to the Six Nations urging that justice be done for Armstrong's murder.

Thomas also warned the General Assembly in July 1744 about Indian traders using "Spirituous Liquors in defiance of the law to cheat Indians of their skins and wampum and involving us in some fatal Quarrel with the Indians."[31]

Thomas' warning was nothing new. In 1685, Thomas Budd wrote how an "Indian King" at a conference warned that the Dutch and Swedes had sold the natives strong liquors and had no eyes to see the harm it did and told the English "the Cask must be sealed up."[32]

The Frankstown Path linking Paxtang at modern Harrisburg, Pa., and the Delaware village of Kittanning on the Allegheny River, emerged as a route for westbound traders and their horse pack trains across Pennsylvania's Ridge and Valley section as early as the 1730s. It was named for trader Frank Stevens who had a trading post at Frankstown. The trail's western section crossing Allegheny Mountain was also known as the Kittanning Path. Geographically, the Frankstown Path crossed the Blue Mountain at Roxbury's Gap, went through the Concord Narrows, by Aughwick Creek and Shade Gap, followed the Juniata

Kittanning Path trace (Author)

River through Jack's Narrows, went by Standing Stone, through a gap in Tussey Mountain at Water Street and then to Frankstown. The modern highways of Routes 641, 11, 522 and 22 follow sections of the path through the modern towns of Carlisle, Roxbury, Shirleysburg, Mount Union, Huntingdon, Alexandria and Water Street.[33]

There were offshoots of the Frankstown Path—the New Path from Carlisle to Aughwick Creek was used by trader George Croghan and his pack horses as a shortcut starting in the late 1740s, for example. Travelers on this path referred to sleeping places where one could rest overnight. It could be a cabin, a bark lean to, or a place identified with an individual such as Hart's Sleeping Place for trader John Hart. A monument to Hart's Sleeping Place is located near modern Patton, Pa., in the area of Chest Creek in Cambria County.

Hart is also associated with Hart's Log, a log trough that Hart used to provide water and salt for his horses. A monument to Hart's Log in located near the Alexandria Memorial Public Library in modern Alexandria, Pa., situated in Hartslog Valley in Huntingdon County.

In 1748 Weiser traveled the Frankstown Path enroute to Logstown on the Ohio River. The journey by this Pennsylvania diplomat marked a shift in interest by the province towards the Ohio Country.

Weiser's journal includes an arresting account of finding the dead body of John Quen who drank too much whiskey. "He smelling very strong we covered him with Stones and Wood & went on our Journey," Weiser wrote.[34]

On the return trip, Weiser's party found that bears had pulled Quen's body out of his makeshift grave and left a few bones and old rags.

Weiser gathered some important intelligence at Logstown: a list of fighting men broken down by the Ohio tribes—163 Seneca, Delaware 165, Mohican 15, etc. This information was given to Weiser during an Indian council in the form of sticks tied in a bundle.[35]

Shadow of Death marker, Shade Gap, PA (Author)

In 1753, trader John Harris Jr., the future founder of Harrisburg, kept a log of the miles from key points on the Frankstown Path. He mentions the distance from Cove Spring to the ominous sounding Shadow of Death as eight miles. The Shadow of Death refers to a spot where the foliage was so thick that sunlight can barely penetrate. It could spark fear if darkness was approaching or one was worried about an ambush. Today the place is known as Shade Gap on Route 522 entering Black Log Valley. A state historical marker denotes the Shadow of Death name.

Harris mentions the Standing Stone near the Juniata River in Huntingdon noting it was fourteen feet high and six inches square. This was a stone pillar with Native American markings that gave its name to the area. Native Americans reportedly took the stone with them when they left the area in the face of white settlement. White surveyors erected a replacement stone in the late 18th century. The current Standing Stone monument in downtown Huntingdon was erected in 1896.

In the 1730s trader Frank Stevens set up operations at Assunepachla, a mixed village of Delaware and Shawnee, on a branch of the Juniata River. This place was eventually called Frankstown, a junction for several trails in western Pennsylvania. A state historical marker for Frankstown is located on Route 22 east of modern Hollidaysburg, Pa.

Stranding Stone monument, Huntingdon, PA (Author)

In 1756 Pennsylvania launched a counterattack against the important Delaware village of Kittanning on the Allegheny River. This attack was in retaliation for Delaware and Shawnee raids on Pennsylvania's western frontier at the start of the French and Indian War in 1755 and the destruction of Fort Granville at modern Lewistown, Pa.

Col. John Armstrong led several hundred troops on the Kittanning expedition starting at Fort Shirley on the Frankstown Path at Shirleysburg. Trader George Croghan had established his Aughwick post here earlier in the decade. When war came he built Fort Shirley. A state historical marker for Fort Shirley is located on Route 522 near Fort Run north of Shirleysburg. Archaeological work under the auspices of Pennsylvania State University, Juniata College and AXIS Research Inc. has found the fort's location and evidence of habitation by pro-British Seneca who arrived there after the French invasion of the Ohio Country in 1754.

Armstrong's attack was successful with the Delaware leader Captain Jacobs killed in battle and eleven English captives freed. But provincial authorities decided to abandon Fort Shirley for a defensive line further east. The Delaware relocated to villages in the Ohio Country.

A section of 80 feet of the Kittanning Path (western section of the Frankstown Path) is preserved near Chest Creek at modern Eckenrode's Mill, Pa. Owned by the Cambria County Historical Society, this is an uphill dirt path lined by trees on a hillside and said to follow its original shape without disruption by plow or wagons.

"The visible marks of the path here have been pointed out by father to son for several generations," wrote Henry M. Gooderham, a president of the Cambria County Historical Society. "The exact location of this particular part of the path can be seen on the survey dated 21st day of June 1773, made for Abiah Taylor in pursuance of a warrant dates the 25th day of May of the same year."[36] The Hart's Sleeping Place monument erected by the county historical society is in this area.

Weiser mentions being in the area of Chest Creek during his 1748 trip:

> "This night we had a great frost; our kettle, standing about four or five feet from the fire, was frozen over with ice, thicker than a brass penny."[37]

Joseph Simon

Joseph Simon of Lancaster was a versatile businessman with many ventures and partners during his long life. His activities cover the gamut of the Indian fur trade. He was a partner, financial backer and middleman for individual traders going with pack horses to the Ohio Country. He went on trading expeditions himself as far as the Mississippi River.

Simon (1712-1804) came to Lancaster in 1740, an emigrant from England. He was the respected patriarch of Lancaster's Jewish

Joseph Simon family grave plot in Lancaster, PA (Congregation Shaarai Shomayim)

community. Lancaster was a center for the fur trade at the time. Simon had a merchandise store in the city's Penn Square.

Traders headed to the Allegheny River region stocked up on goods that Native Americans wanted—glass beads, blankets, combs, etc.—in Lancaster. They came back with the pelts and hides of beaver, deer, fox and other animals that they obtained from Native Americans in exchange for the trade goods.

Simon partnered not only with traders like Donegal's Alexander Lowrey and George Croghan, "King of the Traders," but also with owners of Philadelphia-based import firms like Barnard and Michael Gratz, both of the Jewish faith and emigrants from Prussia. David Franks and Nathan Levy are two other Philadelphia-based importers associated with Simon. He partnered with gunsmith William Henry in selling hardware and employed a silversmith to make the trinkets and brooches favored by Native Americans.[38]

By the 1760s Simon and others had trading posts at British-held Fort Pitt at the Forks of the Ohio. Prior to the American Revolution, he was involved in the formation of several land companies that sought unsuccessfully to promote settlement in the Ohio Valley region. Simon supported the Patriot cause when war came a few years later.

Simon and family members are buried in the Shaarai Shomayim Cemetery on East Liberty Street in Lancaster on land that he helped purchase for use as a burial ground in 1747. This is the fourth oldest Jewish Cemetery in the United States.

Barnabas and Elizabeth Hughes

For nearly two decades, Barnabas Hughes was a player on the Pennsylvania frontier as an Indian fur trader, tavern owner, British Army commissary and founder of Elizabethtown named for his wife.

Hughes' tavern, The Sign of the Bear, stands at 56 North Market Street near Conoy Creek and Conestoga Creek in Elizabethtown. The building has been extensively renovated and used first as a residence and now office space. A monument depicts the original log house on the spot.

The tavern was opened in 1745 by Thomas Harris, a fur trader,

The Sign of the Bear Tavern in Elizabethtown, PA (Author)

and sold in 1751 to Lazarus Lowry, another fur trader. In two years, Lowry sold the tavern to Hughes, an emigrant with his wife Elizabeth from Ireland. It was at a strategic location on the road from Philadelphia to Harris Ferry.

Hughes became prominent in the fur trade receiving trade goods from Philadelphia and sending them by packhorse train to the Native American tribes in the Ohio Country. His business was affected adversely by French incursions into that region in 1754.

Hughes was among residents petitioning Pennsylvania authorities in 1754 for help to defend the area. In 1755 after Braddock's defeat Hughes became a contractor providing supplies to provincial troops at Fort Hunter and Fort Swatara. The Sign of the Bear Tavern was a stopping point for provincial troops headed to the frontier and pro-British Indian refugees ended up there, too.[39]

During the 1758 Forbes campaign against French Fort Duquesne at the Forks of the Ohio, Hughes' tavern served as an important supply depot. Hughes took on a larger role as sutler to the British Army.

"I think it is now time to contract wth (Robert Callender) and Barny Hughes for the 1000 Pack Horses to carry from Bedford to Ligonier, But there is time to consider the (Price we got of) Mr. Hughes & his associates for providing the Carriages as I am not without hopes we can do without them, or at least bring them down to reasonable terms," wrote British Col. Henry Bouquet to Gen. John Stanwix on May 16, 1759, after Fort Duquesne had fallen.[40]

"I have contracted wth Capn Kallender and Mr. Bar: Hughes for 1000 pack horses; to be station'd at Bedford," wrote Stanwix on May 18, 1759.[41]

In 1763 Barnabas and Elizabeth Hughes issued deeds to buyers of lots in their new town, thus putting Elizabethtown on the map like so many other Pennsylvania towns in this postwar period.

A Journey to Lake Erie

In 1790 Pennsylvania's government sent surveyors Samuel Maclay and John Adlum and Timothy Matlack, a state official, to search for navigable waters and sites for future roads in the western wilderness regions of the state.

Their commission mentions the West Branch of the Susquehanna River, Allegheny River, French Creek, Kiskiminetas River and Juniata River in this regard. Maclay's journal helps us trace their steps during this five-month trip from April to September marked by rainy and cold weather. Similar expeditions were sent to explore the headwaters of rivers in other parts of the state. Pennsylvania was securing its modern boundaries at this time.

Maclay records a meeting with the Seneca leader Cornplanter at his village at Jennesadaga, stopping at other Native American villages, baking bread for food, visiting American Fort Franklin and encountering backcountry settlers including David Mead, founder of Meadville. The journey was arduous with Maclay not being able to walk at times. The party ran into difficulty dragging canoes along river bottoms during periods of low water.

The goal of finding a western waterway link to the Ohio region had been around for a long time. In 1743 naturalist John Bartram and mapmaker Lewis Evans wrote about how the Forks of the Susquehanna River at the multi-ethnic village of Shamokin was a gateway to this region during a peacekeeping trip to the Iroquois capital at Onondaga. Bartram wrote about the need to survey the heads and sources of rivers in the region to achieve this goal.[42]

Maclay describes the formidable terrain:

> "The Ground Between the Sinemahoning (Sinnemahoning River) and Little Toby's Creek is a Barren mountain; in some places covered with a poor stunted Growth of Pitch pine, but the far greater part of the mountain has some years ago been covered with small chestnut timber, which has been killed with

fire and is now fallen, and the underwood is grown up among it so thick that in many places it fairly hid the logs, which makes walking both Dangerous and Difficult."[43]

The Sinnemahoning is a tributary of the West Branch of the Susquehanna River. Native Americans and early settlers used land portages from there to carry canoes to the Allegheny River at modern Port Alleghany, Pa.

Maclay and company saw a memorable sight in the Sinnemahoning watershed—the Great Elk Lick—a salt spring covering several acres that drew herds of elk and deer to lick the salt deposits. He wrote on June 30: "Passed the large salt lick and encamped for the night."[44]

Sinnemahoning State Park on Route 872 south of modern Austin, Pa., provides public access and recreation along both sides of the First Fork of Sinnemahoning Creek, an area traveled by the expedition.

"The Cornplanter in a speech told us he was glad to see us, and gave us a welcome to any-thing we could catch in their country," wrote Maclay on July 7 as the expedition reached the Upper Allegheny River.[45]

The party reached Lake Erie, its farthest point, on July 13. Maclay described the lake as smooth as glass that day followed on July 14 by a wind driven swell about three feet high.

Maclay used the surface oil found along French Creek as a balm for his sore back just as the Native Americans had done for generations. "This afternoon I collected a small quantity of oyl from a small oyl spring in the bank of French creek, with which I had my back rubbed before I went to bed."[46]

On the return trip, the party traveled the Kiskiminetas River, went along Stony Creek and used the new Frankstown Road and Juniata River to get to Harrisburg. Maclay and his colleagues issued a report in December suggesting several potential transportation routes to the western waters.

Maclay later became a U.S. Senator representing Pennsylvania, Adlum is remembered as the father of American viticulture at his vineyard in the Washington, D.C., area and Matlack also left his mark on history as the scribe who wrote the Declaration of Independence. A state monument to Maclay and state historical marker are at his grave on Route 45, four miles west of modern Lewisburg, Pa.

Endnotes

1. Charles H. Glatfelter and Arthur Weaner, *The Manor of Maske: Its History and Individual Properties* (Gettysburg, PA: Adams County Historical Society, 1992), 7.
2. Pennsylvania State Library, Pennsylvania Dept. of Public Instruction. Pennsylvania. Secretary of the Commonwealth. (1852) *Pennsylvania Archives*. [S.I.: s.n.] Series 1, Vol. 1, March 30, 2023 accessed. https://www.hathitrust.org. 625.
3. Glatfelter and Weaner, op. cit., 11.
4. William H. Kain, "The Penn Manorial System and the Manors of Springetsbury and Maske," *Pennsylvania History* Vol. X, No. 4 (October 1943), 229.
5. James Logan, 'Letter of Instruction of James Logan to James Steel, on Proprietary Affairs, 1727," *The Pennsylvania Magazine of History and Biography* Vol. 24, Nov. 4 (1900), 495.
6. Evelyn A. Benson, "James Logan as the First Political Boss," *Papers of The Lancaster County Historical Society* Vol. LIX, No. 3 (1955), 73.
7. *Pennsylvania Archives* 1st Series, Vol. 1, op. cit., 295.
8. Ibid., 299.
9. Samuel Hazard, *Pennsylvania Archives* 1st Series, Vol. II (Harrisburg: Printed by Joseph Severn & Co. (1853) April 9, 2023 accessed. https:// www.hathitrust.org 24.
10. Gladfelter and Weaner, op cit., 9.
11. Ibid., 9.
12. *Pennsylvania Archives*, "Papers Relating to Provincial Affairs in Pennsylvania 1682-1750," Second series, Vol. VII, April 9, 2023 accessed. https://www.hathitrust.org. 230.
13. Gladfelter and Weaner, op. cit, 21.
14. *Pennsylvania Archives*, Colonial Records "Minutes of the Provincial Council," (Harrisburg: printed by Theo. Penn. (1851) Vol. 5. April 9, 2023 accessed. https://www.hathitrust.org. 442.
15. Ibid., 443.
16. Ibid., 444.
17. Charles A. Hanna, *The Wilderness Trail*, Vol. 1 (Lewisburg, PA: Wennawoods Publishing. 1995), 177-178.
18. Alexander Lowry. Historical Biographies. Pennsylvania State Senate. April 2, 2023 accessed. https://www.legis.state.pa.us
19. Frank J. Cavaioli, "A Profile of the Paxton Boys: Murderers of the Conestoga Indians," *The Journal of the Lancaster County Historical Society*, Vol. 8.7, No. 3 (1983), 81.
20. Lemay, J.A. Leo ed., *Franklin Writings* (New York: The Library of America, 1987), 556.
21. *James Silver and His Community* (Carlisle, PA: Cumberland County Historical Society and Hamilton Library Association, 1969), 8-15.

22. Robert B. Swift, *The Mid-Appalachian Frontier: A Guide to Historic Sites of the French and Indian War* (Gettysburg, PA: Thomas Publications, 2001), 95.

23. Jean R. Soderlund, Richard S. Dunn and Mary Maples Dunn, eds., *William Penn and the Founding of Pennsylvania 1680-84 A Documentary History* (Philadelphia, PA: University of Pennsylvania Press, Historical Society of Pennsylvania, 1983), 318.

24. Francis Jennings, "The Indian Fur Trade of the Susquehanna Valley," *Proceedings of the American Philosophical Society*, Vol. 110, No. 6 (Dec. 16, 1966) April 2, 2023 accessed. https://www.jstor.org. 406-424.

25. David Brainerd, *The Project eBook of The Life of the Rev. David Brainerd, Chiefly Extracted from His Diary*, by Jonathan Edwards. April 2, 2023 accessed. www.guterberg.org 167.

26. Hanna, op cit., 197.

27. *Prioritizing Berks County Cultural and Historic Resources Within and Nearby the Hopewell Big Woods*. A Study for the Friends of Hopewell Furnace NPS (2016), 107-109; Susan Speros, "Foundations: Unearthing New Facts at Mouns Jones House," *Reading Eagle*, Reading, Pa. May 16, 2018.

28. Hubertis M. Cummings, *Scots Breed and Susquehanna* (Pittsburgh, PA: University of Pittsburgh Press, 1964), 10-17.

29. George Edward Reed, ed., *Papers of the Governors 1681-1747*, Volume I (Harrisburg: Pennsylvania Archives Fourth Series, 1900), 450-451.

30. David Hsiung, "Death on the Juniata: Delawares, Iroquois, and Pennsylvanians in a Colonial Whodunit," *Pennsylvania History*, Vol. 65, No. 4 (Autumn 1998), 445-477.

31. Reed, op cit., 854.

32. Asa Earl Martin and Hiram Herr Shenk, *Pennsylvania History Told by Contemporaries* (New York: The Macmillan Company, 1925), 37-38.

33. Paul A. W. Wallace, *Indian Paths of Pennsylvania* (Harrisburg: Pennsylvania Historical and Museum Commission, 1971), 49-51.

34. Reuben Gold Thwaites, ed., *Early Western Journals 1748-1765* (Lewisburg, PA: Wennawoods Publishing, 1998), 23.

35. Ibid., 31.

36. Henry W. Gooderman, *The Kittanning Path Through Cambria County* (Patton, PA: 1954), 9.

37. Thwaites, op cit., 44.

38. Jerome H. Wood Jr., *Conestoga Crossroads Lancaster Pennsylvania 1730-1790* (Harrisburg: Pennsylvania Historical and Museum Commission, 1979), 98-99, 114-116; David A. Bremer, "Lancaster's First Jewish Community," *The Journal of the Lancaster County Historical Society*, Vol. 80, No. 4 (1976), 241-253.

39. Richard K. MacMaster, *The First Three Centuries* (Elizabethtown, PA: The Elizabethtown Historical Society, 1999), 19-23.

40. Donald H. Kent, Louis M. Waddell and Autumn L. Leonard, eds., *The Papers of Henry*

Bouquet Volume III (Harrisburg: The Pennsylvania Historical and Museum Commission, 1976), 290.

41. Ibid., 294.
42. John Bartram, Lewis Evans and Conrad Weiser, *A Journey from Pennsylvania to Onondaga in 1743* (Barre, MA: The Imprint Society, 1973), 33.
43. Samual Maclay, *Journal of Samuel Maclay* (Lewisburg, PA: Wennawoods Publishing, 1999), 27.
44. Ibid., 30.
45. Ibid., 35.
46. Ibid., 42.

CHAPTER 4

Cherokee Warriors on the Pennsylvania Frontier

Colonel Henry Bouquet was effusive in his praise for the King's allies. "Your friendship is as dear to us as the heat of the Sun in the Spring," the British officer told an assembly of Cherokee and Catawba warriors at Fort Loudoun on the Pennsylvania frontier.[1]

Bouquet spoke of the might of King George II's armies and the rewards awaiting those warriors who helped the king defeat his enemies, the "rapacious" French. The year was 1758 and a British army was marching across the Alleghenies to oust the French from the Forks of the Ohio. Bouquet led the vanguard of an army under the command of Gen. John Forbes.

The Cherokees and the Catawba, were mercenaries of a sort, interested mainly in rewards for their service. But their presence reaffirmed a long-standing alliance with the Crown. Cherokees had fought on the British side before in regional wars. They sent warriors to help North Carolina defeat the hostile Tuscarora in 1713. They aided Georgia in hostilities with Spain in the 1740s.

This alliance brought benefits to both sides. The Cherokees were the largest of the southern tribes with a population of 10,000. They were noted for their skill in battle and long rivalry with the Iroquois in the north. The Cherokees controlled the highlands at the western frontier of Virginia and the Carolinas. They provided a buffer to French and Spanish outposts in the Mississippi River Valley.

The British emissary Lt. Henry Timberlake described the Cherokees as being of "middle stature, of an olive colour, tho' generally

Reenactment of Cherokee Council at Fort Loudoun (Dan Guzy, Conococheague Institute)

painted, and their skins stained with gun-powder, pricked into it in very pretty figures."[2]

Like other tribes, the Cherokees had grown dependent on European trade goods. They relied on a steady stream of guns and powder to pursue their profitable trade in deerskins. British goods were cheaper, plentiful and of good quality. This proved important in the decision by the Cherokee chiefs in 1756 to side with the British. French influence remained strong in some Cherokee towns, however.

The Cherokee warriors who joined the British on the Forbes campaign were hundreds of miles away from their tribal homeland in the Southern Appalachians. They were involved in an imperial contest for empire known as the Seven Years' War. These warriors took an ancient trail known as the Warrior's Path north to rendezvous with Bouquet at Fort Loudoun, a staging depot in the campaign against French Fort Duquesne. A reconstructed Fort Loudoun stands in the shadow of Tuscarora Mountain, the imposing natural barrier to the west. The fort guards the entrance to Path Valley, a narrow north-south passageway between two other mountain ranges.

Two miles north of the fort is Parnell's Knob, a hump-shaped landmark at the end of Kittatinny Mountain easily spotted for miles around. Forbes Road, the military road that carried British troops and supplies through the wilderness, skirted the south end of Parnell's Knob.

At this strategic spot, Bouquet sought to impress upon the Cherokees the importance of the task before them. The colonel charged the French with being "a haughty, ambitious and cruel people" who would enslave the Indians and encroach upon their lands.

> "That rapacious Nation is already in Possession of all the Lakes and Rivers and of the best hunting Country but it is not enough yet for them, they would Sweep us from the Earth, and drown us at once in the Waters of the great Lake."[3]

Bouquet had specific assignments for the warriors. He wanted them to divide into three corps based at the British posts of Fort Loudoun, Fort Lyttelton and Juniata Crossings along Forbes Road. They were to dispatch scouting parties westward to gather intelligence of French strength and bring back French prisoners.

Despite Bouquet's stirring words, the British-Cherokee alliance was troubled. The two sides soon came to distrust and feel let down by the other. In fact, disputes that flared up during the Forbes campaign led to war between the two nations two years later.

Some of these troubles were presaged by events in 1757 when 250 Cherokee warriors fanned out to guard Virginia's long frontier against raids by parties of French and Shawnee warriors. Cherokees under the leadership of Head War-

Fort Loudoun in Fort Loudon, PA (Author)

rior Wawhatchee or Wahachey also made forays against the French in western Pennsylvania.

George Washington, the young 25-year-old commander of Virginia's provincial forces, welcomed the Cherokees' arrival on the scene.

> "They will be of particular service more than twice their number of white men. When they arrive, which I pray may be soon, we may deal with the French in their own way; and, by visiting their country, will keep their Indians at home."[4]

The Cherokees scored some successes on the Pennsylvania frontier in 1757. Cherokee warriors ambushed a French patrol 20 miles

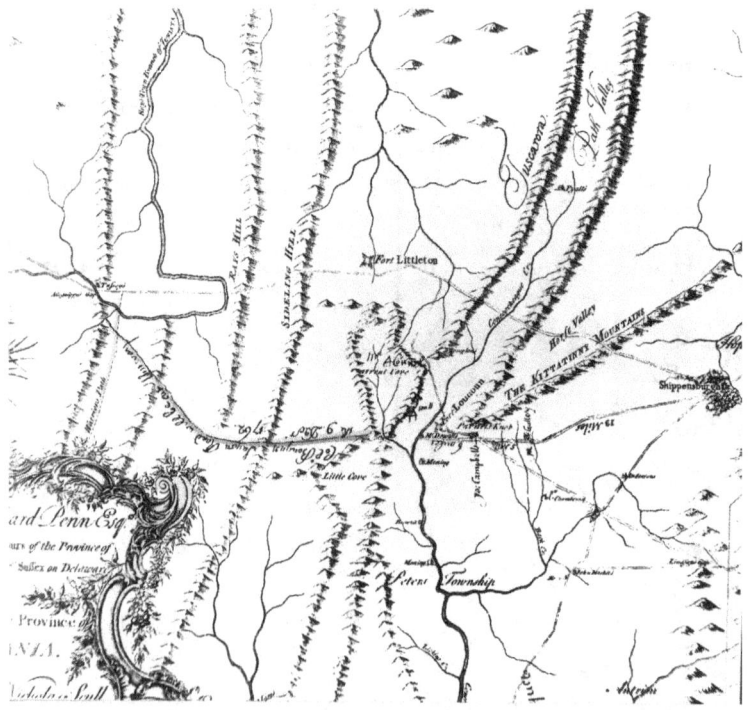

Section of Improved Part of Province of Pennsylvania Nicholas Scull Map 1759 showing Forbes Road (Pennsylvania State Archives MG-11. No. 630. Section Nine 8X10)

east of Fort Duquesne in June. They captured French Ensign Picote de Bellestre, but lost one of their own leaders, Swallow Warrior, in the fight.[5]

But some problems developed. A party of 60 Cherokees entered Pennsylvania's Conococheague Valley in pursuit of pro-French Indians. They were mistaken for enemy raiders themselves. A tragedy was barely averted.

The Cherokees arrived in the area unannounced, but were given lodging for the night in modern Mercersburg. A local resident spotted them and assumed they were hostile. He alerted the garrison at Fort Loudoun and a force of soldiers surrounded the house that night. They waited for dawn to attack, but white traders traveling with the Cherokees spotted the threat in time to clear up the misunderstanding. The Cherokees headed west to Fort Lyttelton. En route they defeated a small party of enemy warriors.[6]

The Cherokees expected presents such as wampum, silver ornaments and glass beads for their services. To British eyes, they appeared greedy. But the Cherokees saw matters in a different light. They received no other compensation for their warriors killed in battle. The warriors fighting for the British were separated from their families and not able to hunt for food and for skins to supply the traders.

However, in 1757, the gift distribution system proved inefficient. This was partly due to squabbling among officials in Virginia, Maryland and Pennsylvania over which colony should pay for specific services rendered by the Cherokees.

Another factor was a turf battle between Sir William Johnson and Edmund Atkin, the British Indian agents for the northern and southern colonies respectively. The Cherokee were a southern tribe, yet they were operating north of the Maryland border that divided the two jurisdictions. Deputies for Johnson and Atkin felt they alone should control the distribution of gifts.

The confusion was such that Wawhatchee's warriors at one point traveled a circuit between Fort Loudoun, Maryland's Fort Frederick

Top: Maryland's Fort Frederick (Author)
Bottom: View of Pennsylvania Ridge and Valley terrain from Maryland (Author)

and Winchester, Va., not knowing if gifts awaited them at each stop or not.

At Fort Frederick, Maryland's imposing stone fort on the Potomac River, Wawhatchee and 60 warriors declared themselves allied with the British after receiving presents in April 1756. Wawhatchee or Wahachey as Marylanders spelled his name danced on the tables in the officers' quarters during a ceremony. The room where the ceremony took place is reconstructed in the fort's East Barracks.[7]

In 1758, as General Forbes readied his campaign against Fort Duquesne, British emissaries set out to recruit far greater numbers of Cherokees than had seen service the year before. The British stockpiled presents and Atkin devised a more efficient system for distributing them. By early spring, some 400 Cherokee warriors had journeyed north. Forbes sought help from North Carolina Gov. Andrew Dobbs in smoothing the way north for the warriors. "I must therefore beg that you will be so good as to give orders that they meet with all kind of good usage in their passing, and hope that Mr. Atkins who has the Charge of Indian Affairs has taken care of their being supplied with provisions & upon their March," he wrote on March 21, 1758.[8]

To join the British at Fort Loudoun and Raystown, the Cherokees journeyed north along the Virginia frontier in parties numbering from 10 to 50 warriors. Relations between the Cherokees and backcountry settlers remained tense. The two clashed over horses that often roamed loose on the frontier. To the English, the Cherokees were no better than horse thieves. The Cherokees found taking horses an easy way to retaliate against untrustworthy traders.

The tensions erupted in deadly clashes in early May between settlers and war parties at the Virginia frontier settlements of Bedford and Otter Creek. The clashes strained the British-Cherokee alliance. Wawhatchee left Carlisle, Pa., for home when he got word of the clashes.

Both sides made an effort to patch things up. Virginia militia escorted northbound parties; Cherokee headmen quieted talk of revenge in their homeland towns. But by July only 50 Cherokees remained with Forbes' army and they were used mainly as scouts.

There were other causes of dissatisfaction. Forbes' slow methodical approach to the campaign frustrated warriors used to quick and decisive military actions of several months or less. They had expected a battle with the French by that summer.

Portrait of Cherokee Chief Cunne Shote (Author)

Forbes believed the best way to cross the Alleghenies was in stages. He sent crews ahead to build a road through the Pennsylvania wilderness. The advance guard then erected a string of forts to secure communications and stockpile supplies for the main army to use.

Forbes was guided by the fate of the British expedition against Fort Duquesne in 1755. General Edward Braddock's army was defeated in a battle within a half-day march of the fort. The British regulars were not prepared for wilderness warfare. They were trained to exchange volleys in open formations, but this proved impractical in the unbroken forest.

While the French and their Indian allies fired from the cover of trees and rocks, the British tried to form battle lines and were shot down. When the battle became a rout, the British had nowhere to regroup. Braddock had decided not to build rear bases. The remnants of his army retreated all the way to Philadelphia and left the frontier settlements open to raids.

A chance for a better British-Cherokee understanding came

when the head Chief Attakullakulla, or Little Carpenter, met with Forbes at Raystown in October. Little Carpenter was considered the most pro-British of the Cherokee leaders. As a young man, he met King George II during a 1730 visit to London. Attakullakulla was a small-built man who spoke good English; the name Little Carpenter was bestowed in recognition of his skills at building good relations between the British and Cherokees.

The naturalist William Bartram wrote about a chance encounter with him during his 1776 journey through Cherokee country:

> "I observed a chief at the head of the caravan, and apprehending him to be the Little Carpenter, emperor or grand chief of the Cherokees, as they came up I turned off from the path to make way, in token of respect, which compliment was accepted and gracefully and magnanimously returned; for his highness with a gracious and cheerful smile came up to me, saying I am Ata-culculla; and heartily shook hands with me..."[9]

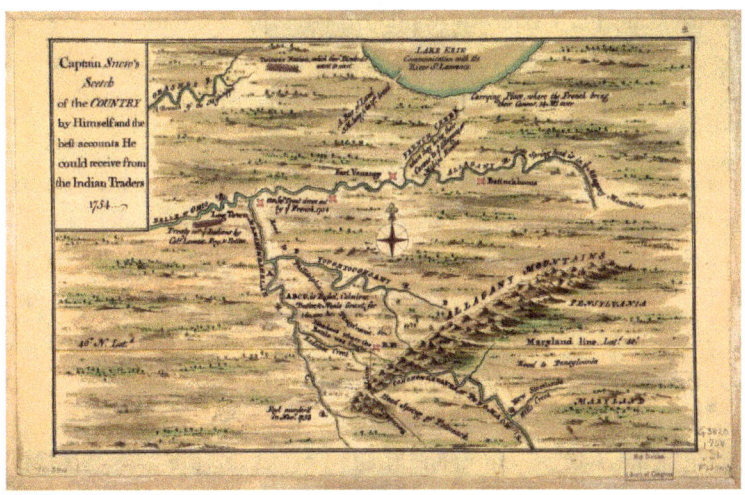

Captain Snow's sketch of the (Ohio) country by himself, and the best accounts he could receive from the Indian traders 1754. (Library of Congress Geography and Map Division. http://hdl.loc/gmd/g3820.ct000.366

The meeting between Little Carpenter and Forbes didn't go well. Forbes was disappointed that Little Carpenter and his warriors wouldn't commit to join the final advance against Fort Duquesne. Little Carpenter had gotten word from the Shawnee the French were preparing to abandon the fort.

The British had just made peace with the Delaware tribes living east of the Susquehanna River and that undercut the French position at the Forks of the Ohio. Fort Duquesne was blown up and abandoned in November. Then events took an unexpected turn. Two years of bitter warfare between the British and Cherokees lay ahead.

In the Carolinas, tensions mounted over white incursions into Cherokee hunting grounds. French agents stirred up discontent. So did emissaries from the neighboring Creek tribe who were pro-French. The situation worsened after a Cherokee war party from the town of Settico went on a raid in 1759 and killed 19 settlers in North Carolina. The British demanded that the Cherokee headmen hand over the errant Settico warriors for execution.

A meeting between the Cherokee war chief Oconastota and South Carolina Governor William Lyttelton at Charleston created new problems. The governor took him and others along as hostages when he marched with a militia to Fort Prince George near the Cherokee town of Keowee. At the fort, Lyttelton told Little Carpenter he would release the hostages once two warriors were turned over. Little Carpenter persuaded the warriors to surrender and the hostages were released.[10]

Hostilities continued, however, and in 1760 South Carolina requested the help of British regulars. British veterans of the Forbes campaign under the command of Col. Archibald Montgomery and Major James Grant were dispatched to the Cherokee frontier. Montgomery met with defeat in an initial invasion and the Cherokees laid siege to the isolated British post of Fort Loudoun near Chota. The garrison under Captain Paul Demere held out for months until food ran out. Demere negotiated a surrender that provided for the gar-

Grave of General Edward Braddock along Route 40, PA (Author)

rison to be escorted to Fort Prince George. En route, the Cherokee attacked the departing soldiers. Demere and thirty-five of his men were killed.

After the fall of Fort Loudoun, the Cherokees were ready to talk peace. But the British thirsted for revenge. In 1761, Grant led a second expedition that destroyed 15 towns and forced the nation to plead for peace. Little Carpenter agreed to terms laid down by Grant at Fort Prince George. These stipulated that all white captives would be returned, Cherokees who killed whites would be tried in Charleston and a boundary would be drawn between the Cherokee towns and white settlements.[11]

The Cherokees had gone from being allies of the British to foes in a few short years. The British effort to forge a friendship with a major native tribe was a complete failure. Yet the Cherokees misjudged the situation, too. They decided to fight the British just as French power waned with the loss of Canada. The Creeks provided no assistance so the Cherokees fought alone. They were premature as the pan-Indian uprising against British rule known as Pontiac's War erupted two years after the Cherokee defeat.

Little Carpenter's fear that his nation would be destroyed wasn't realized. But his people faced great trials. The Americans eventually drove Little Carpenter's descendants from their mountain homeland. The Trail of Tears—the forced removal of the Cherokee nation to Oklahoma—lay seventy years ahead.

French Build Portage Road South From Lake Erie

An army of French soldiers struggled during the summer of 1753 to build a wilderness road linking a natural harbor on Lake Erie with French Creek, a tributary of what the French called the Belle Riviere.

The 2,000 soldiers from Canada pushed themselves to exhaustion cutting the 15-mile road and hauling goods by hand labor through dense forests and miry swamps that had to be bridged with logs in many places. The summer was a hot one and the waterways dried up making them not navigable by canoe. The result of these harsh conditions and a poor diet was an outbreak of illness that led to many French lives lost in this remote gateway to the Ohio Country.

The impetus for the 1753 expedition was an escalation of the French-British rivalry over the Ohio Country, a vast expanse of rich wooded land encompassing the Ohio River and its tributaries such as the Allegheny River. The French had sent two military expeditions to the region in 1739 and 1749; the latter under Capt. Pierre-Joseph Celeron de Blainville encountered English traders as far west as the Miami village of Pickawillany. The British turned their attention to the Ohio Country for trade opportunities after the 1744 Lancaster Conference with the Iroquois.

The French attacked Pickawillany and killed the pro-British leader Memeska in 1752. After that, French officials in Quebec decided to fortify the Ohio region at key points in order to reinforce their claims to that vast area. Fort Niagara at the mouth of the Niagara River was used as a staging point.

Reconstructed British station on Forbes Road, U.S. Army History Education Center, Carlisle, PA (Author)

The Marquis Duquesne, Governor of New France, directed that a fort be built at Presque Isle at modern Erie, Pa., which he described as a "harbor which the largest barks can enter, loaded, and be in perfect safety."[12]

The French built three other forts—at Le Boeuf at modern Waterford, Pa., Machault on the Allegheny at modern Franklin, Pa., and Duquesne at the Forks of the Ohio at modern Pittsburgh, Pa. These forts were all to have been built in 1753, but due to difficulties with the expedition, Forts Machault and Duquesne weren't constructed until later.

Duquesne appointed Pierre Paul de la Malgue, Sieur de Marin, commander of a French fort on Lake Michigan, in charge of the French forces. The French spent the early part of the summer of 1753 building Forts Presque Isle and Le Boeuf and the portage road connecting them.

By August problems were cropping up with a wave of sickness felling Marin's soldiers. French Creek was running dry due to lack of rain while the portage road was very muddy in spots due to the traffic on it. In early September Tanacharison, a Seneca leader, warned the French not to build forts in the region during a council at Presque Isle.

Then Marin fell ill. By October he made a decision to suspend the campaign and send most of the troops back to Montreal. Marin died on Oct. 29 at Fort Le Boeuf.

Duquesne praised the efforts of the Canadians yet observed than many more would have died if the campaign had continued that fall. "The Canadians are the only people in the word who would be capable of sleeping in the open air, and able to endure the immense labor that this detachment performed in transporting baggage on two portages…" he wrote on Nov. 29.[13]

Duquesne thought the late Sieur Marin showed sound judgment in delaying the expedition. He wrote the large number of invalid soldiers left an insufficient force vulnerable to Native American attack if it advanced down the Ohio.[14]

Six weeks after Marin's death, a young George Washington arrived at Fort Le Boeuf with a message from Virginia Gov. Robert Dinwiddie telling the French to withdraw from British territory. The new French commander politely rejected Washington's demand. Washington journeyed to Fort Le Boeuf by way of Nemacolin's Path in Maryland, the Forks of the Ohio, Logstown on the Ohio River and then went north to Le Boeuf.

The next year a new French army descended into the Ohio Country building Forts Machault and Duquesne. The waterways were full making it easy for the French flotilla of bateaux and canoes to reach the Forks. The French ousted a small British party building a storehouse there and set the stage for the outbreak of the French and Indian War.

In 1937 the Pennsylvania Historical Commission in connection with the New Deal era Federal Works Agency conducted a survey of the portage road trace from Erie to Waterford. The survey found the road followed or is close to Route 97. Old logs thought to be part of a bridge were found at two locations as well as defined depressions indicating a roadbed.[15]

In 1954 the Pennsylvania Historical and Museum Commission gained access to documents in the Archives due Seminaire de Quebec giving the French perspective of the 1753-54 invasion. These documents were translated into English and served as the foundation for *The French Invasion of Western Pennsylvania* written by historian Donald H. Kent.

British Army Nurse Weathers Braddock Campaign

The journal of Mrs. Charlotte Browne, head nurse of the hospital for Gen. Edward Braddock's ill-fated campaign to oust the French from the Forks of the Ohio, offers a unique perspective of life at the American towns, army camps and forts that supported the red-coated soldiers marching into the wilderness.

Left: Austenaco, great warrior, Commander in Chief of the Cherokee Nation (Library of Congress Prints and Photographs Division http://hdl.loc.gov/loc.pnp/cph.3b37306)

Right: The Three Cherokees, came over from the head of the River Savanna to London 1762 (The British Museum Prints and Drawings 1982.U3745)

A widow, Browne and her brother who was an apothecary were among a support contingent that cared for the sick, washed clothes and cooked food for Braddock's soldiers. Many wives were among this group, a widespread practice of 18th-century armies.

Browne endured bouts of sickness, miserable weather, physical trials and other deprivations as she first spent four months on a transatlantic voyage to Alexandria, Va., and then followed Braddock's army as it advanced to Fort Cumberland at Wills Creek in Maryland. Browne was at Fort Cumberland in July 1755 when news came of the army's shattering defeat at the hands of the French and Native American allies near Fort Duquesne. Browne then retreated with the demoralized remnants of the army to distant quarters at Albany, N.Y., where her journal ends.

Browne is light on the military details of Braddock's campaign; rather she gives a flavor of the logistics involving in supplying the army and caring for sick soldiers, the social scene in towns such as Lancaster, Philadelphia and Albany where she stayed and the poor roads that she had to travel over, often on foot.

"At 4 in the morning I was call'd up by Mrs. Johnson who came to take her leave of me and at 6 we March'd for Wills's Creek with one Officer, my Brother, self and Servant, 2 Nurses, 2 Cooks and 40 men to guard us. 12 Waggons with the sick. Lame and Blind, my Wagon in the Rear," she wrote on June 1 departing from Alexandria.[16]

On June 5: "My Lodgings not being very clean I had so many Close Companions call'd Ticks that depriv'd me of my Nights Rest," she wrote.[17]

Browne described Fort Cumberland as the "most desolate Place I ever saw." She was lodged in a "Hole that I could see day light through every Log and port Hole for a Window which was as good a Room as any in the Fort."[18]

Browne and her brother were sick most of their stay at Fort Cumberland; on July 11 the first word came that Braddock was dead and many of his soldiers killed by French and Indians who were behind trees. Browne wrote: "it is not possible to describe the Distractions of the poor Women for their Husbands."[19]

Her brother died on July 17 of his illness, and a month later, Browne herself feeling very ill, marched in retreat to Frederick, Md. Browne's horse threw her as they forded the Potomac River and there were scary reports of nearby Indian raiders taking scalps of settlers.

On Oct. 7 she wrote: "An Express is arriv'd from near Fort Cumberland with an Account that the Indians have scalp'd 5 Families and that they are in the greatest Distress having Bread but for 3 days and cannot go out for more."[20]

While staying in Philadelphia, Browne witnessed a striking scene at the Pennsylvania statehouse, now Independence Hall. On Dec. 16 she wrote: "I went to the state house to see 2 men and a Boy that were brought into Town Dead, scalped by the Indians it was the dismallest Sight I ever saw."[21]

What Browne observed was a protest by backcountry settlers against the Quaker-controlled General Assembly for not adequately defending the frontier. The settlers were victims of an onslaught of raids by French-allied Delaware and Shawnee after Braddock's defeat.

The head of Braddock's rear guard, Col. Thomas Dunbar, eventually retreated all the way to Albany leaving the frontiers of Pennsylvania and Maryland basically defenseless against those raids. Dunbar responded to initial orders from Gov. William Shirley, the new British commander-in-chief, to go to Albany. Subsequent orders for Dunbar to remain and garrison the frontier came too late. It wasn't until 1756 that Pennsylvania authorities erected a line of defensive forts and some of those fell to attack.

Browne's journal is also noteworthy for the social invitations she received and the famous people that she met. They include Deborah Franklin, wife of Benjamin; Gov. William Shirley of Massachusetts and Sir William Johnson of New York who invited her to watch an Indian dance. Browne's rank gave her social status, but she wasn't always mingling with high society. She wrote that she had a supper of lamb and bad wine with Col. Thomas Cresap, a colorful Indian trader and commissary to Braddock's army.

Christopher and Thomas Gist: An Eye for Land

Christopher Gist knew how to sell real estate. Here is his enticing description of the Miami River watershed in the Ohio Country while on a 1751 trip for the Ohio Company:

> "...it is well watered with a great Number of little streams or Rivulets, and full of beautiful natural Meadows, covered with wild Rye, blue Grass and Clover, and abounds with Turkeys, Deer, Elks and most Sorts of Game particularly Buffaloes, thirty or forty of which are frequently seen feeding in one Meadow. In short it wants Nothing but Cultivation to make it a most delightfull Country."[22]

Gist wrote that in his journal in February no less.

Gist (1706-1759) and his son Thomas (?-1786) both had experience exploring the wilderness and serving in military expeditions into the interior. Gist was born into a well-to-do Baltimore family yet encountered a series of business losses that led him to the North Carolina frontier. There he learned surveying, trekking and fur-trading skills that served him well in his future career.

Gist's frontier reputation was such that he was hired by the Ohio Company as a land agent in 1750. The company represented a group of wealthy Virginians who obtained a grant from the British King for 200,000 acres of land in the Appalachian region with the provision they find settlers to populate it.

The company hired Gist to search the Ohio River lands and "take an exact Account of the Soil, Quantity, & Product of the Land, and the Wideness and Deepness of the Rivers."[23]

He had explicit instructions for what to do when he found good level land that he thought would suit the company.

> "You are to measure the Breadth of it, in three of four different Places, & take the Courses of the River and Mountains on which it binds in Order to just the Quantity. You are to fix the Beginning & Bounds in such a Manner that they may be easily found again by your Description."[24]

Gist's journey went through southern Pennsylvania to the Forks of the Ohio and Logstown and then headed to the Muskingum River. At a Delaware town called Shannopin, Gist took care not to let the residents see his surveyor's compass.

> "While I was here I took an Opportunity to set my Compass privately, & took the Distance across the River, for I understood it was dangerous to let a Compass be seen among these Indians."[25]

Gist, George Croghan, the prominent Pennsylvania fur trader, and the Native American interpreter Andrew Montour reached the Miami or Twightwee village of Pickawillany in February 1751. They delivered a message from Virginia Governor Robert Dinwiddie to the Miami Chief Memeska who had broken away from the French orbit and sought ties with the British.

Gist's journal is full of accounts of wildlife and big game sightings and useful details such as this about Elk Eye's Creek, which is "good Land, but void of Timber, Meadows upon the Creek, fine Runs for Mills."[26]

In the fall of 1751 Gist set out on a second westbound journey on behalf of the Ohio Company with instructions to look for a route for a road from the company's storehouse at Wills Creek to the Monongahela River. He was to look for about 500 acres of good land on the Ohio River convenient for storehouses and houses. This became Gist's Plantation, a frontier outpost near modern Connellsville, Pa.[27]

This wealth of knowledge and experience made Gist an obvious choice to assist George Washington on his diplomatic journey to French Fort LeBoeuf in 1753. The French burned Gist's Plantation after Washington's defeat at Fort Necessity the next year.

Gist was a guide for British Gen. Edward Braddock when he marched to the Forks of the Ohio in 1755. Gist's sons Thomas and Nathaniel served as guides on that campaign, too. All three escaped the disaster at Turtle Creek and continued fighting for the British.

Thomas was part of a Virginia militia unit in the 1758 Forbes campaign. He was part of a reconnoitering force in September 1758 under Capt. James Grant that left Fort Ligonier in advance of the main army for Fort Duquesne. Grant's force was badly defeated by French and Indian attackers with many captured including Thomas. He was taken with other prisoners to a Huron village near the French fort at Detroit and adopted by a native family with whom he stayed until his escape in the summer of 1759 with two others.

In a journal of his captivity, Thomas recorded the captives' march to Detroit and his escape trek across modern Ontario to reach Fort Niagara, just recently in British hands, in September.

Like his father, Thomas described the lay of the land. "The land on which we encamped every nite appeared to be very rich and level, and well timbered," he wrote enroute to Detroit. "I saw a plenty of wide fowl such as swans, geese, ducks & etc."

"We had very bad swamps to march through, some of which was so thick with a kind of bushes and very… that we obliged to crawl under them; others so very bad we was forced to cut them out of the way," wrote Thomas about the escape.[28]

While Thomas was making his escape, Christopher Gist died of smallpox in July 1759 in Virginia. He was infected with the disease while visiting the Catawba.

General Forbes Last March

Overwhelming arms, a methodical approach and diplomacy as well paid off for British General John Forbes in November 1758 when his army occupied a hastily abandoned French Fort Duquesne at the Forks of the Ohio.

Forbes (1710-1759) led a 6,000-man army on a step-by-step advance from Carlisle, Pa., to the Forks establishing forts and defensive strongholds at strategic points along the way. He even timed the final push with word of a diplomatic achievement with the Ohio Delaware ready to break away from the French at the Treaty of Easton in October 1758. Forbes had been in contact throughout with a Moravian missionary Christian Frederick Post who went on a peace mission to Delaware villages.

After the Treaty, Forbes sent a letter to the Delaware and Shawnee urging them to leave Fort Duquesne and go to their towns "where you may sit by yr Wives and Children, quiet and undisturbed, and smoke your Pipes in safety."[29]

Even so the British army still faced hurdles as it approached Fort Duquesne. An advance force led by Capt. James Grant had been repulsed in September. Winter was approaching and there was a move to halt the final assault until next spring. Then the French attacked a British base at Fort Ligonier on Nov. 12. A French prisoner from that engagement told the British that Fort Duquesne was undermanned with only 500 troops. This piece of information convinced Forbes to send Col. Henry Bouquet and 2,500 soldiers forward and Fort Duquesne fell on Nov. 25.

Forbes directed the 1758 campaign while suffering from an ailment that some historians think was stomach cancer. Forbes called it the bloody flux and made frequent references of his physical sufferings in his letters to British military officers and even civilian authorities. The ailment left him so weak at times that he was unable to walk or ride a horse. But Forbes also experienced rebounds, too, during the long campaign.

"I really can not describe how I have suffer'd both in body and Mind of late," he wrote to Bouquet from Shippensburg on Sept. 2.[30]

Forbes wrote to Gen. James Abercromby on Sept. 4: "my bad state of health, which realy has been in such a condition this month by past from a most violent flux, with most excruciating pains in my Bowells, and I rendered so low and weak that I had oftener than once or twice firmly resolved to have wrote you, to appoint some other person to take this Command, as I absolutely found myself incapable to proceed – But now thank God I am a great deal better, and that my sickness has never retarded my operations one single moment..."[31]

Forbes experienced these medical ups and downs as he attended to the voluminous details of managing and equipping an army in the Pennsylvania wilderness and engaging with higher ups, colonial governors and Native Americans.

Informing British Prime Minister William Pitt of a new town Pittsburgh named in his honor on Nov. 27, Forbes requested that he be given leave to return home to England as soon as he possibly could to reestablish his health. "The physicians and hospital people agree I must go directly to England to save my life," Forbes wrote Pitt.[32]

There followed a grueling two-month journey until Forbes, often carried in a litter, reached Philadelphia. He was concerned during this period with provisioning the British troops left behind to guard the Forks from a French attack.

From Lancaster on Jan. 13, Forbes asked Gen. Jeffrey Amherst to send a doctor to Philadelphia as "I am weaker than a child and recover no Strength."[33]

Forbes drew up a last will and testament on Feb. 13 in Philadelphia. He ordered a gold medal for the officers in the Forks campaign. Forbes died on March 11 of a tedious illness, according to the obituary in the *Pennsylvania Gazette*.[34]

Forbes' funeral and burial at Christ Church, Philadelphia was attended by his soldiers, engineers, surgeons, physicians, clergy and chaplains, the Pennsylvania governor, judges and members of the General Assembly.[35]

Massy Harbison

One of the more dramatic 18th-century captivity narratives is that told by Massy Harbison of her capture by Seneca and Munsee warriors during a final period of frontier warfare in Pennsylvania.

Harbison (1770-1837) and her family lived in 1792 near Reed's Station, a blockhouse near modern Freeport, Pa., on the Allegheny River. Her husband John served with the American Army in the Ohio Country while Massy did camp chores at the station.

In May 1792, while her husband was away, the war party entered the Harbison's cabin, immediately killed one child and departed with Massy and two other children. Harbison said she knew some of her captors and they could speak English. The party crossed the Allegheny River, subjected Harbison to beatings and killed another child. Harbison and a remaining child were led on a march to the Connoquenessing River near modern Butler, Pa. Harbison took her opportunity to escape with her child at night while one captor was sleeping. She hid in a tree at one point. She went without food on a six-day escape that ended when she reached the cabin of a neighbor. She gave an affidavit of her ordeal to Justice John Wilkes at Fort Pitt. A narrative of her story was published in 1825.

Harbison described a close encounter with a rattlesnake at a hiding place:

> "I did not go clear to the log; had I done so, I might have lost my life by the bites of Rattle Snakes; for as I put my hand to the ground, to raise myself to see what was become of the hunters, and who they were, I saw a large heap of Rattle Snakes, and the top one was very large and coiled up very near my face, and quite ready to bite me."[36]

In a later deposition to the Pennsylvania General Assembly seeking government support, Harbison called herself an old soldier's widow:

> "and trust that although I have not shouldered a musket, yet, that my services and sufferings will draw forth the feelings of your Honors, and render me the eve of my life free from penury."[37]

Endnotes

1. S. K. Stevens, Donald H. Kent, and Autumn L. Leonard, eds., *The Papers of Henry Bouquet. Volume II. The Forbes Expedition* (Harrisburg: The Pennsylvania Historical and Museum Commission, 1951), 98.

2. Duane H. King, ed., *The Memoirs of Henry Timberlake The Story of a Soldier, Adventurer, and Emissary to the Cherokees, 1756-1765* (Cherokee, NC: Museum of the Cherokee Indian Nation, 2007), 24.

3. Stevens, Kent and Leonard, op. cit., 98.

4. Frank Donovan, ed., *The George Washington Papers* (New York: Dodd Mead and Company, 1964), 46.

5. David Corkran, *The Cherokee Frontier: Conflict and Survival 1740-62* (Norman: University of Oklahoma Press, 1962), 125.

6. Gary Hawbaker, *Fort Loudon on the Frontier* (York, PA: Pennsylvania Press Inc., 1976), 17.

7. *Maryland in the French and Indian War*. Maryland Forest, Park & Wildlife Service leaflet.

8. Alfred Proctor James, ed., *Writings of General John Forbes Relating to His Service in North America*, The Allegheny County Committee and the Pennsylvania Society of Colonial Dames (Menasha, WI: Collegiate Press, 1938), 61.

9. Mark Van Doren, ed., *Travels of William Bartram* (New York: Dover Publications Inc., 1955), 295.

10. Corkran, op cit., 187-188.

11. Howard Peckham, *The Colonial Wars 1689-1763* (Chicago: The University of Chicago Press, 1964), 204.

12. Sylvester K. Stevens and Donald H. Kent, eds., *Wilderness Chronicles of Northwestern Pennsylvania* (Harrisburg: Pennsylvania Historical Commission, 1941), 49.

13. Ibid., 60.

14. Ibid., 63.

15. Sylvester K. Stevens and Donald H Kent, eds., *The Venango Trail* (Harrisburg: Pennsylvania Historical Commission, 1940), 46-47.

16. Isabel M. Calder, *Colonial Captivities, Marches and Journeys* (Port Washington, NY: Kennikat Press, 1967), 178.

17. Ibid., 180.

18. Ibid., 182-183.

19. Ibid., 184.

20. Ibid., 187.

21. Ibid., 191.

22. William M. Darlington, *Christopher Gist's Journals* (Salem, NH: Ayer Company Publishers Inc., 1991), 47.
23. Ibid., 31.
24. Ibid., 31.
25. Ibid., 34.
26. Ibid., 36.
27. Ibid., 67-68.
28. Howard H. Peckham, "Thomas Gist's Indian Captivity," *The Pennsylvania Magazine of History and Biography*, Vol. 80, No 3 (July 1956), 308.
29. James, op. cit., 252.
30. Ibid., 193.
31. Ibid., 199.
32. Ibid., 269.
33. Ibid., 279.
34. Ibid., 304.
35. Ibid., 305.
36. *A Narrative of the Sufferings of Massy Harbison from Indian Barbarity* (Pittsburgh: printed by S. Engles, 1825) University of Pittsburgh Digital Collection. April 4, 2023 accessed. https://www.digital.library.pitt.edu 39.
37. *Captivity Narrative: Massy Harbison*. April 4, 2023 accessed. https://www.heinzhistorycenter.org/fort-pitt/)

CHAPTER 5

Job Chilloway and His World

For more than two decades on the Pennsylvania frontier, the name of the Delaware Job Chilloway turned up in military correspondence, missionary diaries and even the journals of the Continental Congress.

The writers of these documents drop Chilloway's name like it's the most natural thing in the world.

Yet 260 years later we don't know much about Job Chilloway and a lot written about him especially during the 19th century is sheer fantasy.

What we do know about Chilloway suggests he lived an intriguing life on the Appalachian frontier during a turbulent era that saw two wars and the dislocation of Native American peoples.

A few examples:

-- Chilloway provided first-hand intelligence about the strength of the French garrison at Fort Niagara to Capt. Joseph Shippen at Fort Augusta at the Forks of the Susquehanna River in 1758.

-- He alerted Pennsylvania Gov. John Penn to a choice tract of land initially called Job's Discovery in 1768.

-- Chilloway ended up as the owner of the Moravian mission of Friedenshuetten on the Susquehanna River in 1772. The Native American converts there moved to the Ohio Country that year.

-- General George Washington thought Chilloway the right man for a scouting assignment to reconnoiter the source of the Susquehanna River in New York State in 1779.

Forks of the Susquehanna at Sunbury, PA (Author)

Chilloway traveled widely across a vast wilderness region bounded by the Delaware, Susquehanna and Ohio Rivers during the last half of the 18th century. He belonged to a select group that one prominent historian calls the "go-betweens"—those individuals who traveled back and forth between the Native American and European American worlds to deliver messages, translate speeches, obtain information or help someone in trouble even during wartime.[1]

Chilloway spoke English very well. His proficiency was a key factor in gaining the confidence of British and American military commanders, Pennsylvania governors and Moravian missionaries. While Chilloway is described as speaking English well, his original voice is lost to us. This was the case with most Native Americans of that period. Instead, we read about his deeds and sentiments as conveyed by white interpreters and public officials.

He was called "the friendly Delaware"—a description setting him apart from the pro-French Delaware raiding English backcountry settlements during the French and Indian War and Pontiac's War. Chilloway was a family man with references to his wife, mother, mother-in-law, children, and his brother Billy or William found in chronicles. Chilloway's name is spelled variously as Chelloway, Chillaway, Chilleway, something not unusual in a time of phonetic spelling.

Chilloway was born in the late 1730s at Egg Harbor near modern Atlantic City, N.J. He lived as a remnant Delaware behind the lines of English settlement. The Delaware in southern New Jersey were known as the Unami. Most of them had left for Pennsylvania by the 1750s to escape white encroachment or follow the fur trade. The few who stayed behind were under the sway of Christian missionaries at Crosswicks, south of Trenton.[2]

Chilloway appears in official correspondence in the midst of the French and Indian War, a conflict where the Delaware sided with the French in hopes of regaining lost territory in eastern Pennsylvania. He was used as a messenger and spy. He supplied valuable information about enemy activities to Pennsylvania officials.

Stationed at the strategic Pennsylvania outpost of Fort Augusta, Capt. Shippen described Chilloway in a Jan. 20, 1758, letter to his brother-in-law Major James Burd:

> "he was born & bred at Egg-harbour is a very sensible fellow & speaks the English Language perfectly well. From all the Circumstances of his Conversation & Behavior he appears to be a strict Friend to the English interest."[3]

Chilloway arrived at Fort Augusta with intelligence. He had visited the pro-French Munsee living along the Upper Susquehanna River.

He told Shippen that the Munsee were determined to continue the war against the English. Chilloway related that French soldiers from Fort Niagara were expected to join Munsee warriors soon to launch an apparent attack against Fort Allen in eastern Pennsylvania. Shippen warned provincial authorities, but this rumored attack didn't materialize.

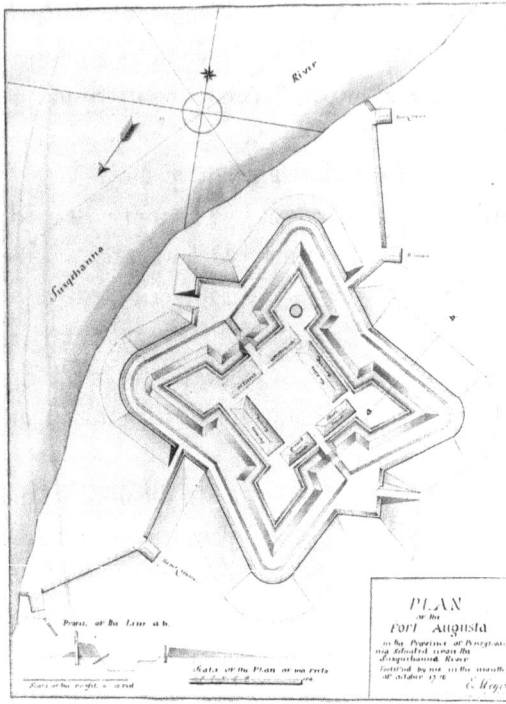

Plan of Fort Augusta at the Forks of the Susquehanna 1756 by Elias Meyer (Pennsylvania State Archives MG-11. No. 115. Section Six 8X10)

Chilloway had traded furs in March 1757 at Fort Niagara located at the mouth of the Niagara River and Lake Ontario. He had an eye for the kind of specific details about Fort Niagara that military officials at Fort Augusta wanted. They lived in constant fear of a French attack coming down the west branch of the Susquehanna.

"...while he was at Niagara there were 5 officers & he computed the number of Soldiers there to be not more than 150, who by his Discription of their appearance & Dress, are Regulars, that they mounted 45 pieces in the Fort, some of wch were the Brass field pieces taken from Gen Braddocks which they intend in the Summer to send to Fort Frontenac & that the Fort was strong & pretty large having in it a great Stone House 3 stories high where the Officers lived," wrote Shippen.[4]

In 1759 Nathanael Holland, a merchant overseeing the Indian

trade at Fort Augusta, relayed information that Chilloway gave about a Mingo-Delaware war council.

"This day Job Chilloway arrived here from up the river & informs that he has been at Maccawson about 8 weeks ago, where a great Council was held by several of the Mingo Nation, that Alopapealon & Paxinoso, Delaware chiefs, where present, when the said Council was opened by singing the Warr Song & handing about a very large War belt…," wrote Holland on April 13, 1759, to the Commissioners for Indian Affairs.[5]

These relationships could have their ups and downs.

A few months earlier Pennsylvania Gov. William Denny received a letter from a soldier at Fort Augusta writing on Chilloway's behalf. Joseph Billings wrote about Chilloway's complaint that Holland had defrauded Indians on the price of trade goods. While giving a formal statement, Chilloway said he made the complaint on behalf of another Indian named Ahoalint. But Ahoalint denied that.[6]

And then there is the matter of Chilloway's horse.

The minutes of a meeting between Pennsylvania Gov. James Hamilton and more than two dozen Indians from Wyalusing on July 12, 1760, in Philadelphia make a reference to this horse. Chilloway is recorded as saying privately that he lent a horse to a British lieutenant who had lost it.[7]

The success of British arms in the French and Indian War and the subsequent Pontiac's War, involving a pan-Indian uprising against the British, opened the Pennsylvania backcountry for white settlement.

The 1768 Treaty of Fort Stanwix led the Iroquois to cede territory from the northern reaches of the Susquehanna River to the Forks of the Ohio River to Pennsylvania. However, the Ohio Valley tribes didn't recognize this treaty.

Chilloway figures in an effort by the Penn family, the proprietors of Pennsylvania, to gain title to a tract of desirable land near modern Muncy, Pa. Chilloway is credited by local historians with telling Gov. John Penn about some choice land along Muncy Creek.

Penn issued a warrant on Nov. 24, 1768, for a survey of this land called Muncy Manor. One survey of the land shows the legend "Job's Discovery."[8] Job's deed put him in good stead with John Penn concerning a separate land transaction the next year.

The end of warfare in 1765 had provided a breather for the Moravian Church's program of building missions for Christian Indian converts in the Pennsylvania interior. These were villages with log huts, gardens, livestock and a chapel for worship.

The lives of Moravian missionaries and converts were in jeopardy during both wars. They lived in a no man's land and were not trusted by either the English or Native Americans who kept their tribal affiliations. One of the first Moravian missions, Gnadenhuetten on the Lehigh River, was destroyed by pro-French Delaware in 1755.

The area around modern Wyalusing, Pa., had attracted attention from missionaries starting in the 1750s. A charismatic Munsee leader, Papunhank, had located a village there along the Susquehanna River and proved receptive to missionary teaching.

Prior to Pontiac's War, both the Moravians and Quakers coveted the allegiance of souls at Wyalusung. In June 1763, two famous missionaries, the Moravian David Zeisberger and Quaker John Woolman, were at Wyalusing at the same time in an effort to win backing from Papunhank's followers. Woolman realized that Zeisberger clearly was the favorite.

In his Journal, Woolman records meeting Chilloway while traveling north by canoe to Wyalusing. Chilloway was traveling south to Fort Augusta, said Woolman, who described him "as an Indian from Wyalusing, who talks good English and is acquainted with several people in and about Philadelphia."[9] Chilloway warned that he had word of three warriors headed south to attack the English in the Juniata River area.

Chilloway's association with Friedenshuetten started early. He lived there in a log house although he didn't become a full-fledged convert like some members of his family. We have more information about Chilloway's life during this period because of the Moravians' habit of documenting everything in their hand-written German script.

The Moravians established the Friedenshuetten Mission in 1765 after Zeisberger baptized Papunhank and won permission from the Iroquois to settle on river bottomland at Wyalusing. The converts who arrived there that spring had been through hell.

Papunhank's villagers and residents of two other Moravian missions had fled the region in late 1763 as Pontiac's War started. They were escorted to Philadelphia and finally resettled on Province Island in the Delaware River to escape the wrath of white vigilante mobs. Smallpox took its deadly toll on the refugees. Finally in 1765, they were allowed to leave and resolved to return to Wyalusing.

The Moravian missionary John Heckewelder described Friedenshuetten in 1767 as having a "large and spacious church, of squared white pine timber, single roofed with a neat cupola and bell on top." He added "at this time there were forty well built houses of squared timber, and shingle roofed, in the village and the gardens back of them were all in good clapboard fence."[10]

A plot of Friedenshuetten that year shows brothers Bill and Job Chilloway living next to each other on house lots with a frontage of 32 feet.[11]

The Moravians' Friedenshuetten diary is full of notations about life at the mission from 1765 to

Friedenshuetten Mission monument (Moravian Historical Society)

1772. It records hunts against marauding wolves, river floods, heavy snowfalls, plagues of grasshoppers and the run of shad in the spring.

An entry for Sept. 13, 1768, reads: "Set watches and kept fires burning through the night, to guard against the depredations of wolves."

And on April 27, 1771, "Daily we have a plentiful supply of wild pigeons, that are taken at the roost in the Swamp."

One finds frequent references to Chilloway and his family who lived there:

> -- Dec. 7, 1766 "Called upon Tamar, Job Chilloway's mother-in-law who is upwards of seventy years of age."

> -- Jan. 7, 1767 "The rite of baptism was administered to a daughter of Job Chilloway, and she was named Augestina"

> -- Jan. 15, 1767 "Billy Chillaway, Job's brother who resides at Zeninge, made application to become an inhabitant of the town"

> -- Jan. 18, 1767 "Tamar departed this life"

> -- Oct. 22, 1767 "Job Chilloway's house was blocked up"

> --Oct. 23, 1767 "It was roofed up."

> -- May 1, 1770 "A white man who had been held prisoner by the New England men at Wyoming upwards of three weeks was brought by Job Chilloway. From him we heard of the calamity which had befallen Capt. Ogden and his brother."[12]

At this time, Pennsylvanians and settlers from Connecticut contested sometimes violently the ownership of lands in the northeast region of the state. Connecticut settlers burned a trading house owned by Amos and Nathan Ogden in April 1770.

The intrusion of Connecticut settlers in the Wyoming Valley was just one of several trouble spots on the horizon for the Friedenshuetten converts.

They were concerned about the loss of their land to white settlers despite reassurances from Gov. John Penn. The sale of liquor to their young people was a constant problem. They petitioned Penn in early 1769 to put their land in a trust.[13]

Penn's response on June 21, 1769, included a strange reference to Chilloway. He said that Chilloway had taken the land to secure it "for himself and the rest of you."

That news caught the Friedenshuetten converts off guard. They replied to Penn that they wished to live in a friendly manner with Chilloway, but "we never desired him to take up any land for us, and upon what account he would call Wyalusing his land, we do not know."[14]

There were tensions among the mission converts. Chilloway was among several who accused Papunhank of witchcraft in 1771 apparently questioning his powers as a healer during a period of deadly sickness.[15]

By 1772, the Moravian missionaries decided to abandon Friedenshuetten. Under the leadership of Rev. John Ettwein, the converts embarked on a historic trek to establish a new mission in the Ohio Country.

Ettwein described locking the chapel door and taking leave of Chilloway and his wife who were both crying at the departure. Chilloway had agreed to look over the mission buildings.[16]

Within two years, the Penns granted a patent to Chilloway for 623 acres of land at Wyalusing. He became one of a handful of Native Americans personally owning land in colonial Pennsylvania. Chilloway sold the land to Henry Pawling in 1775.

During the American Revolution, Chilloway cast his lot with the rebelling American colonists. Fort Augusta was at the fringe of the American defense line and provided refuge to settlers fleeing raids by the British-allied Iroquois. In 1777, fort commander Lt. Samuel

Hunter wrote a letter referring to Chilloway helping to "Reconiter and make Discoverys of any Enimy Indians if within fifty miles of Great Island" at modern Lock Haven, Pa.[17]

Washington was preparing for an American invasion of Iroquois territory in early 1779. He wanted information about the terrain in the Chemung River region so his invading army wouldn't get bogged down in low and swampy ground. Gen. James Clinton led an army through that area in the summer as part of the Sullivan campaign. Washington thought Chilloway the right man for the job.

"There formerly was an Indian near Wyoming, named Job Chilloway, perfectly acquainted with all the Country before mentioned," wrote Washington to Gen. Edward Hand at Fort Pitt on March 21, 1779. "Be pleased to write over to Colonel Butler and desire him to enquire for that Indian, and if he is to be found, and will come down to me, direct him to furnish him with a Horse and to offer him a handsome reward."[18]

That assignment was not to be.

On April 27, 1779, Col. George Morgan, the American Indian agent, reported to a Board of War that Chilloway and his mother had recently died of smallpox at Fort Pitt. Chilloway had reportedly offered his services as interpreter for upcoming negotiations at Fort Pitt with a pro-American Delaware faction. The board directed Morgan to give clothing to Chilloway's children and take steps to provide for their education.[19]

Four months later, an American army camped at the site of the Friedenshuetten mission en route to join Gen. John Sullivan. The Rev. William Rogers, an army chaplain, wrote that the buildings had been destroyed by Indians and by whites salvaging lumber.

He added, "Wyalusing belonged to one Job Chilloway, an Indian, a friend of our cause. Indian Job died last winter. Many handsome things are spoken of him, which makes his manners to be 'By strangers honored, and by strangers mourned.'"[20]

Despite these two respectable sources, some 19th-century historians reported that Chilloway lived until the 1790s in the Ohio region. It's possible this is due to a case of mistaken identity with his brother Billy.

Moravian missionary David Zeisberger, having founded new missions in Canada, wrote in his diary of presiding at the burial of William Chilloway.

"In the evening the helper, William, 61 went very peacefully to his rest after a lingering illness. His remains were interred on the 24th. For the burial we called in the brothers and sisters who were away," wrote Zeisberger on Sept. 22, 1791.

He added: "In the year 1770, he (William) came with his wife, now his widow, to the congregation at Friedenshuetten and resolved immediately upon entry into the congregation – as he himself often said – to remain there all his life and to say goodby to the world, the councils of the Indians, the chiefs with all their activities; and he has really kept his resolution to the very last."[21]

The historian Paul Eugene Miller wrote that Dr. Edmund DeSchweinitz, a 19th-century historian, made an error when he identified the deceased in that 1791 burial as Job Chilloway.[22]

Throughout his life, we see references to Job Chilloway as being friendly or a friend to the whites. Perhaps this led to the romanticizing of his story by Edwin MacMinn in *On The Frontier with Colonel Antes* published in 1900.

MacMinn weaves a dramatic tale of Chilloway and his wife Betsy who loved the wilds but could also dazzle the ladies of Philadelphia. In his telling, Betsy grew tired of her double life and left Chilloway to go back to her people. A good yarn but with no supporting facts. The War Board report appears the most likely end to Chilloway's story.

John Martin Mack and Jeanette Mack

John Martin Mack was one of the most intrepid Moravian missionaries going on arduous wilderness journeys along the Susquehanna River, to the Iroquois capital at Onondaga and on assignments to Moravian missions at Shekomeko in New York, Pachgatgoch in Connecticut and Shamokin at the Forks of the Susquehanna. His wife Jeanette Mack used her fluency with the Mohican language to get the couple out of some life-threatening situations.

John Martin (1715-1784) was born in Wurtemburg, Germany, and joined the Moravians in his teens. He went to America, first to Georgia and then to Bethlehem, Pennsylvania, where he helped clear land for the new Moravian settlement there in 1741.

John Martin's first Native American mission assignment was at Shekomeko at modern Pine Plains, N.Y., where he met Jeanette, daughter of a local German-speaking farmer. They were married in Bethlehem and then accompanied Moravian Church leader Count Nicholas Ludwig Zinzendorf on an exploratory trip to Shamokin and the Wyoming Valley in 1744. During this trip, Shawnee Indians made a threat against Zinzendorf's life and food was scarce. At one point Jeanette was able to obtain much needed corn bread due to her ability to speak Mohican with a Native woman.[23]

John Martin and Jeanette's mission work at Shekomeko and Pachgatgoch near modern Kent, Conn., in the 1740s was strained by English settlers' suspicions of the Moravians as papists or pro-French. At Pachgatgoch, John Martin and two other missionaries were arrested by Connecticut authorities and spent ten days in prison in New Haven in 1743. They were released on condition that they not preach in Connecticut unless the local ministers gave consent.[24]

The next year with a war starting between Great Britain and France, New York officials arrested John Martin at Shekomeko and ordered the mission closed.

John Martin and Jeanette were then assigned to Shamokin. He described the multi-ethnic village as the seat of the Prince of Darkness in a memorable phrase. The couple often hid in the woods at night to escape residents with harmful designs.

"The most of the nights we were obliged to spend in the open air, concealed in the forest, and exposed to all the inclemency of the weather, for we did not venture to kindle a fire. But we enjoyed a blessed fellowship with the Saviour, and were very happy," wrote John Martin.[25]

Moravian Bishop John Christopher Frederick Cammerhoff wrote of a perilous trip to Shamokin in the winter of 1748 where John Martin and two others helped him cross an ice-swollen stream on the Paxtang Path along the east side of the Susquehanna River.

"The rescuers first built a canoe of green wood but it couldn't bear the weight of one person and by 5 p.m.," wrote Cammerhoff, "my heart was gladdened to see Mack, Anton and James Logan, dragging a sled after them upon which was a canoe, which Anton quickly launched and crossed over to me."

"Bro. Mack and his wife are especially held in high esteem, as they speak their (Indian's) language and are always ready to help in cases of sickness," wrote Cammerhoff.[26]

John Martin had the important job of laying out the Gnadenhuetten village for Native American converts, many of them refugees from Shekomeko, at a site north of the Lehigh Water Gap in 1748. Here Jeanette died in 1749.

After a Delaware war party raided Gnadenhuetten at the start of the French and Indian War in 1755, John Martin helped the refugee converts establish a new village at Nain near Bethlehem.

In 1752, John Martin kept a journal of his journey with missionary David Zeisberger to Onondaga by way of the Mohawk River.

"We did not stay here (Canajoharie) long, but continued for eight miles through the woods until

Grave of Moravian Indian convert in Bethlehem, PA (Author)

noon, when we came to the Great Falls, where the settlements again commence. In the afternoon we crossed over the river, which was much swollen by the rain. Here we met about one hundred Indians, mostly from Anajot and Cayuga, who live at present in these parts and dig roots, which are very good in all kinds of sickness. The Indians sell them to the people hereabouts, or exchange them for goods with the traders who come from Albany," he wrote on Aug. 15.[27]

John Martin's later years were spent at Moravian missions in the Danish West Indies.

Great Island

The pastoral Great Island on the West Branch of the Susquehanna River has a mystical aura about it. This 367-acre island is one mile wide and two miles long and is at the mouth of Bald Eagle Creek. The Susquehanna flows around both sides of it. More than a half dozen Indian trails converged on Great Island, sometimes called Big

Great Island Susquehanna West Branch (Author)

Island. Delaware and Shawnee lived there and it was an important gathering site. Missionaries traveled there and on three occasions Great Island was the target of military campaigns.

Moravian missionaries David Zeisberger and John Martin Mack visited Great Island in 1748 during a time of famine and sickness.

"We asked whether we could lodge in a hut over night, were cordially received and a bear skin spread for us to sleep on, but could not obtain anything to eat," the two wrote in a journal. "In the evening we were visited by a number of Indians, Shawnese and Cayugas, among the latter one who spoke Low Dutch from near Albany. In all of the huts there were cases of small-pox, and in one hung a kettle in which grass was being stewed, which they ate with avidity."[28]

Zeisberger and Mack were able to exchange needles and thread for some dried venison the next day.

Pro-French Indians visited the island in the wake of General Braddock's defeat in 1755. Pennsylvania officials received reports of a French army advancing along the West Branch with an aim to attack newly-built provincial Fort Augusta at the Forks of the Susquehanna.

In November 1756, Capt. John Hambright led a force from Fort Augusta to attack and burn Indian villages along the West Branch. Hambright reported that a party sent to Great Island returned by the Allegheny Path without finding any enemy or discovering any paths made in recent months.[29]

In 1763 during Pontiac's War Col. John Arm-

Fort Augusta well (Author)

strong led an expedition from Fort Shirley to attack Great Island and burned villages and crops there. The first surveyors and white settlers arrived in the area in 1769 although Pennsylvania didn't formally acquire the land until the Treaty of Fort Stanwix in 1784.

The Rev. Philip Vickers Fithian visited the estate of John Fleming on the Susquehanna two miles above the mouth of Bald Eagle Creek in 1775. "It is on a Spot of Land which was once an Indian town," Fithian wrote. "There is more than an hundred Acres that had been long cleared. So long that every Stump is wasted all away."[30]

Seven years later Great Island was the scene of more fighting during the American Revolution. An Iroquois war party defeated a smaller American scouting patrol killing nine of them and taking several prisoners, including commander Moses Van Campen.

Van Campen's scout had left Fort Muncy to assist Andrew Culbertson. He was seeking to locate items buried on a farm by his brother, a casualty of Indian raids that depopulated the area. Van Campen's scouts were on Great Island when they were attacked without warning by the Iroquois and overwhelmed after combat.[31]

David Brainerd

David Brainerd was like a shooting star in the short period he spent on missionary work with the Native Americans. His influence carries on through his diary published after his early death at age 29.

Brainerd (1718-1747) was a creature of the Great Awakening, the evangelical religious revival that swept Colonial America in the mid-18th century. Ordained as a Presbyterian minister in 1744, he was hired by a missionary society to preach to Native Americans.

Brainerd was mostly based at Crossweeksung (modern Crosswicks), N.J., where remnant Delaware lived near white settlements. Most Delaware had fled New Jersey and moved west across the Delaware River by then. Brainerd's first convert was the well-known Delaware negotiator Moses Tunda Tatamy who served as an interpreter for him.

Duncan Island where David Brainerd preached (Author)

"He is about fifty years of age, and is pretty well acquainted with the pagan notions and customs of his countrymen; and so is the better able to expose them. He has, I am persuaded, already been, and I trust will yet be, a blessing to other Indians," wrote Brainerd about Tatamy.[32]

He described Crossweeksung as a scattered settlement with "not more than two or three families in a place; and these small settlements were six, ten, fifteen, twenty, or thirty miles, and some more from that place."[33]

What Brainerd is famous for is his account of journeys he made by horseback among Delaware, Iroquois and Nanticoke living along the Delaware and Susquehanna Rivers. Brainerd wrote about his joy and tribulation in trying to preach the Gospel to what he referred to as poor uncultivated pagans. It's also the account of a young man on his first job.

Brainerd's writings are full of references to Bible passages, God, preaching and saving souls, which included white frontier settlers as well. But he said little about the splendors of the natural wilderness that he traveled through.

Brainerd's prejudices concerning Native Americans are jarring to modern ears. "The Indians of this place are counted the most drunken, mischievous, and ruffianly fellows of any in these parts: and Satan seems to have his seat in this town in an eminent manner," wrote Brainerd about Shamokin in 1745.[34]

Brainerd's bane was the practitioner of Native religion—a prime example whom he witnessed during a troubled visit to a Nanticoke village on Juniata Island. He wrote,

> "…none ever excited such images of terror in my mind – as the appearance of one who was a devout and zealous reformer of what he supposed was the ancient religion of the Indians.—He made his appearance in his pontifical garb, which was a coat of bears' skins, dressed with the hair on, and hanging down to his toes, a pair of bear-skin stockings, and a great wooden face, painted the one half black, and the other tawny…He advanced toward me with the instrument in his hand that he used for music in his idolatrous worship."[35]

In October 1745 Brainerd wrote: "I have now rode more than three thousand miles, at which I have kept an exact account, since the beginning of March last, and almost the whole of it has been my own proper business as a missionary."[36]

Brainerd wrote that his travels had impaired his health. He died of tuberculosis two years later. He had been engaged to Jerusha Edwards, daughter of the Great Awakening preacher Jonathan Edwards, and died at Edwards' home before a marriage took place. Edwards arranged the posthumous publication of the diary that made Brainerd famous.

John Brainerd, Brainerd's younger brother, took his place. In 1758 he became superintendent at a reservation that New Jersey established for the remaining Delaware at Brotherton, modern Indian Mills, N.J.

The reservation was established amidst the tensions of the French and Indian War. New Jersey Gov. Francis Bernard settled Indian claims to land around the Raritan River and the state purchased several thousand acres for the reservation. At its peak, a couple hundred Delaware lived at Brotherton in log houses and the community included a meetinghouse, school and gristmill.

The reservation eventually went into decline and in 1801 the remaining inhabitants moved to New York at the invitation of the Stockbridge Indians.[37]

Tree Paintings Tell a Story

The borough of Picture Rocks takes its name from the discovery by the first white settlers of Native American pictures painted on the red shale stone cliffs above Muncy Creek in northcentral Pennsylvania. The pictures didn't survive long, but a bend of Muncy Creek in the vicinity is preserved as a beautiful local park. Picture Rocks was the site of a Munsee village located near the Painted Path or Painted

Picture Rocks (John L. Moore)

Line, called that because of its line of trees with red-and-black paintings of battles, game hunts and other events.

The town of Painted Post, N.Y., takes its name from a wooden post with red-painted figures of men carved on it. The post was discovered by white men in the 1780s. Painted Post is located where the Tioga and Conhocton Rivers merge to form the Chemung River. The site was on the Forbidden Path or Tioga Path guarding the southern doorway to the Iroquois Confederacy. A modern statue shows an Indian warrior before a representation of the original post.

Traders, missionaries and diplomats came upon these tree carvings on the Native American paths they followed on their various pursuits. They took notice of them and described them in their journals. Native Americans made the carvings by peeling a strip of bark from a tree and then painting scenes using red ochre and charcoal. They could be seen for decades.

Moravian missionary David Zeisberger wrote that the carvings could indicate a traveler's tribal status, record of a journey or hunts, or outcome of a battle. "If a party of Indians have spent a night in

Drawing of Native American tree carvings (Tioga Point Museum)

the woods, it may be easily known, not only by the structure of their sleeping huts, but also by their marks on the trees, to what tribe they belong," he wrote.

> "For they always leave a mark behind made either with red pigment or charcoal... Some markings point out the places where a company of Indians have been hunting, showing the number of nights they spent there, the number of deer, bears and other game killed during the hunt. The warriors sometimes paint their own deeds and adventures, the number of prisoners or scalps taken, the number of troops they commanded and how many fell in battle."[38]

In 1745 Moravian Bishop Augustus Spangenberg enroute to Onondaga wrote: "We crossed a creek called Osgochgo and then came to the North Branch of the Susquehanna. Here we found the trees curiously painted by the Indians, representing their wars, the number that had fallen in battle, and the number they had killed.[39]

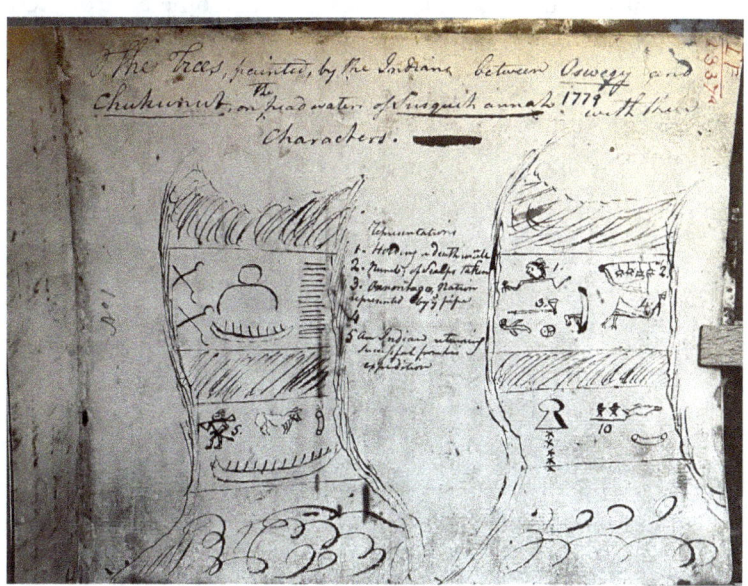

Drawing of tree trunks with carvings (Tioga Point Museum)

During the 1755 Braddock campaign, an unnamed British officer wrote in his journal about a warning sign a few miles west of Fort Necessity: "They (Indians) had drawn many odd figures on ye trees expressing with red paint, ye Scalps and Prisoners they had taken with them; there were three French Names wrote there, Rochefort, Chauraudra & Picuaday."[40]

Moravian missionary John Heckewelder spotted a peeled tree outside the mission town of Pettquotting in Ohio with a verse written in Delaware with charcoal: "The Savior's blood & righteousness."[41]

He described the Indians as having hieroglyphics "on a piece of bark, or on a large tree with the bark taken off for the purpose, by the side of a path, they can and do give the necessary information to those who come by the same way."[42]

The Great Runaway

In the summer of 1778, a strange flotilla headed south along the West Branch of the Susquehanna River. Waterborne craft of every description carried panicked people from their wilderness homes for the relative safety of Fort Augusta at the Forks of the Susquehanna at modern Sunbury, Pa. They fled an onslaught of deadly raids mounted by British-allied Native Americans along Pennsylvania's northern frontier during the American Revolution.

"Boats, canoes, hog troughs, rafts hastily made of dry sticks— every sort of floating article had been put in requisition and were crowded with women, children, and plunder – there were several hundred people in all. Whenever an obstruction occurred at a shoal or riffle, the women would leap out and put their shoulders, not indeed to the wheel, but to the flatboat or raft, and launch it again in deep water," wrote Robert Covenhoven, an American scout.[43]

Armed men walked along the riverbanks to protect their families as the Great Runaway commenced. The exodus came when Fort Augusta's commander Col. Robert Hunter ordered an evacuation of the

West Branch following the Wyoming Valley Massacre and intensifying attacks on outlying forts and homes of settlers.

It was a far cry from the peaceful scene 55 years earlier in 1723 when a group of Palatine families floated in canoes past the Native American village of Shamokin enroute from New York's Schoharie Valley to new homes in Pennsylvania's Tulpehocken Valley.

The contrast between the two journeys reflects the steady movement of Pennsylvania and New Jersey settlers into Iroquois territory in the decades after the French and Indian War. Squatters pushed beyond the lands purchased by Pennsylvania and encroached on Native traditional hunting grounds. The Revolution provided the spark for a renewal of warfare last seen in 1763.

On July 9, 1778, Hunter requested a few hundred troops to help the local defenders and save numbers of lives and prevent the "depredations threatened by the savages on other counties."[44] Fort Augusta had jurisdiction over 14 smaller forts spread out along the Susquehanna's two branches above the Forks. They were manned by militia and sheltered nearby families at times of threat.

Most of these forts were overrun during the next two years, but one that survived was Fort Rice (or Fort Montgomery) near modern Turbotville, Pa. Fort Rice was built in 1779-80 of grey limestone blocks and it stands today surrounded by farmland.[45]

The German Regiment of the American Army, a

Fort Rice (Author)

unit sent to bolster the militia units guarding the region, built Fort Rice. The German Regiment was part of the 1779 Sullivan expedition into Iroquois territory.

The fort is two and one-half stories tall with thick walls and situated over a spring from the headwaters of Chillisquaque Creek. After the German Regiment left the region to rejoin the main American army in the fall of 1780, the militia defending Fort Rice came under attack from a force of loyalists and Indians, but the fort's defenses held and proved their strength.

The West Branch wasn't fully repopulated until after the Revolution ended in 1783.

End Notes

1. James H. Merrill, *Into the American Woods Negotiators on the Pennsylvania Frontier* (New York: W.W. Norton & Company, 1999), 19.
2. Dorothy Cross, *New Jersey Indians* (Trenton, NJ: New Jersey State Museum, 1976), 84.
3. "Military Letters of Capt. Jos. Shippen," *The Pennsylvania Magazine of History and Biography*, Vol. 36, No. 4 (1912), 454.
4. Ibid., 455.
5. *Pennsylvania Archives, 1st Series, Vol. III* (Philadelphia: printed by Joseph Severns & Co. (1853) April 10, 2023 accessed. https://www.hathitrust.org. 583-584.
6. William A. Hunter, *Forts on the Pennsylvania Frontier, 1753-1758* (Harrisburg: The Pennsylvania Historical and Museum Commission, 1960), 557.
7. Robert S. Grumet, ed., *Journey on the Forbidden Path: Chronicles of a Diplomatic Mission to the Allegheny Country, March-September, 1760* (Philadelphia: American Philosophical Society, 1999), 127.
8. Kenneth Wood, "Job Chilloway The Friendly Delaware," *Now and Then*, Vol. 5 (1936), 59.
9. Phillips P. Moulton, ed., *The Journal and Major Essays of John Woolman* (New York: Oxford University Press, 1971), 131-132.
10. John Heckewelder, *A Narrative of the Mission of the United Brethren Among the Delaware and Mohegan Indians, from Its Commencement, in the Year 1740, to the Close of the Year 1808, Comprising All the Remarkable Incidents Which Took Place at Their Missionary Stations During That Period, Interspersed With Anecdotes, Historical Facts, Speeches of Indians and Other Interesting Matter.* (Philadelphia: M'Carty & Davis, 1820), 97.
11. William C. Reichel, "Wyalusing and the Moravian Mission at Friedenshuetten," *Transactions of the Moravian Historical Society* 1, no. 5 (1871) Dec. 28, 2020 accessed. https://www.jstor.org. 313.
12. Ibid., 197-203.
13. Ibid., 214.
14. Ibid., 217.
15. Richard W. Pointer, *Pacifist Prophet Papunhank and the Quest for Peace in Early America* (Lincoln, NE: University of Nebraska Press, 2020), 240-242.
16. Wood, op. cit., 62-63.
17. Samuel Hazard, *Pennsylvania Archives, 1st Series, Vol. 5*. April 10, 2023 accessed. (Philadelphia: printed by Joseph Severns & Co. 1858) https://www.hathitrust.org. 717-718.
18. "From George Washington to Brigadier General Edward Hand, 21 March 1779." Founders Online. Sept. 29, 2019 accessed. https://founders.archives.gov/documents/Washington.

19. Worthington C. Ford, et al., *Journals of the Continental Congress, 1774-1789* (Washington, DC: 1904-37), 19:137. 645.

20. Frederick Cook, *Journals of the Military Expedition of General John Sullivan Campaign Against the Six Nations of Indians in 1779* (Auburn, NY: Knapp, Peck and Thomson, printer, 1887), 257-258.

21. Paul Eugene Miller, "David Zeisberger's Official Diary, Fairfield, 1791-1795," *Transactions of the Moravian Historical Society*, Vol. 19, no. 1 (1963) Dec. 28, 2020 accessed. https://www.jstor.org. 62-64.

22. Ibid., 61.

23. "John Martin Mack, Bishop of the Brethren's Church," *Transactions of the Moravian Historical Society*, Vol. II (Whitefield House, Nazareth: 1886), 237.

24. Ibid., 240.

25. Ibid., 240.

26. John Jordan, "Bishop Cammerhoff's Journey to Shamokin, Pa. 1748," *Pennsylvania Magazine of History and Biography*, Vol. 29, No. 2 (1905), 171-173.

27. John Jordan, "Rev. John Martin Mack's Narrative of a Journey to Onondaga in 1752," *Pennsylvania Magazine of History and Biography*, Vol. 29, No. 3 (1905), 344-345.

28. David Zeisberger and John Martin Mack, "An account of the famine among the Indians of the north and west ranch of the Susquehanna, in the summer of 1748," *Pennsylvania Magazine of History and Biography*, Vol. 16, Nov. 4 (January 1893), 431.

29. William A. Hunter, *Forts on the Pennsylvania Frontier, 1753-1758* (Harrisburg, PA: The Pennsylvania Historical and Museum Commission, 1960), 512-513.

30. Robert Greenhalgh Albion and Leonidas Dodson, eds., *Philip Vickers Fithian: Journal, 1775-1776* (Princeton: Princeton University Press, 1934), 71.

31. John L. Moore, *Murder at Killbuck Island* (Mechanicsburg, PA: Sunbury Press Inc., 2020), 87-90.

32. *The Project Gutenberg ebook of the Life of Rev. David Brainerd, Chiefly Extracted From His Diary*, by Jonathan Edwards. e book #65006. 2021 https://www.gutenberg.org. 164.

33. Ibid., 134.

34. Ibid., 167.

35. Ibid., 173.

36. Ibid., 192.

37. Cross, op. cit., 85-86.

38. Archer Butler Hubert, ed., *David Zeisberger's History of the Northern American Indians* (Lewisburg, PA: Wennawoods Publishing, 1999), 114.

39. Rev. Wm. M. Beauchamp, ed., *Moravian Journals Relating to Central New York, 1745-1766* (Bowie, MD: Heritage Books Inc., 1999), 11.

40. Charles Hamilton, ed., *Braddock's Defeat* (Norman: University of Oklahoma Press, 1959), 45.
41. Paul A. W. Wallace, ed., *Thirty Thousand Miles With John Heckewelder* (University of Pittsburgh Press, 1958), 248.
42. John Heckewelder, *History, Manners, and Customs of the Indian Nations* (Arno Press & The New York Times, 1971), 130.
43. John Meginness, *The Early History of Lycoming County* (Lewisburg, PA: Wennawoods Publishing, 2005), 117.
44. Ibid., 118.
45. Brian J. Mast. "Fort Rice," *The Pennsylvania Magazine of History and Biography*, Volume CXXXVI, No. 4 (October 2012), 503-505.

CHAPTER 6

Seneca Ordeal at Fort Niagara

A frozen and starving encampment of Native Americans huddled along eight miles of the east bank of the Niagara River from Fort Niagara south to modern Lewistown, N.Y., during the unusually harsh winter of 1779.

They were refugees driven from prosperous villages in the Genesee River Valley and elsewhere in New York by invading American armies during the previous summer. The Americans destroyed the homes, fields of corn, squash, beans and other crops and orchards that were meant to tide the Seneca and other nations of the Haudenosaunee or Iroquois Confederacy over the winter months when game was scarce.

The 400-man British garrison at Fort Niagara was short on rations and supplies for itself let alone a refugee diaspora numbering 5,000. The naval supply route along Lake Ontario from British-held Canada was impassable due to winter storms and ice jams. As a result, hundreds of Seneca, Cayuga, Onondagas and members of other tribes died of starvation and exposure to the elements in their rude huts and ice caves that long winter.

Sheltering at Gardeau Flats on the Genesee River, white captive turned Seneca matron Mary Jemison reminisced years later:

> "The snow fell about five feet deep, and remained so for a long time, and the weather was extremely cold; so much so indeed, that almost all the game that the Indians depended upon for subsistence, perished and reduced them almost to a state of starvation through that and three or four succeeding years...

Many of our people barely escaped with their lives, and some actually died of hunger and freezing."[1]

The full horror of the deaths became known in the spring when the British garrison sent out parties to cover the remains of Native Americans in earthen caves with quick lime and seal them to prevent disease from spreading.[2]

The Seneca ordeal at Fort Niagara is not as familiar as other episodes of the American Revolution. It marked a low ebb for the fortunes of the Iroquois Confederacy. The Iroquois held the balance of power earlier in the 18th century between the French and British in the eastern Great Lakes region because they offered a united front. But the American Revolution split the Confederacy apart between British and American factions. Warriors from the Seneca and Oneida Nations actually fought on opposite sides at the Battle of Oriskany in 1777.

The idea of members of the Confederacy opposed to fighting each other would have seemed far-fetched three years earlier when Sir William Johnson, the British superintendent of Indian Affairs in the Northern Colonies, addressed an Iroquois council for the last time outside his home at Johnson Hall in the Mohawk River Valley.

Johnson sought Iroquois help in stopping a border war between Virginians and the Shawnee in Ohio even as rebellious American colonists formed the First Continental Congress. Johnson died suddenly during the council and the Iroquois lost a powerful advocate even though members of his family sought to carry on his work.

A united Confederacy could field some 2,000 warriors in 1774, but during the next two years fissures appeared in an initial neutral policy as the rival Americans and British and loyalists sent envoys to woo the member nations to their side.[3]

By 1776 with the declaration of American Independence, the fighting in the Mohawk Valley resembled a civil war between patriots and loyalists. Guy Johnson, the new British Indian superintendent, and Sir John Johnson fled to Canada that year while Molly Brant, William Johnson's Mohawk wife, fled to Fort Niagara a year later following the Oriskany battle. Molly Brant and her brother Joseph Brant were very influential in swaying the western Iroquois nations to join the British side.

The British plan in 1777 for a three-way invasion of New York in order to separate New England from the rest of the American colonies ended the hesitancy for many Iroquois. They picked the British to keep the trade goods flowing and as the best bet to keep their lands from being encroached upon by white settlers.

The Seneca chief Old Smoke said that the Rebels "wish for nothing more, than to extirpate us from the Earth, that they may possess our Lands, the Desire of attaining which we are convinced is the Cause of the present War between the King and his disobedient children."[4]

The American victory at Saratoga over Gen. John Burgoyne's army ended the invasion plan. The pro-British Iroquois were a major

18th-Century Map of New York (The New York Public Library, Lionel Pincus Princess Firyal Map Division https://digital collections.nypl.org/items.ffledfb0-34b7-0134-663c-00505686a51c)

part of the army of Lt. Col. Barry St. Leger invading east from Oswego on Lake Ontario.

Sizeable numbers of Seneca, including war leaders Old Smoke or Sayenqueraghta and Cornplanter, participated in the unsuccessful siege of Fort Stanwix under St. Leger. The bloodshed at nearby Oriskany hardened attitudes between the majority of Iroquois aligned with the British and a minority, mostly Oneida, siding with the Americans. Thereafter, Fort Niagara became the main British base for launching raids against American settlements in the Mohawk Valley and on the Pennsylvania frontier.

Fort Niagara occupied a strategic chokepoint for military control and trade linking the inland waterway of Lake Ontario with the rest of the Great Lakes via the Niagara River. British governors at Quebec exercised jurisdiction over Fort Niagara. This fort served as the supply connection to British posts farther west at Detroit and Fort Michilimackinac. The fort was also a center for the Iroquois to gather for conferences, trade furs for manufactured goods and bring muskets for repairs.

In 1778, the fortifications at Fort Niagara included the stone Castle, five bastions and two blockhouses manned by its 400-man garrison.

Col. Mason Bolton, the British commander at Fort Niagara starting in 1777, spent much of his time supplying the Iroquois gathered at the fort

Joseph Brant (Library of Congress Prints and Photographs Division http://hdl.loc.gov/loc.pnp/ppmsca.15712)

Fort Niagara (The New York Public Library, The Miriam and Ira D. Wallach Division of Art, Prints and Photographs: Print Collection https://digital collections.nypl.org/items/501d47da-2168-a3d9-e040-e00a18064a99)

with rations, cattle, rum and other sundries worth thousands of pounds to keep their allegiance.[5]

Molly Brant exerted considerable influence over the councils at Fort Niagara given her status as Johnson's widow and member of a prominent Mohawk family.

Joseph Brant led a raid against American settlements in the Mohawk Valley from the town of Onoquaga in the spring of 1778, the first in a spiraling series of tit-for-tat reprisals that continued for four years. Brant often partnered with Major John Butler, leader of a group of loyalist rangers.

Two 1778 raids in particular proved devastating to Americans living on the frontier. The first in July under Butler led to the near wipeout of American militia in the Wyoming Valley in Pennsylvania venturing from a fortified stockade at Forty Fort to defend their homes.

The second raid that November by Butler and Brant at Cherry Valley in New York resulted in the killing of 30 civilians even though the local fort held out. These raids had strategic implications as well since the Mohawk and Wyoming Valleys served as granaries for the American armies.

The raids led American General George Washington to order an expedition in 1779 into the Iroquois homeland to bring about the Confederacy's "total destruction and devastation."[6] This campaign earned Washington the Iroquois nickname of Town Destroyer.

The two-pronged invasion involved troops under Gen. John Sullivan coming from Easton, Pa., and troops under Gen. James Clinton coming from the Mohawk Valley. They met at modern Athens, Pa. Sullivan commanded a combined army of 4,000 soldiers when it defeated a much smaller force of about 700 Iroquois and Butler's rangers at Newtown in late August. This was the only major engagement between the two sides during the campaign.

Another invading American army under Col. Daniel Brodhead moved north from Fort Pitt that summer to attack Seneca villages on the upper Allegheny River. The victory at Newtown opened the way for Sullivan's army to invade the numerous Seneca heartland villages located along the Finger Lakes and Genesee River Valley.

This was a procession of plunder, ruin and total destruction like Washington wanted. It

Groveland massacre monument (John L. Moore)

was hindered only by the ambush of an advance party under Lt. Thomas Boyd on Sept. 13 near modern Groveland, N.Y. The army arrived in early September right at harvest time and found the Seneca fields full of ripening crops. Their villages consisted of wood-framed houses built in the European manner.

"The land exceeds any that I have ever seen," wrote Major John Burrows, "some corn stalks measured eighteen feet, and a cob one foot and a half long. Beans, cucumbers, watermelons, muskmelons, cimblens are in great quantity."[7]

The first target after Newtown was the deserted Catharine's Town, home of Catharine Montour of the celebrated Montour family, where the army burned 30 houses and destroyed crops and fruit orchards.

On Sept. 9 at Seneca Castle, Sgt. Moses Fellows wrote "what Corn, Beans, peas, Squashes, Potatoes, Inions, turnips, Cabage, Cowcumbers, watermilions, Carrots, parsnips &c., our men and horses Cattle &c we could not Eat was Destroyed this Morning before we march..."[8]

At Genesee Castle or Little Beard's Town on Sept. 15, Lt. Col. Adam Hubley found 107 well-finished houses, rich soil and fields of corn, beans, potatoes and all kinds of vegetables. The tortured bodies of Lt. Boyd and Sgt. Michael Parker had been discovered the day before.

> "This morning the whole army, excepting a covering party, were engaged in destroying the corn, beans, potatoes, and other vegetables which were in quantity immense, and in goodness, unequaled by any I ever yet saw. Agreeable to a moderate calculation, there was not less than two hundred acres, the whole of which was pulled and piled up in large heaps, mixed with dry wood, taken from the houses, and consumed in ashes."[9]

Regarding the same episode, Fellows weighed in on the impact of the destruction for the Tories:

> "it is thought we Destroyed 15,000 bushels of Corn, Besides Beans, Squashes, Potatoes in abundance, a great Part of this Corn was Planted By the tories under Butler and Intend's for a magazine to aid them to Carry on their war against our Frontiers as we are informed By Some Prisoners."[10]

Genesee Castle at modern Cuylerville, N.Y., was the farthest advance of Sullivan's army although detachments from there went east to destroy villages along Seneca and Cayuga Lakes. Sullivan decided not to advance westward and attack Fort Niagara about eighty miles away. Sullivan worried about adequate supplies and rations and the lateness of the season as he noted in his official report on Sept. 30. "The number of towns destroyed by this army amounted to 40 besides scattering houses," wrote Sullivan. "The quantity of corn destroyed, at a moderate computation, must amount to 160,000 bushels, with a vast quantity of vegetables of every kind."[11]

But Major Jeremiah Fogg was prescient with his summation: "The nests are destroyed, but the birds are still on the wing."[12]

Loyalist Col. Butler tried in vain to obtain reinforcements from the British and Iroquois for another round with Sullivan. Instead, a diaspora of thousands of homeless Iroquois headed to Fort Niagara, already burdened with refugees and scarce food supplies as a result of the 1778 campaigns.

The Seneca matron Mary Jemison described in her life narrative years later how in the destroyed Iroquois villages:

> "there was not a mouthful of any kind of substance left, not even enough to keep a child one day from perishing with hunger. I immediately resolved to take children and look out for myself, without delay. With this intention I took two of my little ones on my back, bade the other three follow, and the same night arrived at the Gardeau flats, where I have ever since resided."[13]

Jemison took refuge with two escaped black slaves who lived in a cabin.

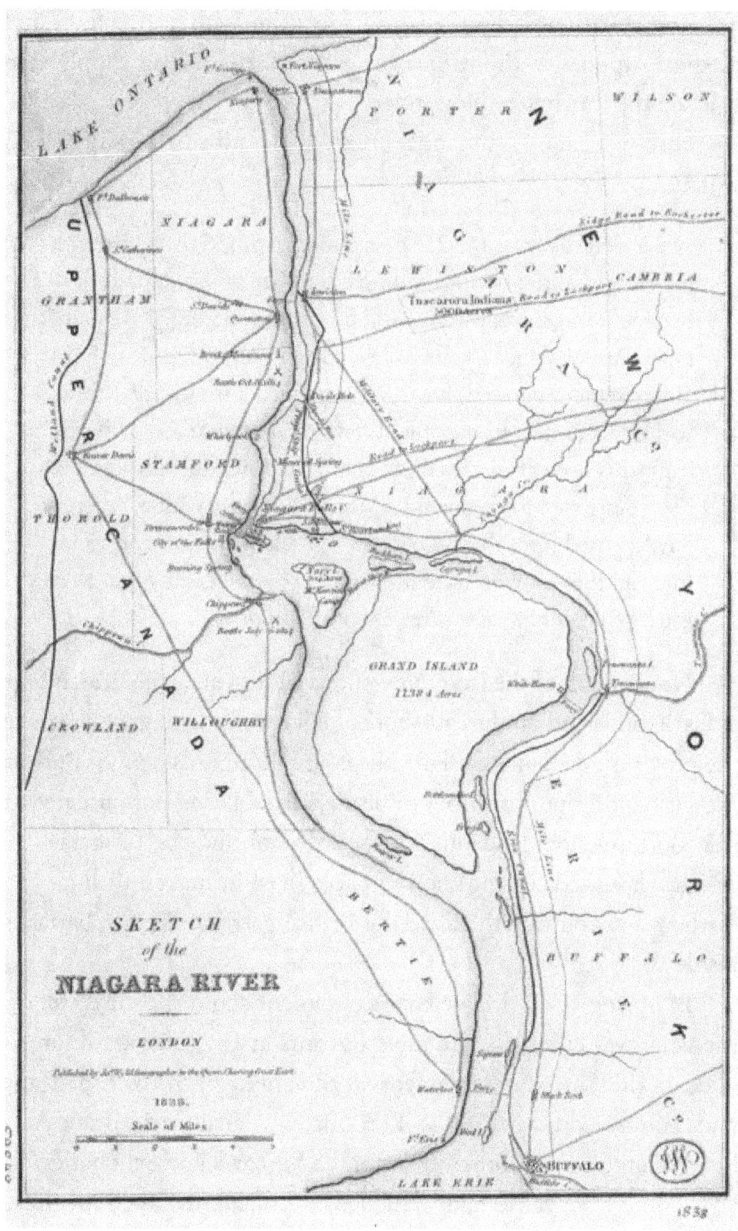

Sketch of Niagara River (The New York Public Library Digital Collections https://nypl.getarchive.net)

The situation at Fort Niagara was grim with scarce food and medical supplies as the winter closed in. A last British supply ship reached the fort in late November.

Fort Niagara commander Bolton described the dire food situation:

> "we had at this Post the 21st of last month 5,036 to supply with provisions, and notwithstanding a number of parties that have been sent out since, we have still on the ground 3,678 to maintain. I am convinced your Excellency will not be surprised, if I am extremely alarmed, for to support such a multitude I think will be absolutely impossible. I have requested of Major Butler to try his utmost to prevail on the Indians whose villages have been destroyed to go down to Montreal for the winter, where I have assured him, they would be well taken care of; and to inform all the rest who have not suffered by the enemy that they must return home and take care of their corn."[14]

Not enough of the Iroquois went to Montreal or the British base at Carleton Island on the east shore of Lake Ontario to greatly reduce the provision demands on Fort Niagara. During this period, Butler's Rangers and important Iroquois leaders lived in log huts situated at The Bottoms, low land outside the fort fronting the Niagara River. The thousands of common refugees lived in makeshift huts and earthen caves outside the fort. The British garrison lived in barracks inside the fort.[15]

By spring 1780, Major Fogg's comment about the birds still on the wing was evident as Iroquois warriors at Fort Niagara resumed raids on the American settlements at the urging of the British. These raids continued from 1780 to 1782 hitting Canajoharie, Stone Arabia, Warrenbush and other towns in the Mohawk and Schoharie Valleys. Some were cattle raids designed to procure livestock for those drawing British rations at Fort Niagara.

To lessen dependency on Fort Niagara's rations, Quebec Gov. Sir

Frederick Haldimand encouraged the resettlement of Iroquois refugees to Buffalo Creek at the site of modern Buffalo, N.Y. The refugees traveled south along the Niagara Falls Portage to lands once farmed by the French agent Chabert Joncaire. The British provided seed corn and hoes so they could start planting, but supplies were limited.

"We broke up the sod with hoes; we had no plows or cattle or work horses, so we had to do the best we could about planting things. We obtained the hoes, which the British government furnished us, and some money and hunting utensils were also furnished to us at that time," related Seneca Chief Chainbreaker in a memoir published years later.[16]

In May 1780, British Indian Superintendent Guy Johnson said that more than 1,000 Iroquois relocated to Buffalo Creek.[17] This is the genesis of what became the Seneca Buffalo Creek Reservation. The Seneca lost most of their lands west of the Genesee River at the Treaty of Big Tree in 1797. Buffalo Creek was one of nine initial Seneca reservations. The Seneca lost Buffalo Creek in 1845 to speculators who wanted their land because it was in the path of the expanding city of Buffalo.

Colonel Bolton at Fort Niagara

A career soldier in the British Army, Lt. Col. Mason Bolton commanded at Fort Niagara during the perilous years between 1777 and 1780. He dealt with a series of crises that taxed his health—starving Iroquois refugees and the costly expense of providing them with the limited goods available, lack of medicines, fear of American attack and discord between Loyalist Col. John Butler and Indian Superintendent Guy Johnson.

Bolton (?-1780) counted 30 years of service with the British army mainly in Florida and the West Indies before arriving at Fort Niagara. He was Lt. Colonel of the King's or 8th Regiment of Foot, the regiment charged with garrisoning forts along the Great Lakes.[18]

The 8th regiment was stationed at Quebec and Montreal until 1774 when it was assigned to guard the Great Lakes posts at Oswegatchie, Niagara, Detroit and Michilimackinac.

The regiment's garrison duties at Fort Niagara included handling the vast quantity of goods moving through the post to forts in the west. Small detachments of the 8th participated in the attack against American settlers at Cherry Valley in 1778, the Battle of Newtown in 1779 and attacks in the Mohawk and Schoharie Valleys in 1780 and 1781.[19]

After years of disrepair, Fort Niagara's earthwork and stockade defenses were strengthened with construction in 1770-71 of the south and north stone redoubts that stand guard to this day. The redoubts featured a guard room on the second floor and smaller cannon on the third floor. The redoubts have unique Chinese-style roofs with flaring eaves.

Even before the Sullivan campaign, Bolton had dealt with the problems of supporting Loyalist refugees from the Mohawk Valley and refugees from Iroquois towns whose seasonal planting had been disrupted by war.

He reported in May 1778 that he spent nearly 18,000 pounds on goods for the Iroquois, "2,700 being assembled at a time when I little expected such a number, obliged me to send to Detroit for a supply of provisions, and to buy up all the cattle, etc., that could possibly be procured."[20]

Officials of the British Northern Indian Department relayed the requests to Bolton for goods and presents to help retain the loyalty of the Iroquois. Initially the spending requests came from Loyalist Col. Butler in his dual capacity as deputy superintendent.

The Indian Department had been thrown in turmoil at the Revolution's start. The new Superintendent Guy Johnson, William Johnson's nephew, and associate Daniel Claus, William Johnson's son-in-law, fled the Mohawk Valley for Canada in 1775 to avoid arrest by Patriot militia.

Johnson, Claus and Mohawk leader Joseph Brant traveled to London in 1776 to lobby to keep their positions after an army officer was appointed as Superintendent for Indian Affairs in Canada.[21] Guy Johnson eventually returned to New York City, but he didn't appear at Fort Niagara, the main site for Indian conferences, until 1779.

In the interim, Butler exercised the dual roles of Deputy Indian Superintendent and commander of Butler's Rangers, a development that hindered the Department's effectiveness. The Johnson family was critical of Butler's performance and he lost influence when Guy Johnson arrived at Fort Niagara.

Bolton's tenure was also marked by competition among the commercial traders for primacy in supplying the Army and its Iroquois allies. Butler's favorites were sidelined when Guy Johnson appeared on the scene.[22]

The question of whether Fort Niagara with its 400-man garrison could have withstood an attack by Sullivan's 4,000-man army equipped with artillery in the fall of 1779 wasn't put to a test. Sullivan's army withdrew after coming within 80 miles from Fort Niagara. For Bolton, the difficulties of command during the succeeding winter were compounded by his sickness. Many in Bolton's command were ill that winter, too. He requested leave in September 1779.

He left Niagara at the end of October aboard the newly-built *Ontario*, a sloop-of-war with 22 guns, and largest vessel on the Great Lakes until that date. The *Ontario* sank in a fierce storm on the night of Oct. 31 on Lake Ontario taking the lives of Bolton and at least 87 other passengers. Only six bodies were recovered and the *Ontario's* whereabouts remained a mystery until discovery by divers in 1995. The story of the lost *Ontario* is superbly told in *Legend of the Lake: The 22-Gun Brig-Sloop Ontario* by Arthur Britton Smith.[23]

Catharine Montour

As Gen. John Sullivan's army marched north after the Battle of Newtown, they came to Catharine's Town, a deserted Seneca village except for an elderly woman. This town at modern-day Montour Falls, N.Y., was named for Catharine Montour, a member of a prominent family on the New York-Pennsylvania frontier.

"Catharine's town is pleasantly situated on a creek, three miles from Seneca lake; it contained 50 houses, in general, very good, --the country near is excellent. We found several very fine corn-fields, which afforded the greatest plenty of corn, beans, &c., of which, after our fatiguing march, we had an agreeable repast," wrote Lt. Col. Adam Hubley of Sullivan's expedition.[24]

"The Queen's Pallace was a gambril ruft house about 30 feet long and 18 feet wide," wrote Lt. William Kendry.[25]

Sullivan's troops camped at the town on Sept. 1 and burnt the houses and destroyed crops and orchards there the next day before departing. Catharine Montour had fled the town along with the inhabitants as Sullivan's army approached. With that, the Montour family begins its fade out from recorded history.

For three generations, the Montour family was influential in the interactions between the Iroquois, French and British. Their legacy is remembered in place names in Pennsylvania and New York. The members of this extended family are mentioned in the journals of missionaries, traders and military officers. Yet they are shrouded in legend, too. Much of the information about their ancestry, birth dates and death dates is contradictory.

The matriarchal figure of the family was Madame Montour, also known as Isabelle Montour or Elizabeth Couc. She was of French-Algonquin ancestry from Quebec, but gained a reputation as an interpreter at provincial conferences with Native Americans in New York and Pennsylvania.

In 1742, the Moravian Church leader Count Nicholas Ludwig

Von Zinzendorf visited Madame Montour at the village of Ostonwakin at modern Montoursville, Pa., on the Susquehanna River. The Count wrote unsympathetically about Madame Montour saying she was ignorant of Jesus' life despite having been brought up as a Christian. He observed she was displeased when he wouldn't grant her request to baptize two children.[26]

Zinzendorf recorded a fuller description of Andrew Montour, the Madame's son, and a renowned interpreter and frontier scout for the British in his own right. Andrew's face was adorned with bear fat, yet he wore a waistcoat and breeches, wrote Zinzendorf.[27]

Madame Montour had a relative (variously described as a sister, niece or daughter) named French Margaret who lived at a village bearing her name at the mouth of Lycoming Creek at modern Williamsport, Pa. The Moravian missionary John Martin Mack visited French Margaret in 1753. She served Mack and his party milk and watermelon.

"French Margaret is also held in high esteem by the Indians, and allows no drunkard in her town. Her husband is a Mohawk, who understands French well, as also their children, but they do not speak it," wrote Mack.[28]

John Hays, a Pennsylvania militia lieutenant, reported he ate breakfast with French Margaret during a diplomatic journey in 1760, but she is said to be living then on the Chemung River near modern Elmira, N.Y.[29]

French Margaret's two daughters are known as Catharine Montour and Queen Esther. They figure in the accounts of Revolutionary War campaigns in 1778 and 1779.

Queen Esther's Town was located near the Iroquois southern gateway town of Tioga at the juncture of the Chemung River and Susquehanna River. An American army under Col. Thomas Hartley destroyed the town during an upriver expedition following the Wyoming Valley Massacre in 1778. Queen Esther is the subject of an early legend that she personally tomahawked American prisoners to death during the massacre.

The Pennsylvania Historical and Museum Commission erected a historical marker in 1962 in Wyoming, Pa., recognizing The Bloody Rock as where a woman "traditionally but not certainly identified as Queen Esther" murdered the prisoners.[30] But there is much dispute about whether Queen Esther or any Native American woman was even at the scene.

Catharine Montour's legacy is remembered at Montour Falls, but reports of her fate after the flight from Catharine's Town are fragmentary. The modern Catharine Valley trail marks the town's site, a monument to Catharine Montour in Cook Cemetery Memorial Park and the remnants of the 19th-century Chemung Canal.

Old Smoke

Old Smoke was a Seneca leader known by a variety of names. These include Old King, the Seneca King, Sayenqueraghta and Kaien'kwaahton. He fought on the British side in the French and Indian War and American Revolution.[31]

Old Smoke plays a role in a turning point in the Seneca matron Mary Jemison's long life. Following the end of Pontiac's War in 1764, there was a determined effort by the British to secure the return of hundreds of white captives taken during a decade of conflict.

Taken captive as a teenager during a Delaware raid on her family's home in Adams County, Pa., in 1758, Jemison was a young mother living contentedly with her Seneca family in the Genesee Valley by then. Old Smoke attempted to return Jemison to British-held Fort Niagara, but her brother sent her to a hiding place while he told Old Smoke to call off his search.

"In the morning after I fled, as was expected, the old King (as Old Smoke is referred to here) came to our house in search of me, and to take me off; but, as I was not to be found, he gave up and went to Niagara with the prisoners he had already got into in his possession," related Jemison in her life narrative decades later.[32]

During the Revolution, Old Smoke fought at the Battle of Oriskany in 1778, the Wyoming Massacre in 1778 and the Battle of Newtown in 1779. He was among the thousands of Seneca refugees at Fort Niagara during the winter of 1779-80. But Old Smoke probably fared better than many others during this grim period. The British built log houses for key Seneca leaders at the Bottoms as Col. Mason Bolton noted.[33]

Old Smoke and his family were among the first of the Seneca to settle with British support in the spring of 1780 at Buffalo Creek. They lived there in a log cabin and planted corn, potatoes and squash while also drawing supplies from Fort Niagara. This became the genesis of the Buffalo Creek Reservation.[34]

Old Smoke died in 1786 and Smokes Creek in modern Lackawanna, N.Y is named for him.

Mary Jemison at Gardeau Flats

Mary Jemison fled to the isolated Gardeau Flats along the Genesee River in modern Letchworth State Park to find food for her young family after American General John Sullivan's destructive march in 1779. The Seneca captive lived there for five decades eventually becoming known as the "White Woman of the Genesee."

Gardeau was as remote as the Pennsylvania backcountry cabin where Jemison lived with her Scots-Irish family until captured during a Delaware raid in 1758.

Jemison was in her thirties by the time she reached Gardeau. She had survived the murder of her parents as a teenager, a captive's march, been adopted by the Seneca as Deh-ge-wa-nus in the Ohio Country, then migrated to the Genesee Valley and raised a family with two husbands.

Jemison initially found shelter at first with two runaway Black slaves living in a cabin. She helped them harvest their corn crop and shared their cabin until she built her own hut. Hiakotoo, Jemison's Seneca warrior husband, was away leading retaliatory campaigns against the Americans during these wartime years. The two Blacks left after several years leaving Jemison squatter's rights to the bottom land.

Jemison established herself as a self-sufficient homesteader to the extent that she was awarded a 17,000-acre land tract known as the Gardeau Reservation by the 1797 Treaty of Big Tree. This treaty marked a large cession of Seneca territory following American Independence. The Seneca had nearby smaller reservations at Big Tree, Little Beard's and Squakie Hill for a while as a result of this treaty.

"My land derived its name, Gardow, from a hill that is within its limits, which is called in the Seneca language Kautam. Kautam when interpreted signifies up and down, or down and up, and is applied to a hill that you will ascend and descend when passing it," wrote Jemison in her life narrative.[35]

The arrival of white settlers during the next decade brought both opportunity and trouble for Jemison. With Hiakotoo's death in 1811 at an advanced age, Jemison was truly on her own.

Societal changes that greatly disrupted the Iroquois way of life were hard on her family. Three of her sons met with violent deaths. That was one of Jemison's greatest trials because one of the sons, John, killed the other two Thomas and Jesse in separate incidents. Three daughters outlived her.

Jemison became familiar to the white settlers giving them food if they were destitute, leasing them farmland and even carrying boards from Ebenezer Allen's sawmill for her daughter's log cabin.[36]

She was a target of land speculators. In one instance, a man named George Jemison claiming to be her cousin lived on her land for a number of years. George Jemison eventually asked her to deed him some of the tract. In her narrative, Mary Jemison wrote of her reluctance to sign the deed without a witness "knowing my ignorance of writing." The suspect deed, she related, contained 400 acres rather than the 40 acres she intended to transfer. She soon cast him out.[37]

The year 1817 brought a geological phenomenon known as the Big Slide to Gardeau. This was a collapse of a high bank of land on the Genesee near the home of Jemison's daughter Polly.

At this time Jemison and two white men she counted as advisors started making arrangements for the sale of her coveted land. A key step was taken when the New York legislature made her a naturalized United States citizen. In 1823 Jemison sold most of her land except for a small portion following assent at a Seneca-U.S. government council. Rev. Timothy Alden, a Seneca missionary, described her in 1820 as living in a "comfortably Indian style" and being able to converse in English yet showing the reserve of a Seneca about her.[38]

Jemison spent the last two years of her life at the Seneca Buffalo Creek Reservation dying in 1833 at age 88. Jemison left her mark on posterity when she spent three days in 1823 relating her life story to Dr. James Seaver at Whaley Tavern at modern Castile, N.Y. Her story was published as *A Narrative of the Life of Mary Jemison* and became an early bestseller. The book remains in print today having gone through numerous editions with much supplementary material added and deleted over the years.

This book didn't come about happenstance. A group of locals met at Whaley Tavern, home of the area's first white settlers Robert and Janet Whaley, to discuss approaching Jemison about the project. Seaver who dabbled in poetry was hired to interview her.[39]

"My strength has been great for a woman of my size, otherwise I must long ago have died under the burdens which I was obliged to carry," reflected Jemison at the narrative's end.

> "I learned to carry loads on my back, in a strap placed across my forehead, soon after my captivity, and continue to carry in the same way…I have planted, hoed and harvested every season but one since I was taken prisoner. Even this present fall I have husked my corn and backed it into the house."[40]

Gardeau Overlook Mary Jemison homestead (Author)

One can speculate about how much Seaver truly captured of Jemison's voice, but the book nevertheless lifted her into legend.

This much was guaranteed in 1874 when philanthropist William Letchworth removed Jemison's remains from the Buffalo Creek graveyard threatened by urbanization and reinterred them in a grove near his home at what eventually became Letchworth State Park.

Nearby the grave topped with a bronze statue of a young Dehge-wa-nus is the relocated log cabin owned by Jemison's daughter Nancy and a relocated Seneca Council House that was built before the Revolution. A New York State historical marker marks the site of Whaley Tavern on Route 39 west of Castile. A 19th-century photo shows a three-sectioned tavern with a low overhanging roof.

The Gardeau Overlook at Letchworth State Park offers a panoramic view of the flats. Today Gardeau is a remote area of the park where excess floodwater is stored for the U.S. Army Corps of Engineers Mount Morris Dam and Recreation Area. The area was farmed until the dam was built in the early 1950s. Some twenty feet of silt covers the farm that Jemison lived on.

Three Captives Shape Genesee History

Seneca matron Mary Jemison isn't the only white captive who left a legacy in her adoptive homeland.

Horatio Jones (1763-1836), Sarah Whitmore (1768-c. 1792) and Jasper Parrish (1767-1836) came to the region as Seneca captives during the American Revolution.

Jones and Whitmore shared an unusual love story. Both Jones and Parrish knew Jemison and played roles in key moments of her life. Parrish was influential for decades as an Indian agent for the U.S. government. They were all young when taken captive to the Genesee region and each decided to remain in the area after the Revolution ended. The stories of Jones, Whitmore and Parrish are told in the narrative history *Life of Horatio Jones* published in 1903.

At age 16, Jones was captured in 1781 when his American ranger unit was overrun by a Seneca war party near Bedford, Pa. Jones exhibited courage when he and other prisoners ran a gauntlet of Seneca wielding clubs at a village in the Genesee River region. The scene apparently took place at the Caneadea Council House, relocated a century later by William Letchworth to what is now Letchworth State Park. A historical plaque at the council house states that prisoners ran the gauntlet there. A relative of the Seneca leader Cornplanter adopted Jones. He adapted to Seneca customs, learned their language and became an interpreter for them.

Jones and Whitmore met at a communal passenger pigeon hunt near Seneca Lake. Whitmore had been taken captive during a raid on her family's homestead in eastern Pennsylvania. Age 15, she was caring for two younger brothers and a baby at their cabin while her family was away boiling sap to make maple syrup. A war party raided the cabin and took them prisoner. They killed the baby and Whitmore was separated from her brothers.[41]

A Seneca family from the Genesee region adopted Whitmore. At the pigeon hunt, Whitmore asked Jones for advice on dealing with a marriage proposal from a Seneca chief. Jones suggested that he and Whitmore get married on a temporary basis until both were free. She agreed and they married only to later affirm their vows as free individuals before a minister in Schenectady, N.Y., in 1784. The Treaty of Fort Stanwix signed that same year had freed all Seneca-held captives.

The couple lived in the Genesee region where Jones ran a trading post and maintained his close contacts with the Seneca. They had four children but Whitmore died at an early age and Jones later remarried.[42]

Jones encountered Parrish, taken captive in 1778, for the first time at British-held Fort Niagara early in their captivity. At age eleven, Parrish and his father were captured by a party of Munsee while working in their cornfield on the Delaware River in southern New York State.[43]

Parrish was adopted by a Mohawk family and eventually freed with the Treaty of Stanwix. He returned to his birth family and faced some difficulty readjusting to white life. Parrish's fluency with Native American languages led to him becoming an interpreter for the U.S. Government in 1790. He was based at Canandaigua, N.Y. Jones was appointed U.S. sub-agent to the Six Nations in 1803 and served in the post until 1829.

Jones and Parrish served as interpreters at the 1797 Treaty of Big Tree where the Seneca ceded most of their land in western New York. They are credited with persuading American financier Rob-

Portrait of Jasper Parrish, Indian agent (Jasper Parrish Papers, Vassar College Digital Library)

ert Morris and Seneca leaders to grant Mary Jemison the Gardeau Tract where she had lived since 1779.

"Red Jacket (the prominent Seneca leader) not only opposed my claim at the council, but he withheld my money two or three years, on the account of my lands having been granted without his consent," related Jemison in her life narrative. "Parrish and Jones at length convinced him that it was the white people and not the Indians who have given me the land and compelled him to pay over all the money which he had retained in my account."[44]

When Jemison decided in 1823 to sell most of her Gardeau Tract to white settlers, a council of American officials and Seneca leaders met to give needed approval. Jones was present as an interpreter and Parrish in his role as sub-agent.[45] The Seneca gave Jones and Parrish two tracts of land in modern Buffalo, N.Y., for their services at Big Tree.[46]

Yet the two operated for decades in an environment where the Seneca eventually lost most of their original land and much of the reservation acreage carved out for them at Big Tree. One report to the Quaker Indian Committee mentions Jones and Parrish working in 1816 for the Ogden Land Co., a firm that sought for decades to obtain the remaining Seneca land.[47]

Both Jones and Parrish died in 1836 at Geneseo, N.Y., and Canandaigua respectively as respected survivors of the Revolutionary War era.

Cherry Valley and Stone Arabia

The 1779 Sullivan campaign didn't end the British Tory/Iroquois attacks on American towns along the New York and Pennsylvania frontiers as Major Jeremiah Fogg foresaw in his comment about the birds being still on the wing. The Haudenosaunee or Iroquois staged raids in revenge for the destruction of their villages and crops starting in the spring of 1780.

Indeed, the Revolution in these backcountry regions was a series of retaliatory actions, tit for tat as both sides mobilized to extract punishment for previous atrocities. Two British raids—the November 1778 raid on Cherry Valley and 1780 attack on Stone Arabia both in the Mohawk River Valley—stand out.

A force of Loyalists and Iroquois under Capt. Walter Butler and Joseph Brant swooped down on Cherry Valley named for its cherry orchards. The local Fort Alden held out against the attack, but the commander Col. Ichabod Alden was killed at the house outside the fort where he was staying.

Cherry Valley earned notoriety because of the deaths of 32 civilians, mainly women and children, who were killed by Seneca warriors in some cases at their homes outside the fort. The death toll included some Loyalists and 15 American soldiers.[48]

The Americans decried the deaths by tomahawk while the overall responsibility of Butler and Brant for the massacre has been debated since it ended. There are accounts of the two leaders acting to save individuals in harm's way and questions about whether they could have done more. An 1878 monument marking the spot where the dead are buried is located in the Cherry Valley Cemetery on Alden Street in Cherry Valley, N.Y.

Stone Arabia

The Palatines left their homes in the German Rhineland in the early 18th century to escape continual religious warfare and eventually settled in New York. By 1723, a group of 28 Palatine families settled at modern Palatine Bridge, N.Y., in the Mohawk River Valley. They were attracted by a land patent for 17,000 acres of rich farmland in an area called Stone Arabia.

The Palatines built up a peaceful wheat-growing agriculture community for the next five decades until the American Revolution broke out. They experienced the turmoil of the "The Bloody Mohawk" a name for the civil war between Patriots and Loyalists that gripped the region. In October 1780, the warfare directly touched Stone Arabia.

Sir John Johnson, the exiled son of the late Sir William Johnson, invaded the American-controlled Mohawk Valley with a force of some 1,500 Loyalists, Iroquois and some British Army units. Lt. Col. John Butler of Butler's Rangers and Joseph Brant were part of this campaign. Johnson sailed from the British base on Carleton Island on Lake Ontario, landed at Oswego and then spent a month fighting several battles and destroying homes, barns, mills and bushels of wheat on a scale similar to the Sullivan campaign.[49]

The Battle of Stone Arabia occurred on Oct. 19 when Johnson's force encountered several hundred American soldiers under command of Col. John Brown based at local Fort Paris. Johnson's force burnt homes and barns in Stone Arabia and soundly defeated Brown's force, killing him and about 100 of his soldiers.[50]

Johnson's forces burned the heart of the community, a wooden frame Dutch Reformed Church. In 1788 the Palatines built a beautiful limestone church that stands today on Route 10 north of Palatine Bridge. A monument in the church cemetery marks where Col. Brown and a number of his soldiers are buried.

Joseph Brant Leads Exodus to Canada

Joseph Brant lived a long and eventful life starting as a protégé of Sir William Johnson and then exercising influence with his sister Molly Brant in Six Nations councils, fighting on the British side during the American Revolution and later creating a Six Nations settlement in Canada.

The contemporaries of Brant or Thayendanegea (1742-1807) often misunderstood his motives. He was like other prominent Native Americans who moved between two worlds in the 18th century. Brant's travels took him to Connecticut for schooling, Montreal, London twice, Fort Niagara, Quebec, Philadelphia, Detroit, the Grand River region of Canada and modern Brantford, Ontario. He was a Mohawk, a member of the eastern tribe of the Iroquois Confederacy who lived closest to white settlements in the Mohawk River Valley.

Brant was born in the Ohio Country where his parents emigrated, but his mother returned to her family home in the Mohawk Valley after her husband died. As a teenager, Brant was on British Army campaigns during the French and Indian War, including the 1759 campaign that captured French-held Fort Niagara.[51]

Brant's association with Sir William Johnson began when the latter visited his family's home in Canajoharie, N.Y. Those ties were strengthened when Molly Brant became Johnson's wife in 1759. Johnson sent Joseph Brant to an "Indian" school run by Rev. Eleazar Wheelock in Columbus, Conn. Brant's language skills put him in demand as an interpreter at British-Six Nations conferences.

Brant's ties to the Johnson family kept him loyal to King George III when the Revolution broke out. Brant fled to Montreal with Johnson's heirs when Patriot militia threatened the family's position in the Mohawk Valley. He went to London in 1775-1776 to seek British help in safeguarding Mohawk lands. The British replied that the American rebellion must be crushed first.

London treated Brant as a celebrity. He was painted by artist George Romney and interviewed by future literary icon James Boswell for *The London Magazine*. Boswell reported that Brant was educated and spoke English well, was not a savage, and would raise three thousand men for the British.[52]

Brant urged the Six Nations to declare for the British in 1777 and led forces, consisting of Native Americans and white Loyalists, in many of the major frontier engagements—Oriskany, German Flats, Cherry Valley, Minisink, Newtown, Stone Arabia—of the war during the next five years. Molly Brant gave the British useful intelligence prior to Oriskany and fled her Mohawk Valley home for Fort

Niagara after that. The raids that Brant helped lead wreaked havoc and destruction among American settlements. He was often accused in early Patriot accounts of committing atrocities. Brant got widely blamed for the Wyoming Valley Massacre, but his chief biographer points out he wasn't at the scene.[53]

Brant's southernmost raid culminated in the Battle at Minisink Ford near modern Barryville, N.Y., on July 22, 1779. Brant had raided settlements at Mahackamack in the Neversink River Valley at modern Port Jervis, N.Y. American militia then pursued Brant's forces along the Upper Delaware River. The Americans planned to ambush Brant at Minisink Ford on the Delaware, but Brant was alerted to their presence. He outflanked the Americans and they retreated up to a hill on the New York side. The Americans and Brant's forces fought for several hours with the former eventually making a last stand at Hospital Rock, so named because that is where American Lt. Col. Benjamin Tusten and 17 wounded soldiers were killed. Hospital Rock is among the topographic features at Minisink Battleground Park maintained by Sullivan County.

Hospital Rock Battle of Minisink Ford (Author)

A 1778 meeting with Canadian Governor Sir Frederick Haldimand in Quebec proved important for Brant's course following the war. Haldimand told Brant the Mohawks would be granted land if they couldn't return home to the Mohawk Valley following the war.[54]

Brant endured the horrific winter at Fort Niagara in 1779 and led more raids for several years after that. With the Revolution's end, he turned his attention towards obtaining the promise of land for the pro-British Mohawk in Canada. The Six Nations were stunned to learn that the British transferred their lands to the Americans in the 1783 peace treaty.

Brant pursued a two-track strategy of obtaining a land grant along the Grand River in 1784 at Brantford, and trying unsuccessfully to create a new confederation of the Six Nations and the Ohio Country tribes to confront the Americans.

The new grant attracted some 1,800 residents, including 400 Mohawk, several hundred Cayugas and Onondagas and smaller groups from a half-dozen other tribes.[55] Brant fought verbal and legal battles with Canadian officials in the ensuing years over land rights at Grand River and ultimately the settlement survived as his chief legacy.

About two-thirds of the Six Nations remained in the United States. The Seneca were established first at Buffalo Creek, and then following the 1797 Treaty of Big Tree at scattered reservations. These were eventually consolidated into three reservations at Tonawanda, Cattaraugus and Allegany in western New York.

Over time, the Six Nations living in New York and Canada drew apart as they faced the difficult challenges of accommodating and negotiating with the American and British governments respectively. By 1803, the two groups had established separate council fires at Buffalo Creek for the Seneca remaining in New York and at Grand River for Brant's followers. The War of 1812 between Britain and the United States further strained ties between the two groups.

The lore of Letchworth State Park in the Genesee Valley region includes the 1872 council where descendants of the Iroquois leaders at the time of the Revolution reunited. The occasion was the rededication of a Seneca Council House that William Letchworth relocated to his estate. Grandsons of Joseph Brant and Cornplanter shook hands at the ceremony.

Today the nine Six Nations communities in New York and seven Six Nations communities in Ontario maintain close ties.

Jemima Wilkinson—The Public Universal Friend

This charismatic leader of a religious cult preached on several occasions to the Seneca as she established a communal society in their own homelands. Accounts differ on whether Wilkinson, known as "The Public Universal Friend," made a good impression on them.

Wilkinson (1752-1819) began her calling as a teenager after contracting a fever, awakening from a coma and then proclaiming herself a new person neither female or male and taking the name of The Public Universal Friend. The Friend broke with a Quaker family background and wore a mix of male and female clothing as she took up preaching.

"She called herself, the 'Universal Friend,' and would not permit herself to be designated by any other appellation," wrote Thomas Morris, son of American financier Robert Morris. "She pretended to have had revelations from Heaven, in which she had been directed to devote her labors to the conversion of sinners."[56]

By the 1780s, The Friend had attracted a group of followers and looked for a site in western New York to build a new religious community. The society called their first settlement City Hill on the site of an old Seneca village. They then moved in 1792 to a second place called Jerusalem Town on Keuka Lake.

In 1791 The Friend preached to a gathering of Seneca at Seneca Lake. The white interpreters Horatio Jones and Jasper Parrish were with this group and likely interpreted for her. But an account of this event mentions one of the Seneca being disgruntled because The Friend also relied on an interpreter to know what the Seneca were saying.[57]

The Friend also preached during the 1794 Treaty of Canandaigua that established a formal peace between the Six Nations and the United States. The Friend died in 1819 at age 67 and the celibate society left behind didn't hold together for long.

The Friend was part of the first of a wave of religious prophets, seekers and spiritualists who appeared throughout the 19th century and gave the nickname the "Burned-over District" to Western and Central New York. The Friend is even remembered today as a nonbinary religious leader.

Buffalo Creek Reservation

The Seneca knew it as "the place of basswoods" for the basswood trees along the banks of the creek.[58] Evidence of prehistoric occupation here was found in refuse heaps excavated in the 19th century. But the real importance of what became known as the Buffalo Creek Reservation is that it was the principal Seneca settlement in the United States for six decades.

"The Buffalo Creek Reservation was in general a flat plain tilted upward to the east," wrote Frederick Houghton in *The History of the Buffalo Creek Reservation*. "This tilted plain is bisected by Buffalo Creek and by its main branches, Cazenovia Creek and Cayuga Creek. Its southern portion is cut by Smoke's Creek which enters it on its southern edge and continues in it to its mouth."[59]

The first historic occupants at Buffalo Creek, a tributary of the Buffalo River, were the Seneca leader Old Smoke and others relocated by the British in the spring of 1780 to lessen the refugee crisis at Fort Niagara in the aftermath of the Sullivan campaign. The population grew to more than 1,500 a year later. The British also encouraged white Loyalist refugees to start farmsteads on the west side of the Niagara River in the vicinity of modern Niagara-on-the Lake, Ontario, in order to reduce Fort Niagara's dependence on supplies from Montreal.

The Iroquois felt betrayed that the 1783 peace treaty recognizing the independence of the United States didn't recognize their land rights, but Buffalo Creek remained in the British orbit until 1796 when King George III gave up control over Fort Niagara under the Jay Treaty.

An American diplomat, Col. Thomas Proctor, speculated on April 27, 1791, during a visit that the Seneca at Buffalo Creek were better clothed than those in villages farther away due to interactions with the British at Fort Niagara.[60]

In 1797 at the Treaty of Big Tree, the Seneca sold virtually all their land west of the Genesee River to American land speculators. The treaty carved out eleven reservations for the Seneca, including the 130-square mile Buffalo Creek Reservation. The inhabitants of Buffalo Creek lived in log cabins in separate villages associated with tribal leaders or in scattered clearings. In time, frame wooden houses replaced many of the log cabins.

The Seneca orator Red Jacket lived close to the Seneca Mission Church near the present Seneca Indian Park at Indian Church Road in South Buffalo. Jack Berry's town was in modern Gardenville, N.Y. Big Kettle lived at modern East Elma, N.Y. A band of Cayuga

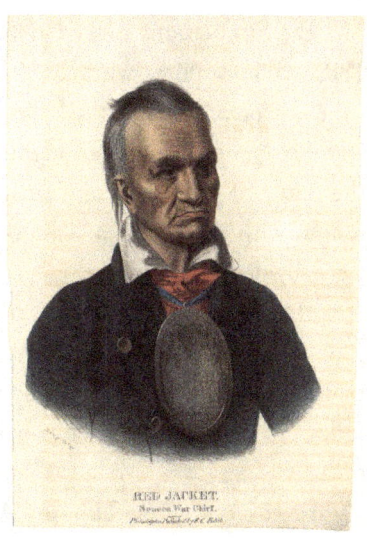

Red Jacket, Seneca war chief (Library of Congress Prints & Photographs Division https://lcn.gov/2013644353)

lived on Cayuga Creek. The Onondaga led by Big Sky lived near the site of the future German communal settlement of Ebenezer.[61]

Red Jacket (1750-1830) is the most famous of the Seneca leaders at Buffalo Creek. He was an advocate of traditional Iroquois values. Red Jacket told the land speculator Ogden Richardson that if the Seneca sold their lands and moved to the setting sun, they would be looked upon as foreigners and strangers and be despised by both red and white men.[62] The Seneca Council House where treaties were negotiated was near an old confluence of the Buffalo River and Cazenovia Creek at the intersection of Seneca and Elk Streets in Buffalo.[63]

With the establishment of the village of Buffalo (initially called New Amsterdam) in 1804, white settlers moved in nearby and this sometimes led to altercations. The American Indian agent Erastus Granger dealt with complaints from the Seneca at Buffalo Creek over the terms of timber sale contracts with whites. The Tuscarora living near modern Lewiston, N.Y., complained of thefts of timber, hogs and horses.[64]

The Six Nations moved their council fire to Buffalo Creek in 1803 while disputes with Joseph Brant and his Mohawk followers led to a separate council fire being established at Grand River in Canada. Six Nations warriors fought and died for the American side at the Battle of Chippawa on Canadian soil in 1814. Brant's son John fought with the British at Chippawa, but the Grand River Iroquois were divided in loyalties.

The spread of Handsome Lake's revival message led to religious splits at Buffalo Creek between his followers and converts to Christianity. This fueled dissension on land sales with Handsome Lake followers generally being in opposition and Christians supportive of them.

In 1817, the Rev. Timothy Alden, a missionary, visited Buffalo Creek and reported "there are about seven hundred Senecas, sixteen Munsees, some Onondagas, some Cayuga and some Squakees" living there.[65] He spoke at the school house crowded with inhabitants while others stood outside at the doors and windows. Ten Seneca chiefs were present including the "celebrated" Red Jacket.[66]

Within two years of Alden's visit, the Ogden Land Co. made the first of its ultimately successful efforts to purchase the Buffalo Creek Reservation for white settlement. Red Jacket and others rebuffed an 1819 purchase offer from Ogden, but in 1826 the Seneca sold a strip of land on the reservation to Ogden.

In 1838 Ogden struck again, this time with a fraudulent treaty that only a few Seneca chiefs signed to purchase the reservations at Buffalo Creek, Cattaraugus and Allegany and force the Seneca to relocate to Kansas west of the Mississippi River. This treaty caused an uproar that reached Washington, D.C. It was resolved with a "compromise" treaty in 1842 that saved the Cattaraugus and Allegany reservations for the Seneca yet forfeited Buffalo Creek in the path of the expanding city of Buffalo.[67] The Tonawanda Reservation was under great threat, too, during these land grabs, but it ultimately survived to become the Seneca Nation community today near Lockport, N.Y.

Many of the Buffalo Creek Seneca relocated to Cattaraugus and Allegany. The removal process entailed paying individuals for the land and any improvements such as houses, barns and saw mills. Thomas Jemison, the grandson of Mary Jemison known as "Buffalo Tom," had lived at Buffalo Creek since 1826. He moved to Cattaraugus in 1844 and was paid $2,609 ($109,291 in 2024) for 179 acres he owned at Buffalo Creek.[68]

Some of the relocated Buffalo Creek residents would return to fish in Cazenovia Creek in the spring or visit the graves of their family members. A few reminders of Buffalo Creek exist today. The Seneca Indian Park in a South Buffalo residential neighborhood is on the site of the cemetery where Mary Jemison, Red Jacket and others were initially buried.

Jemison's remains were transferred in 1874 to what eventually became Letchworth State Park. Red Jacket's remains were moved first to the Cattaraugus Reservation in 1852. In 1884, the remains of Red

Jacket and several Seneca chiefs were reinterred at Buffalo's prestigious Forest Lawn Cemetery. A statue of Red Jacket was erected in 1890. The other chiefs buried there are The Young King, Captain Pollard, Little Billy, Tall Peter and Destroy Town.

The Charles E. Burchfield Nature Center and Art Center is located on part of the old reservation along Buffalo Creek in modern West Seneca, N.Y. A monument to the 1842 Buffalo Creek Treaty was dedicated there in 2004.

Passenger Pigeons

The journey to a roosting ground of passenger pigeons rewarded its participants with one of the great spectacles—and great opportunities for a feast—in 18th-century America. The passenger pigeons were so numerous their flocks darkened the sky for hours while in flight. The meat of a pigeon and especially the young squabs was very tasty. And passenger pigeons especially when roosting were easy to hunt and kill.

The Seneca and other Native Americans relied on roasted and stewed passenger pigeon meat as an important contribution to their diet. The pigeon was featured on restaurant menus throughout the 19th century. Despite flocks numbering in the hundreds of millions, the passenger pigeon was hunted to extinction during the next 100 years. The last one named Martha died in 1914 at a zoo in Cincinnati.

The Moravian missionary David Zeisberger described a flight of passenger pigeons:

> "In some years in the fall, or even spring, they flock together in such numbers that the air is darkened by their flight. Three years ago they appeared in such great numbers that the ground under their roosting-place was covered with their dung, above a foot high, during one night."[69]

One memorable account of a pigeon hunt occurred when Seneca captive Horatio Jones met the newly captured American solider

Moses Van Campen during a hunting encampment along the Genesee River in 1782.⁷⁰ Several hundred Seneca, with entire families participating, gathered at the site after runners came to their villages telling of a great pigeon roost in a forest. The pigeons had built nests in the trees and the young squabs were hatching. The sound of the mass of birds at feeding time was overwhelming. The collective weight of the pigeons caused the tree branches they assembled on to break and fall to the ground.

The Seneca had built lean-tos to stay in. They cut down the roosting trees to kill thousands of the squabs unable to fly yet. The

Above inset: Passenger Pigeon 1829 by John James Audobon (National Gallery of Art)

Right: Passenger Pigeon monument Codorus State Park, Hanover, PA (Author)

Seneca suspended the squabs on poles over fires, smoked them and carried them in baskets back to their villages.

On May 3, 1791, American negotiator Col. Thomas Proctor described eating pigeon meat at a feast provided by Onondaga Chief Big Sky at the Buffalo Creek Reservation:

> "...the feast, which principally consisted of young pigeons, some boiled, some stewed, and the mode of dishing them up was, that a hank of six were tied with a deer's sinew around their necks, their bills pointing outwards; they were plucked, but of pen feathers there plenty remained; the inside was taken out, but it appeared from the soup made of them, that water had not touched them before. The repast being the best I had seen for a long time, I ate of it very heartily."[71]

An early Western New York historian quoted a Springville resident, C. C. Smith, relating that he had seen Native American women cut down trees getting fifty or sixty nests containing squabs from one tree. The squabs were scalded, salted and dried by the thousands.[72]

A monument to the extinct passenger pigeon in the "interest of the preservation of wildlife" is located on a hill overlooking the marina at Pennsylvania's Codorus State Park near Hanover, Pa. The hills north of Hanover were reported roosting grounds of the passenger pigeon through most of the 19th century.

End Notes

1. June Namias, ed., *A Narrative of the Life of Mary Jemison* by James E. Seaver (Norman: University of Oklahoma Press, 1992), 105.
2. Robert West Howard, *Thundergate: The Forts of Niagara* (Englewood Cliffs, NJ: Prentice-Hall Inc., 1968), 141.
3. William T. Hagan, *Longhouse Diplomacy and Frontier Warfare* (New York State American Revolution Bicentennial Commission, 1976), 2.
4. Colin G. Calloway, *The American Revolution in Indian Country* (Cambridge: Cambridge University Press, 1995), 132.
5. Frank H. Severance, *Old Trails on the Niagara Frontier* (Cleveland: The Burrow Brothers Company, 1903), 62.
6. John B. B. Trussell Jr., *The Sullivan and Brodhead Expeditions*, Historical Pennsylvania Leaflet No. 41 (Harrisburg: Pennsylvania Historical and Museum Commission, 1976), 1.
7. *Journals of the Military Expedition of Major General John Sullivan Against the Six Nations of Indians in 1779* (Reprint Glendale, NY: Benchmark Publishing Company Inc., 1970), 45.
8. Ibid., 90.
9. Ibid., 163.
10. Ibid., 91.
11. Ibid., 303.
12. Ibid., 101.
13. Namias, op. cit., 105.
14. Severance, op. cit., 60.
15. *A Native Interpretive Center for Old Fort Niagara* (Youngstown, NY: Old Fort Niagara Association), 24-26.
16. Jeanne Winston Adler, ed., *Chainbreaker's War* (Hensonville, NY: Black Dome Press Corp., 2002), 110-111.
17. Timothy T. Shaw, "Refugees of Niagara 1779-1780" April 11, 2023 accessed. https://www.clintonsullivan.com
18. Old Fort Niagara exhibit.
19. William L. Potter, *Redcoats on the Frontier: King's Regiment in the Revolutionary War* National Park Service. Selected Papers From The 1983 and 1984 George Rogers Clark Trans-Appalachian Frontier History Conference, 2-5.
20. Severance, op. cit., 62.
21. Jonathan G. Rossie, "The Northern Indian Department and The American Revolution," Niagara Frontier Buffalo & Erie County Historical Society Buffalo, New York (Autumn 1973) Volume 20, Number 3, 56-57.

22. Bruce Wilson, "The Struggle for Wealth and Power at Fort Niagara 1775-1783," *Ontario History*, Vol. 68 (September, 1976), 145.

23. Arthur Britton Smith, *Legend of the Lake: The 22-gun Brig-Sloop Ontario 1780* (Kingston, Ontario: Quarry Press, 1997).

24. Sullivan, op. cit., 158.

25. Ibid., 204.

26. William Reichel, ed., *Memorials of the Moravian Church* (Philadelphia: The Moravian Book Association, J. B. Lippincott & Son, 1870), 97-98.

27. Ibid., 95-96.

28. "A Missionary's Tour to Shamokin and The West Branch of the Susquehanna 1753" *The Pennsylvania Magazine of History and Biography* Vol. 35 (1915), 442-444.

29. Robert S. Grumet, ed., *Journey on the Forbidden Path: Chronicles of a Diplomatic Mission to the Allegheny Country, March-September, 1760* (Philadelphia: American Philosophical Society, 1999), 108.

30. Pennsylvania Historical and Museum Commission marker text.

31. Thomas S. Abler, "KAIEN'KWAAHTON," in *Dictionary of Canadian Biography*, vol. 4, University of Toronto/Universite Laval, 2003-, accessed September 26, 2021, http:www.biographi.ca/en/bio/kaienkwaahton_4E.html.

32. Namias, op. cit., 94.

33. Fort Niagara, op. cit., 25-26.

34. Frederick Houghton, *History of the Buffalo Creek Reservation* (Buffalo, NY: Buffalo Historical Society Publications, 1920), Volume XXIV, 71-72.

35. Namias, op. cit., 121.

36. Mildred Lee Hills Anderson, *Genesee Echoes* (Castile, NY: 1958), 69.

37. Namias, op. cit., 145-146.

38. Timothy Alden, *An Account of Sundry Missions Performed Among the Senecas and Munsees; in a series of letters. With an appendix* (NY: J. Seymour, 1827), 111.

39. Katherine Barnes, *The Genesee Country* (1972), 24.

40. Namias, op. cit., 159.

41. Saverio Bruni, *From Seneca Slave to Indian Chief* (Niagara-on-the-Lake, Ontario: Newark Publishers, 1974), 32-34.

42. George H. Harris, *Captured by the Indians The Seldom Told Stories of Horatio Jones and The Benjamin Gilbert Family* (Lewisburg, PA: Wennawoods Publishing, 2003), 520.

43. *Jasper Parrish Papers*. Vassar College Digital Library https://digitallibrary.vassar.edu/islandora/object/vassar:parrish.

44. Namias, op. cit., 121.

45. Ibid., 155.

46. Harris, op cit., 500-502.
47. Christopher Densmore, *Red Jacket. Iroquois Diplomat and Orator* (Syracuse, NY: Syracuse University Press, 1999), 89.
48. David Goodnough, *The Cherry Valley Massacre November 11, 1778: The Frontier Atrocity That Shocked a Young Nation* (NY: Franklin Watts Inc., 1968), 9.
49. Richard Berleth, *Bloody Mohawk The French and Indian War & American Revolution on New York's Frontier* (Hensonville, NY: Black Dome Press Corp., 2010), 292.
50. Ibid., 291.
51. Barbara Graymont, "THAYENDANEGEA," in *Dictionary of Canadian Biography*, vol. 5, University of Toronto/Universitie Laval, (2003) July 4, 2016 accessed. http://www.biographi.ca/ca/en/bio/thayendanegea_5E.html.
52. Isabel Thompson Kelsay, *Joseph Brant 1743-1807 Man of Two Worlds* (Syracuse, NY: Syracuse University Press, 1984), 171.
53. Ibid., 220-222.
54. James W. Paxton, *Joseph Brant and His World* (Toronto: James W. Lorimer & Company Ltd., 2008), 44-45.
55. Graymont, op. cit., 6.
56. Carl Carmer, ed., *The Tavern Lamps Are Burning* (NY: Van Rees Press, 1964), 399.
57. Harris, op. cit., 494.
58. Houghton, op. cit., 64.
59. Ibid., 6.
60. *Narrative of the Journey of Col. Thomas Proctor to the Indians of the Northwest 1791*. Pennsylvania Archives second series. Vol. IV. April 10, 2023 accessed. http://www.files.usgwarchives. 22.
61. Houghton, op. cit., 115-116.
62. Robert B. Swift, *By Great Rivers: Lives on the Appalachian Frontier* (Charlestown, SC: America Through Time, 2019), 107.
63. *Buffalo River Urban Canoe Trail Guide*. N.Y. Department of Environmental Conservation and Erie County Department of Environmental and Planning, 1994.
64. Charles M. Snyder, ed., *Red and White on the New York Frontier* (Harrison, NY: Harbor Hill Books, 1978), 31-35.
65. Alden, op cit., 42.
66. Ibid., 34.
67. Swift, op. cit., 108.
68. Houghton, op cit., 178.

69. Archer Butler Hubert, ed., *David Zeisberger's History of the North American Indians in 18th Century Ohio, New York & Pennsylvania* (Lewisburg, PA: Wennawoods Publishing, 1999), 66.

70. Harris, op. cit., 449-451.

71. Pennsylvania Archives, "Narrative of the Journey of Col. Thomas Proctor to the Indians of the Northwest 1791." Second Series, Vol. IV, 497.

72. Clayton Mau, *The Development of Central and Western New York* (Dansville, NY: F.A. Owen Publishing Company, 1958), 149.

Bibliography

A

Abler, Thomas H. *Cornplanter Chief Warrior of the Allegheny Senecas.* Syracuse, NY: Syracuse University Press, 2007.

Adler, Jeanne Winston, ed. *Chainbreaker's War A Seneca Chief Remembers The American Revolution.* Hensonville, NY: Black Dome Press Corp., 2002.

Albion, Robert Greenhalgh and Leonidas Dodson, eds. *Philip Vickers Fithian: Journal 1775-76 Written on the Virginia-Pennsylvania Frontier and in the Army Around New York.* Princeton: Princeton University Press, 1934.

Alden, Timothy. *An Account of Sundry Missions Performed Among the Senecas and Munsees; in a series of letters. With an appendix.* New York: J. Seymour, 1827.

Amrhein, Cindy. *A History of Native American Land Rights in Upstate New York.* Charleston, SC: The History Press, 2016.

Anderson, Mildred Lee Hills. *Genesee Echoes.* Castile, NY: 1956.

B

Barnes, Katherine. *The Genesee Country.* 1972.

Bartram, John, Lewis Evans and Conrad Weiser. *A Journey from Pennsylvania to Onondaga in 1743.* Barre, MA: The Imprint Society Inc., 1973.

Beauchamp, Rev. Wm. M. *Moravian Journals Relating to Central New York, 1745-1766.* Bowie, MD: Heritage Books Inc., 1999.

Becker, Marshall J. "The Okehocking: A Remnant Band of Delaware Indians." *Pennsylvania Archaeologist.* Vol. 46. Issue 3, 1976.

Benson, Adolph B., ed. *Peter Kalm's Travels in North America.* NY: Dover Publications Inc., 1966.

Berleth, Richard. *Bloody Mohawk. The French and Indian War & American Revolution on New York's Frontier.* Hensonville, NY: Black Dome Press Corp., 2012.

Biddle, Gretchen B. and Sarah D. Lowrie, eds. *Notable Women of Pennsylvania.* Philadelphia: University of Pennsylvania Pres, 1942.

Bilharz, Joy A. *The Allegany Senecas and Kinzua Dam.* Lincoln and London: University of Nebraska Press, 1998.

Blethen Tyler and Curtis Wood Jr. *From Ulster to Carolina: The Migration of the Scotch-Irish to Southwestern North Carolina.* Chapel Hill, NC: 1998.

Bouquet, Henry. *The Papers of Henry Bouquet. Volume II The Forbes Expedition.* Edited by S.K. Stevens, Donald H. Kent and Autumn L. Leonard, Harrisburg. The Pennsylvania Historical and Museum Commission, 1951.

Bremer, David A. "Lancaster's First Jewish Community." *The Journal of the Lancaster County Historical Society.* Vol. 80, No. 4, 1976.

Bruni, Saviero. *From Seneca Slave to Indian Chief.* Niagara-on-the-Lake, Ontario: Newark Publishers, 1974.

Byrne, Thomas E., ed. *A Bicentennial Remembrance of the Sullivan-Clinton Expedition 1779 in Pennsylvania and New York.* Elmira, NY: Sullivan-Clinton, 1979.

C

Calder, Isabel M. *Colonial Captivities, Marches and Journeys.* Port Washington, NY: Kennikat Press, 1967.

Calloway Colin G. *The American Revolution in Indian Country.* Cambridge: Cambridge University Press, 1995.

Carmer, Carl, ed. *The Tavern Lamps Are Burning.* NY: Van Rees Press, 1964.

Carter, John H. "The Shamokin Indian Traders." *Proceedings of the Northumberland County Historical Society.* Vol. XV, 1946.

Cavaioli, Frank J. "A Profile of the Paxton Boys: Murderers of the Conestoga Indians." *The Journal of the Lancaster County Historical Society.* Vol. 87, No. 3, 1983.

Clune, Henry W. *The Genesee.* NY: Holt, Reinhart and Winston, 1963.

Colden, Cadwallader, *The History of the Five Indian Nations.* Cornell University Press, 1964.

Colonial Records. Minutes of the Provincial Council of Pennsylvania. Vol. III. May 31, 1717 to January 23, 1736. Harrisburg: The State of Pennsylvania, 1840.

Crist, Robert G. *George Croghan of Pennsboro.* Harrisburg: Dauphin Deposit Trust Co., 1965.

Cross, Dorothy. *New Jersey's Indians.* Trenton, NJ: New Jersey State Museum, 1976.

Cummings, Hubertis M. *Scots Breed and Susquehanna.* Pittsburgh: University of Pittsburgh Press, 1964.

D

Darlington, William M., ed. *Christopher Gist's Journals.* Reprint Edition. Salem, NH: Ayer Company Publishers, 1991.

Dictionary of Canadian Biography. Vol. I-Vol. XXII. University of Toronto/Universite Laval, 2003-2018.

Doblin, Helga and William A. Starna, eds. *The Journals of Christian Daniel Claus and Conrad Weiser. A Journey to Onondaga, 1750.* Independence Square, Philadelphia: The American Philosophical Society, 1994.

E

Eshelman, H. Frank. *Annals of the Susquehannocks and Other Indian Tribes of Pennsylvania, 1500-1763.* Lewisburg, PA: Wennawoods Publishing, 2000.

F

Fenton, William A., ed. *Parker on the Iroquois.* Syracuse, NY: Syracuse University Press, 1968.

Flexner, James Thomas. *Mohawk Baronet.* Syracuse, NY: Syracuse University Press, 1979.

———. *First Flowers of Our Wilderness American Painting, The Colonial Period.* NY: Dover Publications Inc, 1969.

G

Gehring, Charles T. and William A. Starna. *A Journey into Mohawk and Oneida Country, 1634-1635.* Syracuse, NY: Syracuse University Press, 1988.

Goodnaugh, David. *Cherry Valley Massacre Nov. 11, 1778: The Frontier Atrocity That Shocked a Young Nation.* NY: Franklin Watts Inc., 1968.

Graham, Lloyd. *Niagara Country.* NY: Duell, Sloan & Pearce, 1949.

Gray, Elma E. *Wilderness Christians The Moravian Mission to the Delaware Indians.* Toronto: The MacMillan Company of Canada Limited, 1956.

Graymont, Barbara. *The Iroquois in the American Revolution.* Syracuse, NY: Syracuse University Press, 1972.

Grumet, Robert S., ed. *Northeastern Indian Lives 1631-1816.* Amherst: University of Massachusetts Press, 1996.

———. *Journey on the Forbidden Path: Chronicles of a Diplomatic Mission to the Allegheny Country, March-September, 1760.* Philadelphia: American Philosophical Society, 1999.

———. *The Lenapes.* NY: Chelsea House Publishers, 1989.

H

Hagan, William T. *Longhouse Diplomacy and Frontier Warfare.* The New York State Bicentennial Commission.

Hamilton, Charles. *Braddock's Defeat.* Norman: University of Oklahoma Press, 1959.

Hanna, Charles A. *The Wilderness Trail.* Volumes One and Two. Lewisburg, PA: Wennawoods Publishing, 1995.

Harshbarger, Jean P. *Hartslog Heritage.* American Bicentennial Association, 1976.

Hazard, Samuel, ed. *Pennsylvania Archives. Vol. 1. 1664-1747.* Joseph Severns & Co. Philadelphia, 1852.

Heckewelder, John. *History, Manners, and Customs of the Indian Nations.* Arno Press & The New York Times, 1971.

Hinman, Marjory Barnum. *Onaquaga: Hub of the Border Wars.* Valley Offset Inc., 1975.

Hoffman, Ronald, Mechal Sobel and Frederika J. Teute, eds. *Through A Glass Darkly Reflections on Personal Identity in Early America.* Omohundro Institute of Early American History and Culture. Williamsburg, VA: University of North Carolina Press. 1997.

Hosenm Frederick E. *Rifle, Blanket and Kettle Selected Indian Treaties and Laws.* Jefferson, NC: McFarland & Company, 1985.

Houghton, Frederic. "History of the Buffalo Creek Reservation." *Publications of the Buffalo Historical Society.* Volume XXIV, 1920.

Hsiung, David C. "Death on the Juniata: Delaware, Iroquois and Pennsylvanians in a Colonial Whodunit." *Pennsylvania History.* Vol. 65, No. 4, Autumn 1998.

Hubert, Archer Butler, ed. *David Zeisberger's History of the North American Indians in 18th Century Ohio, New York & Pennsylvania.* Lewisburg, PA: Wennawoods Publishing, 1999.

J

James, Alfred Proctor, ed. *Writings of General John Forbes.* The Allegheny County Committee of the Pennsylvania Society of the Colonial Dames of America. Menasha, Wisconsin: The Collegiate Press, 1938

Jemison, G. Peter & Schein, Anna M., eds. *Treaty of Canandaigua 1794 200 Years of Treaty Relations Between the Iroquois Confederacy and the United States.* Santa Fe, NM: Clear Light Publishers, 2000.

Jennings, Francis. *The Ambiguous Iroquois Empire.* NY: W. W. Norton & Company, 1984.

———. "Incident at Tulpehocken." *Pennsylvania History.* Vol. XXXV, No 4, October 1968.

Jordan, John W. "Bishop J.F.C. Cammerhoff's Narrative of a Journey to Shamokin, Penna., in the Winter of 1748." *Pennsylvania Magazine of History and Biography.* Vol. 29, Issue 2, 1905.

———. "Rev. John Martin Mack's Narrative of a Visit to Onondaga, 1758." *Pennsylvania Magazine of History and Biography.* Vol. XXIX, Issue 3, 1905.

Journals of the Military Expedition of Major General John Sullivan 1779. Glendale, NY: Benchmark Publishing Company Inc., Reprint 1970.

K

Kelsay, Isabel Thompson. *Joseph Brant 1743-1807 Man of Two Worlds.* Syracuse, NY: Syracuse University Press, 1984.

Kenny, Kevin. *Peaceable Kingdom Lost The Paxton Boys and the Destruction of William Penn's Holy Experiment.* NY: Oxford University Press, 2009.

Kent, Donald H. *The French Invasion of Western Pennsylvania.* Harrisburg: Pennsylvania Historical and Museum Commission, 1981.

Kraft, Herbert C. *The Lenape Archaeology, History and Ethnography.* Newark: New Jersey Historical Society, 1986.

L

Lancaster County 300th Anniversary Committee. *Lancaster County Observes Pennsylvania's Tercentenary.* Reprint 1982.

Lancaster County Historical Society. "The Site of Conestoga Indian Town." *Papers of the Lancaster County Historical Society.* Vol. XXVIII, No. 7, 1924.

Landis, David. "Conoy Town and Peter Bezaillion." *Papers of the Lancaster County Historical Society.* Vol. 37, 1933.

Lemay, J. A. Leo, ed. *Franklin Writings*. NY: The Library of America, 1987.

Leonard, Autumn L. "The Presque Isle Portage and the Venango Trail." *Pennsylvania Archaeology.* Vol. XV, No. 3, July 1945.

Loudon, Archibald. *A Selection of Some of the Most Interesting Narratives of Outrages Committed by the Indians in Their Wars with the White People*. NY: Arno Press & The New York Times, Reprint 1971.

M

Maclay, Samuel, *Journal of Samuel Maclay.* Published by John Meginness. Lewisburg, PA: Wennawoods Publishing, 1999.

MacMaster, Richard. *The First Three Centuries*. Elizabethtown, PA: The Elizabethtown Historical Society, 1999.

Martin, Asa Earl and Shenk, Hiram Herr. *Pennsylvania History Told By Contemporaries*. NY: The Macmillan Company, 1925.

Mast, Brian J. "Fort Rice." *The Pennsylvania Magazine of History and Biography*. The Historical Society of Pennsylvania. Volume CXXXVI, No. 4, 2012.

Mau, Clayton. *The Development of Central and Western New York*. Dansville, NY: F.A. Owen Publishing Company, 1958.

McIlnay, Dennis P. *Juniata, River of Sorrows*. Hollidaysburg, PA: Live Oak Press, 2003.

Meehan, Susan E. *Life Along the Big Spring*. Carlisle, PA: Cumberland County Historical Society, 2019.

Meginness, John. *The Early History of Lycoming County.* Lewisburg, PA: Wennawoods Publishing, 2005.

Merrell, James H. *Into The American Woods: Negotiators on the Pennsylvania Frontier.* NY: W.W. Norton & Co., 1999.

Merrell, James H., ed. *The Lancaster Treaty of 1744*. Boston and New York: Bedford/St. Martin's, 2008.

Merrill, Arch. *The White Woman and Her Valley*. Rochester, NY: Seneca Book Bindery Company, 1968.

———. *Pioneer Profiles*. Rochester, NY: Seneca Book Bindery Company, 1957.

Miller, Isabel Winner. *Old Town A History of Early Lock Haven*. Lock Haven: Anne Halenbake Ross Library, 1966.

Mintz, Max X. *Seeds of Empire. The American Revolutionary Conquest of the Iroquois*. New York and London: New York University Press, 1999.

Moore, John L. *Scorched Earth General Sullivan and the Senecas*. Mechanicsburg, PA: Sunbury Press, 2018.

———. *Murder at Killbuck Island*. Mechanicsburg, PA: Sunbury Press, 2020.

N

Namias, June, ed. *A Narrative of the Life of Mrs. Mary Jemison by James E. Seaver.* Norman: University of Oklahoma Press, 1992.

P

Paxton, James W. *Joseph Brant and His World.* Toronto: James Lorimer & Company, 2008.

Peckham, Howard. H. "Thomas Gist's Indian Captivity." *The Pennsylvania Magazine of History and Biography.* Vol. 80, No. 3, July 1956.

Pencak, William A. and Richter, Daniel K. eds. *Friends & Enemies in Penn's Woods Indians, Colonists and the Racial Construction of Pennsylvania.* University Park, PA: The Pennsylvania State University Press, 2004.

Porter, Frank W. III. "A Century of Accomodation: The Nanticoke Indians in Colonial Maryland" *Maryland Historical Magazine.* Vol. 74, No. 2, Summer 1979.

———. "Behind the Frontier: Indian Survivals in Maryland." *Maryland Historical Magazine.* Vol. 75, No. 1, Spring 1980.

Printup, Bryan and Patterson Jr., Neil. *Tuscarora Nation.* Charlestown, SC: Arcadia Publishing, 2007.

Q

Quimby, Ian M. G. ed. *American Painting to 1776 A Reappraisal.* Charlottesville: The University Press of Virginia, 1974.

R

Reichel, William. *Memorials of the Moravian Church.* Philadelphia: The Moravian Book Association, J.B. Lippincott & Son, 1870.

Rossie, Jonathan G. "The Northern Indian Department and The American Revolution." *Niagara Frontier.* Buffalo & Erie County Historical Society. Buffalo, NY: Vol. 20, No. 3, Autumn 1973.

S

Schwartz, Seymour I. *Cadwallader Colden A Biography.* Amherst, NY: Humanity Books, 2013.

Severance, Frank H. *Old Trails on the Niagara Frontier.* Cleveland: The Burrows Brothers Company, 1903.

Shirk Jr., Willis L. "The Scots-Irish of Donegal Township 1716-1815." *The Journal of the Lancaster County Historical Society.* Vol. 101, No. 1, Winter 1999.

Simonson, Lee. *Tuscarora Heroes.* Lewiston, NY: Historical Association of Lewiston, Inc. 2014.

Sipe, C. Hale. *The Indian Chiefs of Pennsylvania.* Lewisburg, PA: Wennawoods Publishing, 1994.

Smith, Arthur Britton. *Legend of the Lake The 22-gun Brig-Sloop Ontario 1780.* Kingston, Ontario: Quarry Press Inc., 1997.

Snyder, Charles M. ed. *Red and White on the New York Frontier.* Harrison, NY: Harbor Hill Books, 1978.

Spittal, Wm. Guy, ed. *Iroquois Women An Anthology.* Ontario, Canada: Iroqrafts. Ltd. 1990.

Stevens, Sylvester K. and Donald H. Kent, eds. *The Venango Trail.* Harrisburg: Pennsylvania Historical Commission, 1940.

———. *Wilderness Chronicles of Northwestern Pennsylvania.* Harrisburg: Pennsylvania Historical Commission, 1941.

Swain, William T. "Primitive Passageways to Future Newville." *Cumberland County History.* Vol. VI, No. 1, Summer 1989.

Swift, Robert B. *The Mid-Appalachian Frontier: A Guide to Historic Sites of the French and Indian War.* Gettysburg, PA: Thomas Publications, 2001.

———. *By Great Rivers Lives on the Appalachian Frontier.* Charlestown, SC: America Through Time, 2019.

T

Thomas, Earle. *Sir John Johnson Loyalist Baronet.* Toronto and Reading: Dundurn Press, 1986.

Thompson, Allan D. *The Meeting House Springs Graveyard.* Carlisle, PA: 1927.

Thwaites, Reuben Gold. *Early Western Journals: 1748-1765.* Lewisburg, PA: Wennawoods Publishing, 1998.

Tome, Philip. *Pioneer Life or Thirty Years a Hunter.* Mechanicsburg, PA: Stackpole Books, 2006.

Transactions of the Moravian Historical Society. Whitefield House, Nazareth. Volume II, 1886.

V

Vincens, Simone. *Madame Montour & The Fur Trade (1667-1752).* Xlibris Corporation, 2011.

W

Wainwright, Nicholas B. *George Croghan Wilderness Diplomat.* Chapel Hill: The University of North Carolina Press, 1959.

Wallace, Anthony F. C., ed. "Halliday Jackson's Journal to the Seneca Indians." *Pennsylvania History.* Vol. XIX, No. 2, April, 1952.

———. *The Death and Rebirth of the Seneca.* New York: Alfred A. Knopf, 1970.

———. *Tuscarora a History.* Albany: State University of New York Press, 2012.

Wallace, Paul. A. W. *Thirty Thousand Miles With John Heckewelder.* University of Pittsburgh Press, 1958.

———. *Conrad Weiser Friend of Colonist and Mohawk.* NY: Russell & Russell, 1971.

———. *Indian Paths of Pennsylvania.* Harrisburg, PA: Pennsylvania Historical and Museum Commission, 1971.

———. *Indians in Pennsylvania.* Harrisburg, PA: Pennsylvania Historical and Museum Commission, 1981.

Wennawoods Publishing. *Captured by the Indians. The Seldom Told Stories of Horatio Jones and the Benjamin Gilbert Family.* Lewisburg, PA: 2003.

Weslager, C. W. *The Delaware Indians. A History.* New Brunswick, NJ: Rutgers University Press, 1991.

Williams, John Page. *Chesapeake Exploring The Water Trail of Captain John Smith.* Washington D.C.: National Geographic Society, 2006.

Williams, Ted C. *The Reservation.* Syracuse, NY: Syracuse University Press, 1976.

Wilson, Bruce. "The Struggle for Wealth and Power at Fort Niagara 1775-1783." *Ontario History.* Vol. 68, September 1976.

Wolf, George D. *The Fair Play Settlers of the West Branch Valley.* Harrisburg, PA: Pennsylvania Historical and Museum Commission, 1969.

Wood, Jerome H. Jr. *Conestoga Crossroads. Lancaster Pennsylvania 1730-1790.* Harrisburg: Pennsylvania Historical and Museum Commission, 1979.

Index

A

Abeel (also spelled O'Bail), John, 8
Abercromby, James, Gen., 126
Acrelius, Israel, Pastor, 19
Adams County, 174
Adlum, John, 98, 100
Agnew, James, 66
Ahoalint, 135
Albany, ix, 42, 55, 120, 121, 144, 145
Alden, Ichabod, Col., 182
Alden, Timothy, Rev., 6, 177, 190, 191
Alexandria, 91, 120
Allegany, 186, 191
Allegany Reservation, 15
Alleghenies, 105, 112
Allegheny College, 207
Allegheny Mountain, 85, 90
Allegheny Path, 82, 145
Allegheny River, 2, 6, 7, 10, 11, 14, 16, 60, 86, 88, 90, 93, 95, 98, 99, 116, 117, 127, 164
Allen, Ebenezer, 176
Allummapees, 85
Alopapealon, 135
American Revolution, 13, 42, 59, 68, 75, 95, 146, 152, 160, 174, 179, 182, 183
Amherst, Jeffrey, Gen., 126
Amity Township, 86
Anajot, 144
Antes, Colonel, 141
Appalachian Frontier, ix, 207
Appalachian Plateau, 55
Appalachian Ridge and Valley, 68
Appalachians, 38
Armstrong, Alexander, 89
Armstrong, Jack, 88, 90
Armstrong, John, 67
Armstrong, John, Col., 93, 145, 146
Assunepachla, 93
Atkin, Edmund, 109, 111

Atlantic City, 133
Attakullakulla, Chief, 48, 113
Audobon, John James, 193
Aughwick, 74, 93
Aughwick Creek, 90, 91
Augusta County, 83
Augusta Stone Presbyterian Church, 83
Austenaco, 119

B

Bahama Islands, 60
Bald Eagle Creek, 144, 146
Barryville, 185
Bartram, John, x, xi, 21, 37, 39, 54, 59, 85, 98
Bartram, William, 113
Battle at Minisink Ford, 185
Battle of Chippawa, 190
Battle of Newtown, 170, 172, 175
Battle of Oriskany, 42, 160, 175
Battle of Stone Arabia, 183
Bear Tavern, 14
Bedford, 97, 11, 179
Belle Riviere, 116
Berks County, 45
Bernard, Francis, Gov., 149
Berry, Jack, 189
Bethlehem, 39, 142
Big Cove, 74
Big Island, 144, 145
Big Kettle, 189
Big Sky, 190, 194
Big Slide, 177
Big Spring Presbyterian Church, 76, 82
Big Spring Run, 82
Big Tree, 176, 180, 181, 186
Billings, Joseph, 135
Binghamton, 24
Black Log Valley, 92
Blacksnake, 9
Bloody Mohawk, The, 182, 183

Bloody Rock, 174
Blue Mountain, 17, 35, 72, 75, 80, 90
Blunston, Samuel, 71, 82
Bolton, Mason, Col., 162, 168, 169, 170, 175
Boswell, James, 184
Bottoms, The, 168, 175
Bouquet, Henry, Col., 77, 97, 105, 106, 107, 125, 126
Boyd, Thomas, Lt., 165
Braddock Expedition, xiv
Braddock, Edward, Gen., 97, 112, 115, 119, 120, 121, 122, 124, 134, 145, 152
Brainerd, David, 21, 85, 146, 147, 148
Brainerd, John, 148
Brandywine, 77
Brant, John, 190
Brant, Joseph, xiv, 26, 47, 49, 161, 162, 163, 164, 171, 182, 183, 184, 185, 186, 187, 190
Brant, Molly, 161, 163, 183, 184
Brantford, 184, 186
Broad Creek, 20
Brodhead, Daniel, Col., 164
Brotherton, 148, 149
Brown, John, Col., 183
Browne, Charlotte, xiv, 119, 120, 121
Budd, Thomas, 90
Buffalo, 169, 181, 190, 191
Buffalo Creek, 42, 169, 175, 178, 186, 188, 189, 190, 191, 192
Buffalo Creek Reservation, 175, 176, 177, 188, 189, 191, 194
Buffalo History Museum, iii
Buffalo River, 188, 190
Buffalo Tom, 191
Burd, James, Major, 133
Burgoyne, John, Gen., 161
Burned-over-District, 188
Burnet, William, Gov., 50
Burnt Cabins, 72, 75
Burrows, John, Major, 165
Butcher, Zachary, 65
Butler, John, Col., 140, 166, 169, 170, 183
Butler, John, Major, 163, 164, 168
Butler, Walter, Capt., 182

C

Callender, Robert, 97
Calloway, George, 74
Calloway, William, 74
Calvert Family, 69
Cambria County, 91
Cammerhoff, Bishop, 51
Cammerhoff, John Christopher Frederick, x, 41, 60, 143
Canajoharie, 143, 168, 184
Canandaigua, 180, 181, 188
Canasatego, xiii, 21, 38, 41, 53, 54, 55
Captain Pollard, 192
Carleton Island, 168, 183
Carlisle, 80, 82, 91, 111, 125
Cartlidge, Edmund, 87
Cartlidge, John, 87
Castile, 177, 178
Catawba, 124
Catesby, Mark, 60
Catharine Valley, 174
Catharine's Town, 165, 172, 174
Cattaraugus, 186, 191
Cattaraugus Reservation, 12, 15, 191
Cayuga Creek, 188, 190
Cayuga Lake, 59, 166
Cazenovia Creek, 188, 190, 191
Chainbreaker, Chief, 169
Chambers, Benjamin, 83
Chambers, Ranald, 81, 82
Chambersburg, 83
Charles E. Burchfield Nature Center and Art Center, 192
Charleston, 114, 115
Charlotte Creek, 45
Chartier, Peter, 71
Chartier's Town, 2
Chauraudra, 152
Chelloway, 133
Chemung Canal, 174
Chemung River, 41, 140, 150, 173
Cherry Valley, 164, 170, 181, 182, 184
Cherry Valley Cemetery, 182
Chesapeake Bay, 19, 23
Chest Creek, 91, 94
Chester County, 87

Chicony Reserve, 20
Chief Memeska, 123
Chillaway, 133
Chillaway, Billy, 138
Chilleway, 133
Chillisquaque, xi
Chillisquaque Creek, 154
Chilloway, Augestina, 138
Chilloway, Betsy, 141
Chilloway, Billy, 133, 137, 141
Chilloway, Job, xiv, 6, 131, 132, 133, 134, 135, 137, 138, 139, 140, 141
Chilloway, William, 133, 141
Chippawa, 190
Chota, 114
Christ Church, 126
Cincinnati, 192
City Hill, 187
Claus, Christian Daniel, 41, 42
Claus, Daniel, 170, 171
Clinton, James, Gen., 140, 164
Codorus State Park, 193, 194
Cohoon, George, 74
Cold Spring, 14
Colden, Cadwallader, 50, 51
Colden, Jane, x, 50
Coldengham, 51
Columbus, 184
Concord Narrows, 90
Conejohela, 71
Conestoga, 69, 70, 72, 79
Conestoga Creek, 96
Conestoga Manor, 70, 71
Conhocton River, 150
Connecticut, 138
Connellsville, 123
Connoquenessing River, 127
Conococheague Creek, 83
Conococheague Institute, iii
Conococheague Valley, 109
Conodoguinet Creek, 71, 80, 81, 82
Conoy Creek, 96
Conrad Weiser Homestead, 46
Cook Cemetery Memorial Park, 174
Coope or Cope, Benjamin, 9, 14
Coope or Cope, Rachel, 9, 10, 14

Cornplanter, 7, 8, 9, 10, 12, 15, 16, 60, 98, 99, 162, 179, 187
Cornplanter Run, 10
Cornplanter Seneca, 11
Cornplanter Tract, 1, 3, 6, 7, 11, 14, 15
Cornplanter's Town, 60
Couc, Elizabeth, 172
Cove Spring, 92
Covenhoven, Robert, 152
Craig, John, Rev., 83
Cresap, Thomas, Col., 71, 122
Crissop, 71
Croghan, George, 80, 91, 93, 95, 123
Crossweeksung (modern Crosswicks), 146, 147
Crosswicks, 133, 146
Culbertson, Andrew, 146
Cumberland County, 71, 73, 76, 80
Cunne Shote, Chief, 112
Cuskarawaok, 20
Cuylerville, 166

D

Danish West Indies, 144
Dauphin County, 76
De Bellestre, Picote, 109
De Blainville, Pierre-Joseph Celeron, Capt., 116
De Graffenried, Christoph, Baron, 24, 25
De la Malgue, Pierre Paul, 117
Deh-ge-wa-nus, 175, 178
Delaplane, Gene, 86
Delaware River, xi, 2, 17, 34, 42, 46, 68, 132, 137, 146, 147, 180
Delaware Valley, 84
Delaware Water Gap, 42
Demere, Paul, Captain, 114, 115
Denny, William, Gov., 135
Derry Presbyterian Church, 76
DeSchweinitz, Edmund, Dr., 141
Destroy Town, 192
Detroit, 124, 162, 170, 184
Dinwiddie, Robert, Gov., 118, 123
Dobbs, Andrew, Gov., 111
Donegal, 46, 70, 77, 79, 95
Donegal Presbyterian Church, 76
Donegal Spring, 77

Donegal Township, 77
Double Eagle, 36
Douglassville, 86
Duckett, Thomas, 5
Dudick, Joseph, iii
Dumond, Isaac, 59
Dunbar, Thomas, Col., 121
Duncan Island, 21, 147
Duquesne, Marquis, 117, 118
Dutch Reformed Church, 183

E

Eagle Peak, 47
East Elma, 189
Eastern Shore, 20
Easton, 125, 164
Ebenezer, 190
Eckenrode's Mill, 94
Edwards, Jerusha, 148
Edwards, Jonathan, 148
Egg Harbor, 133
Elder, John, Rev., 78, 79
Elizabethtown, 14, 96, 97
Elk Eye's Creek, 123
Elmira, 173
Emerson, Robert, iii
England, 126
Ephrata, 22
Erie, 117, 118
Etowaucum, 47
Evans, Lewis, 37, 39, 40, 54, 98

F

Falling Spring Creek, 83
Falling Spring Presbyterian Church, 76, 83
Fauquier, William Francis, Gov., 49
Fellows, Moses, Sgt., 165
Fenton, William, 6, 10, 11, 16
Finger Lakes, 2, 164
Fithian, Philip Vickers, Rev., 146
Five Nations, 34, 50, 51, 54
Fleming, John, 146
Fogg, Jeremiah, Major, 166, 168, 181
Forbes, John, Gen., xiv, 77, 105, 111, 112, 113, 114, 124, 125, 126
Forbidden Path, 150
Forest Lawn Cemetery, 192

Fort Alden, 182
Fort Allen, 133
Fort Augusta, 131, 133, 134, 135, 136, 145, 152
Fort Bull, 58
Fort Cumberland, 120, 121
Fort Defiance, 83
Fort Duquesne, 97, 106, 109, 111, 112, 114, 117, 118, 120, 124, 125
Fort Franklin, 98
Fort Frederick, 109, 110, 111
Fort Frontenac, 134
Fort Granville, 93
Fort Hunter, 48, 97
Fort Johnson, 42, 57
Fort Le Boeuf, 117, 118, 124
Fort Ligonier, 124, 125
Fort Loudoun, 105, 106, 107, 109, 111, 114, 115
Fort Loudon, Pa., 25, 107
Fort Lyttleton, 107
Fort Machault, 117, 118
Fort Michilimackinac, 162
Fort Montgomery, 153
Fort Muncy, 146
Fort Necessity, 124, 152
Fort Niagara, ix, xiv, 19, 26, 34, 42, 56, 58, 116, 124, 131, 133, 134, 159, 160, 161, 162, 163, 166, 168, 169, 170, 174, 175, 180, 184, 185, 186, 188, 189
Fort Ontario, 58
Fort Oswego, 34
Fort Paris, 183
Fort Pitt, 95, 127, 140, 164
Fort Presque Isle, 117
Fort Prince George, 114, 115
Fort Rice (or Fort Montgomery), 153, 154
Fort Shirley, 93, 146
Fort Stanwix, 2, 58, 59, 135, 146, 162, 180
Fort Swatara, 97
Forty Fort, 163
Franklin County, 76
Franklin, Benjamin, 50, 59, 61, 79, 121
Franklin, Deborah, 121
Franklin, Pa., 117
Franks, David, 95
Frankstown, 90, 91

Frankstown Path, 88, 90, 91, 92, 93, 94
Frederick, 121
Fredericksburg, 42
Freeport, 127
French and Indian War, 19, 42, 47, 49, 57, 68, 75, 78, 80, 82, 83, 93, 118, 133, 135, 143, 149, 153, 174, 184, 207
French Creek, 87, 98, 99, 116, 117
French Margaret, 173
Friedenshuetten, 23, 41, 131, 136, 139, 140, 141
Friedenshuetten Mission, 137
Friend, The, 187, 188
Fulton County, 75

G

Gahonto (Wyalusing), 41
Gardeau, 175, 177
Gardeau Flats, 159, 175
Gardeau Overlook, 178
Gardeau Reservation, 176
Gardeau Tract, 181
Gardenville, 189
Gardow, 176
Gayantgogwus, 8, 11, 12
Genesee, 177, 179, 179 180, 181
Genesee Castle, 165, 166
Genesee River, 3, 8, 159, 169, 175, 179, 189, 193
Genesee River Valley, 159, 164, 174, 186
German Flats, 184
Germantown, 73
Gettysburg, 65, 67
Gist, Christopher, x, 122, 123, 124
Gist, Nathaniel, 124
Gist, Thomas, 122, 124
Gnadenhuetten, 136, 143
Gooderham, Henry M., 94
Gooseberry Hill, 35, 37
Gordon, Charlie, 10
Gordon, Patrick, Gov., 87
Grand Reserve, 43
Grand River, 19, 184, 186, 190
Granger, Erastus, 190
Grant, James, Capt., 124, 125
Grant, James, Major, 114, 115
Grantham, 207

Gratz, Barnard, 77, 95
Gratz, Michael, 95
Great Awakening, 146
Great Elk Lick, 99
Great Falls, 144
Great Island, xiv, 144, 145, 146
Great Lakes, 160, 169, 170, 171
Great Minquas Path, 84
Great Plains, 3
Great Road, 80, 82
Great Runaway, 152
Great Spring, 82
Great Valley, 75, 76
Greb, Erin, iii, 1
Griffing, Robert, ii
Grill Creek, 28
Groveland, 165
Guzy, Dan, 106

H

Haldimand, Frederick, Gov., 169, 186
Hall, Johnson, 56
Hambright, John, Capt., 145
Hamilton, James, Gov., 74, 135
Hand, Edward, Gen., 140
Handsome Lake, 6, 8, 9, 11, 12, 16, 43, 190
Hannah (Indian woman), 87
Hanover, 193, 194
Harbison, John, 127
Harbison, Massy, 127, 128
Harris, John, Jr., 78, 92
Harris, Thomas, 96
Harris Ferry (future Harrisburg), 80, 82, 97
Harrisburg, 78, 80, 90, 92, 99
Hart, John, 91
Hart's Log, 91
Hart's Sleeping Place, 91, 94
Hartley, Thomas, Col., 173
Hartslog Valley, 91
Haudenosaunee, 24
Haverford College, 14
Hays, John, 173
Heckewelder, John, Rev., 23, 137, 152
Hendrick, 47
Henry, William, 95
Hesselius, Gustavus, 17, 18, 19
Hiakotoo, 175, 176

Hiddleston, David, 74
Hinderaker, Eric, 48
Hinepaugh, Peter, 59
Hislop, Codman, 55
Hockendaqua, 18
Holland Land Company, 26
Holland, Nathanael, 134, 135
Hollidaysburg, 93
Hooswick, Thomas, 73
Hooswik, Thomas, 65
Hosack (or Hooswik), Thomas, 65
Hospital Rock, 185
Houghton, Frederick, 188
Hsiung, David, 89
Hubley, Adam, Lt. Col., 165, 172
Hudson River, 44, 51, 55
Hudson Valley, 42
Hughes, Barnabas, 96, 97
Hughes, Elizabeth, 96, 97, 97
Hunter, Robert, Col., 152, 153
Hunter, Robert, Gov., 44
Hunter, Samuel, Lt., 139, 140
Huntingdon, 91, 92, 93
Huntingdon County, 91

I

Independence Hall, 121
Indian Mills, 148
Indian Run, 22
Indiantown Mennonite Church, 22
Ireland, 75
Ithaca, 59, 60

J

Jack's Mountain, 88
Jack's Narrows, 88, 91
Jackson, Halliday, 8, 9
Jacobs, Captain, 93
Jacobs, Havey, 10
James, Arthur, Gov., 15, 16
Jay Treaty, 189
Jemison, George, 176
Jemison, Jesse, 176
Jemison, John, 176
Jemison, Mary, xiv, 13, 159, 166, 174, 175, 176, 177, 178, 179, 181, 191
Jemison, Nancy, 178

Jemison, Polly, 177
Jemison, Thomas, 176, 191
Jennesadaga, 7, 8, 9
Jennings, Francis, 53, 84
Jerusalem Town, 187
Johnson, Guy, 49, 160, 169, 170, 171
Johnson, John, Sir, 161, 183
Johnson, Mrs., 120
Johnson, William, Sir, xiii, 42, 55, 56, 57, 58, 59, 109, 121, 160, 161, 163, 170, 171, 183, 184
Johnson Family, 171
Johnson Hall, 57, 59
Jonaidy River, 72
Joncaire, Chabert, 169
Jones, Horatio, 179, 181, 187, 192
Joniady (Juniata), 72
Juniata, 89
Juniata College, 93
Juniata Crossings, 107
Juniata Island (now Duncan Island), 12, 148
Juniata River, xi, 21, 25, 71, 74, 88, 90, 91, 92, 93, 98, 99

K

Kaien'kwaahton, 174
Kallender, Capt., 97
Kalm, Peter, 19
Kautam, 176
Keith, William, Gov., 45, 69, 70
Kendry, William, Lt., 172
Kennedy, President, 11
Kent, Conn., 142
Kent, Donald H., 119
Keowee, 114
Keuka Lake, 187
King George II, 48, 105, 113
King George III, 49, 184, 189
King George's War, 54, 89, 90
King James I, 75
Kingsessing, 87
Kingston, 59
Kinzua Dam, 10, 11, 15, 16
Kinzua Reservoir, 7
Kiskiminetas River, 98, 99
Kittanning, 2, 82, 90, 93
Kittanning Path, 90, 94
Kittatinny Mountain, 107

L

Lackawanna, 175
Lake Erie, 61, 98, 99, 116
Lake George, 57
Lake Michigan, 117
Lake Ontario, 33, 55, 58, 134, 159, 162, 168, 171, 183
Lancaster, 79, 82, 89, 120, 126
Lancaster County, 76, 87
Lappawinsoe, 17
Laughlin Mill, 82
Lawson, John, 24, 25
Le Boeuf, 117, 118
Lehigh River, 136
Lehigh Water Gap, 143
Letchworth State Park, 175, 178, 179, 186, 191
Letchworth, William, 178, 179
Letort, Anne, 85
Letort, Jacques, 85
Letort, James, 85
Levy, Nathan, 95
Lewisburg, 100
Lewiston, 26, 190
Lewistown, 93, 159
Lichtenthaeler, Frank E., 46
Ligonier, 97
Limestone Springs, 75
Little Beard's, 176
Little Beard's Town, 165
Little Billy, 192
Little Carpenter, 48, 113, 114, 115, 116
Little Toby's Creek, 98
Lock Haven, 140
Lockport, 191
Logan, Anton, 143
Logan, James, Secretary, 4, 18, 35, 37, 39, 46, 70, 73, 77
Logan, Mack, 143
Logstown, 39, 91, 118, 123
London, 48, 49, 113, 119, 171, 184
Lowrey, Alexander, 77, 95
Lowrey, Alexander, Sr., 77
Lowrey, Daniel, 77
Lowrey, James, 77
Lowrey, John, 77
Lowrey, Lazarus, 77, 97
Lowrey Family, 77
Lusk, William, 82, 83
Lycoming Creek, 35, 36, 38, 173
Lycon, Andrew, 74
Lyttleton, William, Governor, 114

M

Maccawson, 135
Machault, 117
Mack, Jeanette, 141, 142
Mack, John Martin, 141, 145, 173
Maclay, Samuel, 98, 98, 99, 100
Maclay, William, Sen., 78
MacMinn, Edwin, 141
Mahackamack, 185
Manatawny, 87
Manor of Maske, 65, 72, 73
Marin, Sieur, 117, 118
Marsh Creek, 65, 66, 72, 73
Marsh Creek Cemetery, 67
Marsh Creek Settlement, 65
Marshall, Edward, 18
Marshe, Witham, 53, 54
Martha the Passenger Pigeon, 192
Martin, Jeanette, 143
Martin, John, 142, 143, 144
Massachusetts, 121
Massy, 127
Matlack, Timothy, 98, 100
Mead, David, 98
Meadville, 98
Mechanicsburg, 80
Meeting House Springs, 81, 82
Meeting House Springs Presbyterian Church, 76, 80
Memeska, 116
Menakihikon, 18
Mercersburg, 109
Meyer, Elias, 134
Miami, 116, 123
Miami River, 122
Michilimackinac, 170
Mid-Appalachian Frontier, 207
Middle Spring Presbyterian Church, 76
Middletown, 14, 46
Miller, Paul Eugene, 141

Minisink, 184
Minisink Battleground Park, 185
Minisink Ford, 185
Mississippi River, 85, 94, 191
Mississippi River Valley, 105
Mohawk River, 42, 55, 143
Mohawk River Gateway, xiii, 55
Mohawk River Valley, 42, 44, 50, 182, 184
Mohawk Valley, 8, 56, 57, 71, 164, 168, 170, 183, 184, 186
Monocacy River, 25
Monongahela River, 123
Montgomery, Archibald, Col., 114
Montour, Andrew, 5, 123, 173
Montour, Catharine, xiv, 165, 172, 173, 174
Montour, Isabelle, 172
Montour, Madame, 35
Montour Falls, 172, 174
Montour Family, 165, 172
Montoursville, 173
Montreal, 118, 168, 183, 189
Moore, John L., iii, 164
Moravian Church, x
Morgan, George, Col, 140
Morlatton Village, iii
Morris, Robert, 180, 181, 187
Morris, Thomas, 187
Mouns Jones House, 86, 87
Mount Joy, 77
Mount Morris Dam and Recreation Area, 178
Mount Union, 88, 91
Muncy, 135
Muncy Creek, 135, 149
Muncy Manor, 136
Munoz, Kelly, iii, 88
Muschkoss, 23
Mushemeelin, 88, 89
Muskingum River, 2, 123

N

Nanticoke Creek, 20
Nanticoke Indian Museum, 24
Nanticoke Path, 23
Nanticoke Village, 22
Narrows, x, 89
Nemacolin's Path, 118

Neuse River, 24
Neversink River Valley, 185
New Amsterdam, 190
New Bern, 25
New France, 50, 117
New Haven, 142
New Jersey, 133
New Path, 6, 80, 91
New Sweden, 87
New World, x
New York, 121, 131
Newtown, 164, 165, 184
Newville, 82
Niagara, 134, 170, 171, 174
Niagara Escarpment, 25, 26
Niagara Falls, 59
Niagara Falls Portage, 34, 169
Niagara Power Project, 27
Niagara River, 43, 58, 59, 116, 134, 159, 167, 168, 189
Niagara-on-the Lake, 189
Nicholls, Issac, 20
Nilsson, Jonas, 87
Northampton, 18
Nutimus, 18

O

Oconastota, 114
Odjiskwathe, 12
Ogden Land Co., 181, 191
Ogden, Amos, 138
Ogden, Nathan, 138
Ogilvie, John, Rev., 57, 58
Ohio River, 3, 39, 91, 116, 118, 122, 132, 135
Ohio Valley, 54
Okehocking, 1, 4, 5, 6
Okehocking Reservation, 3, 15
Old Fort Niagara, iii
Old King, 174
Old Morlatton Village, 86
Old Smoke, 161, 162, 174, 175, 188
Onandaga, 38
Onaquaga or Oquaga, 25, 26
Onatario, 24
Oneida, 25, 26, 162
Oneida Carry, 55, 58

Oneida Lake, 55
Onondaga, ix, xiii, 21, 33, 34, 35, 36, 37, 39, 41, 42, 43, 50, 51, 53, 54, 55, 59, 60, 98, 142, 143, 151, 190
Ononquaga, 163
Ontario, 124, 171, 184, 187, 189
Oriskany, 162, 184
Ostenaco, 49
Osteningo, 24, 35
Ostonwakin, 35, 38, 173
Oswegatchie, 170
Oswego, 55, 56, 58, 162, 183
Oswego River, 55
Otter Creek, 111
Owego, 35

P

Pachgatgoch, 142
Painted Line, 149, 150
Painted Path, 149
Painted Post, 150
Palatinate, 44
Palatine Bridge, 182, 183
Pamlico Sound, 24
Papunhank, 136, 137
Parker, Arthur C., 12
Parker, Michael, Sgt., 165
Parnell's Knob, 107
Parrish, Jasper, 179, 180, 181, 187
Parsons, William, 66
Path Valley, 25, 74, 106
Path Valley Tuscarora, 27
Patton, Pa., 91
Pawling, Henry, 6
Paxinoso, 135
Paxtang, 78, 90
Paxtang Path, 143
Paxton, Pa., 89
Paxton Boys, 79
Paxton Church, 78
Paxton Presbyterian Church, 76, 78
Paxton Rangers, 79
Peckstang, 79
Penn, John, Gov., 6, 17, 70, 73, 79, 131, 135, 136, 139
Penn, Springett, 69
Penn, Thomas, 17, 65, 69, 72

Penn, William, 2, 3, 4, 33, 48, 68, 69, 71, 79, 84
Penn Family, 5, 17, 18, 45, 46, 47, 53, 68, 70, 71, 72, 73, 75, 82, 135
Penn Square, 95
Peshtang, 78
Peters, Richard, Sec., 66, 73, 74, 75
Pettquotting, 152
Philadelphia, ix, xi, 33, 79, 84, 87, 88, 89, 97, 112, 120, 121, 126, 135, 136, 137, 141, 184
Pickawillany, 116, 123
Picture Rocks, 149
Picuaday, 152
Pierce, John, 8
Pilger Ruh (Pilgrim's Rest), 36
Pine Creek Valley, 60
Pine Plains, 142
Pitt, William, British Prime Minister, 126
Pittsburgh, 117, 126
Poland, 85
Pontiac, Chief, 58
Pontiac's War, 58, 78, 79, 115, 133, 135, 136, 137, 145, 174
Port Alleghany, 99
Port Jervis, 185
Portage Road, 116
Post, Frederick, 125
Potomac River, 80, 82, 111, 121
Pratt, Joseph, 5
Presque Isle, 117, 118
Proctor, Thomas, Col., 189, 194
Province Island, 137
Province of Pennsylvania, 108
Prussia, 95
Public Universal Friend, The, 187

Q

Quebec, ix, 44, 47, 48, 116, 162, 170, 172, 184, 186
Queen Anne, 44, 47, 48
Queen Anne Chapel, 48
Queen Esther, 173, 174
Quen, John, 91
Quilee (Indian Woman), 87

R

Randle, Martha Champion, 14
Raritan River, 149
Raystown, 111, 113
Red Jacket, 13, 181, 189, 190, 191, 192
Reed's Station, 127
Revolutionary War, xiv, 59, 77, 82, 173, 181
Reynolds, Joshua, Sir, 49
Rhine River Valley, 44
Rhineland, 44
Richardson, Ogden, 190
Rider, John, Capt., 20
Ridge and Valley, 90, 110
Ridge Road, 26
Ridley Creek, 4, 5
Ridley Creek State Park, 5
River Mohawk, 57
River Savanna, 119
Riverview-Corydon Cemetery, 16
Robert Livingston's Manor, 44
Rochefort, 152
Rogers, William, Rev., 140
Rome, 55, 58
Romney, George, 49, 184
Roxbury, 91
Roxbury's Gap, 90
Runesassa, 14

S

Sadowski, Anthony, 85, 86, 87
Saint Gabriel's Episcopal Church, 86
Sassoonan, 47, 85, 87
Savery, William, 13
Sawantaeny, 87
Sayenqueraghta, 162, 174
Schenectady, 180
Schoharie, 45, 46, 153
Schoharie River, 44
Schoharie Valley, 43, 168, 170
Schohary, 43
Schull, William, III, 85
Schuylkill River, xi, xiii, 35, 84, 85, 86
Schuyller, Peter, 47
Schwadara, 43
Scotland, 7
Scull, Edward, 85
Scull, John, 85, 87
Scull, Nicholas, 87, 107
Scull, Nicholas, I, 85
Scull, Nicholas, II, 85
Scull, Nicholas, III, 85
Seaver, James, Dr., 177, 178
Second Mountain, x
Seneca Castle, 165
Seneca Indian Park, 189
Seneca Iroquois National Museum, 12
Seneca Lake, 166, 187
Seneca Mission Church, 189
Seneca Ordeal, 159
Seven Years' War, 106
Shaarai Shomayim Cemetery, 96
Shade Gap, 90, 92
Shadow of Death, 92
Shakespear, 47
Shamokin, x, 25, 34, 35, 38, 47, 53, 84, 85, 86, 87, 88, 89, 98, 142, 148, 153
Shannopin, 123
Shannopin's Town, x
Sharpless, Joshua, 14
Shekomeko, 142, 143
Shenandoah Valley, 25, 83
Sherman's Creek, 72, 74
Sheshequin Path, 35, 36
Shikellamy, 34, 35, 36, 38, 39, 41, 54, 73, 85, 88, 89
Shikellamy, Chieftain, 36
Shikellimo, 54
Shippen, Joseph, Capt., 131, 133
Shippensburg, 126
Shirley, William, Gov., 121
Shirleysburg, 91, 93
Sign of the Bear Tavern, The, 96, 97
Silver, James, 80
Silver Spring Church, 80
Silver Spring Presbyterian Church, 76, 80
Simon, Joseph, 77, 94, 95, 96
Sinemahoning (Sinnemahoning River), 98
Sinnemahoning Creek, 99
Six Nations, 90, 180, 183, 186, 187, 188, 190
Six Nations Reservation, 24
Smith, Arthur Britton, 171
Smith, C. C., 194

Smith, John, Captain, 19, 20
Smith, Steve, iii
Smoke's Creek, 188
Smokes Creek, 175
Snake Mountain, 60
Snow, Captain, 113
South Buffalo, 189
Southern Appalachians, 106
Spain, 105
Spangenberg, Augustus, Bishop, 36, 151
Springettsbury Manor, 69
Squakie Hill, 176
St. Lawrence River, 55
St. Leger, Barry, Lt. Col., 162
Standing Stone, 91, 92, 93
Stanwix, John, Gen., 97
Staring (or Starns), Frederick, 71
Steel, James, 70
Stevens, Frank, 90, 93
Stevenson, George, 66
Stockholm, 19
Stone Arabia, 45, 168, 181, 182, 183, 184
Stony Creek, 99
Sullivan, John, Gen., 8, 140, 154, 164, 166, 170, 172, 175, 181, 183, 188
Sullivan Campaign, xiv
Sullivan County, 185
Sunbury, 84, 132, 152
Susquehanna, x, 43, 45, 60, 67, 73, 132, 134
Susquehanna River, xi, xiii, xiv, 3, 14, 19, 21, 23, 25, 34, 38, 41, 45, 46, 69, 70, 71, 72, 78, 80, 82, 84, 88, 98, 99, 114, 131, 132, 135, 136, 141, 142, 143, 144, 147, 152, 173
Susquehanna River Valley, 33, 65
Susquehanna Valley, 18
Swallow Warrior, 109
Swarthmore College, 14
Swatara Creek, 43, 45, 46
Swift, Brian, iii, 88
Swift, David, iii
Swift, Judy, iii
Swift, Robert B., 219
Syracuse, xi, 33

T

Tall Peter, 192
Tamar, 138
Tanacharison, 118
Tatamy, Moses Tunda, 5, 146, 147
Taylor, Abiah, 94
Thames River, 47
Thayendanegea, 183
Thomas, George, Gov., 89, 90
Thompson, Janet, 82
Thousand Steps Trail, 88
Timberlake, Henry, Lt., 49, 105
Tioga, 35, 173
Tioga Path, 150
Tioga Point Museum, iii
Tioga River, 150
Tishcohan, 17, 18
Tohashwuhdionny, 41, 42
Tome, Philip, 60
Tonawanda, 186
Tonawanda Reservation, 191
Tooker, Elisabeth, 13
Towanda Creek, 35
Tower of London, 48
Town Destroyer, 164
Trail of Tears, The, 116
Treaty of Big Tree, 189
Trenton, 133
Tulpehocken, 44, 45
Tulpehocken Creek, 35
Tulpehocken Path, 35, 36, 38, 47, 85
Tulpehocken Valley, xiii, 34, 35, 43, 45, 46, 153
Tunesassa, 9, 14, 15
Turbotville, 153
Turtle Creek, 124
Tuscarora Creek, 25
Tuscarora Heroes, 26
Tuscarora Mountain, 25, 74, 80, 106
Tuscarora Nation Reservation, 24, 26
Tuscarora Path, 25
Tussey Mountain, xi, 91
Tusten, Benjamin, Lt. Col., 185
Twightwee, 123

U

Ulster, 68, 70, 75
Universal Friend, 187
Upper Allegheny River, 3, 99
Upper Delaware River, 185
Upper Susquehanna River, 133

V

Van Campen, Moses, 146, 193
Van den Bogaert, Harmen Meyndertsz, 55
Van Schaick, Goose, American General, 42
Vienna, 20
Von Zinzendorf, Nicholas Ludwig, Count, 38, 142, 172, 173

W

Wahachey, 107, 111
Walking Purchase, 2, 17, 18, 19, 34, 39, 53, 68, 85
Wallace, Paul A. W., iii, 23, 26, 41
Wallach, Ira D., 57, 163
Wallach, Miriam, 57, 163
Warrahijagey, 56
Warrenbush, 168
Warrior's Path, 106
War of 1812, 26
Washington, George, General, 108, 118, 124, 131, 164
Washington, George, President, 7
Water Street, xi, 90, 91
Waterford, 117, 118
Wawhatchee or Wahachey, 107, 109, 111
Weaver, Kyle, 46
Weiser, Conrad, ix, xiii, 21, 26, 34, 35, 36, 38, 41, 42, 43, 44, 45, 47, 53, 54, 55, 72, 73, 85, 88, 89, 91, 94
Weld, Isaac, Jr., 61
West Seneca, 192
Westminster Abbey, 48
Whaley, Janet, 177
Whaley, Robert, 177
Whaley Tavern, 177, 178
Wheelock, Eleazar, Rev., 184
White, William, 74
Whitmore, Sarah, 179, 180
Wilkes, John, Justice, 127
Wilkinson, Jemima, 187
Williams, Ted C., 28
Williamsburg, ix, 49
Williamsport, 14, 173
Willistown Township, 4
Wills Creek, 120, 123
Winchester, 111
Windfall, 36
Winnsoccum Island, 21
Winter, John, 87
Winter, William, 87
Wolf Clan mother, 16
Womelsdorf, 35, 47, 85
Wood Creek, 55
Woolman, John, 136
World War II, 11
Wurtemburg, 142
Wyalusing, 6, 23, 41, 135, 1136, 37, 139, 140
Wyoming, 138, 140, 174
Wyoming Valley, 8, 18, 21, 41, 53, 138, 142, 163, 164
Wyoming Valley Massacre, 153, 173, 175, 185

Y

Yaple, Jacob, 59
Yarnell, Amos, 5
Yarnell, Mordecai, 5
Yellow Breeches Creek, 71
Young King, The, 192

Z

Zeisberger, David, 41, 136, 137, 141, 143, 145, 150, 192
Zeninge (Osteningo), 23, 138
Zilla Woolie, 21

About the Author

Robert B. Swift is a native of western New York and the author of *By Great Rivers Lives on the Appalachian Frontier* (2019) and *The Mid-Appalachian Frontier: A Guide to Historic Sites of the French and Indian War* (2001).

He has spent most of his 50-year career as a journalist covering the Pennsylvania statehouse. He graduated from Allegheny College with a bachelor's degree in American Studies in 1974. He lives in Grantham, PA.

www.ingramcontent.com/pod-product-compliance
Lightning Source LLC
Chambersburg PA
CBHW070054080526
44586CB00013B/1056